WESTMAR COLLEGE LIBRARY

W9-BTI-807

Religion Goes to School

Religion Goes to School

A Practical Handbook for Teachers

James V. Panoch

David L. Barr

HARPER & ROW, PUBLISHERS
NEW YORK, EVANSTON and LONDON

1817

377.1 LC
P195 405
.P3

75025

To
Jean
who couldn't know

Religion Goes to School. Copyright © 1968 by Religious Instruction Association. Printed in the United States of America. All rights reserved. No part of this book may be used or reproduced in any manner whatsoever without written permission except in the case of brief quotations embodied in critical articles and reviews. For information address Harper & Row, Publishers, Incorporated, 49 East 33rd Street, New York, N.Y. 10016.

FIRST EDITION

H-S

LIBRARY OF CONGRESS CATALOG CARD NUMBER: 68-17598

PREFACE

This book is written for the classroom teacher. It is intended (1) to clarify the relation between religion and public education, and (2) to suggest methods and materials adaptable for classroom use. In the years immediately following the court decisions on prayer and Bible reading in the public schools, the legal aspects of the issue were the subject of discussion in countless meetings and articles. In recent years there has been less emphasis on the legal phase and more interest in the practical. As the legal limits were increasingly defined and understood it became apparent that the valid question was not whether religion could be included in the public school curriculum—but *how*. The purpose of this book is to give the concerned teacher help on how to include religion and religious literature significantly and properly in the curriculum within the legal limits and in keeping with the goals of education.

The authors are indebted to countless individuals and groups who over a period of many years have given moral and financial support to the organization they represent. Royalties from this book will go to that organization. We wish to extend a sincere "Thank-you" to Lilly Endowment, Inc., without whose help neither this book nor our own extended activities would have been possible.

JAMES V. PANOCH
DAVID L. BARR

Contents

I GUIDE

1 WHAT IS THIS ALL ABOUT?

THE SCHOOL teaches religion whether it teaches religion or not. The school teaches in one way by what it includes, and teaches in quite another way by what it excludes. But one way or the other, it teaches something about religion. Your school is doing something with your religion whether you know it or not.

The school that excludes religion teaches by inference that religion has not been an important area of human concern—an inference not borne out by facts. The school that seeks to be neutral toward religion by excluding it has confused neutrality with sterility. To exclude everything over which people disagree would render the school completely sterile. On the other hand, the school that includes religion runs the risk of being misunderstood. There are right ways and wrong ways for a school to handle religion, but confusion persists over which is which. In the resulting confusion both religion and education suffer. The purpose of this book is to identify and implement what may be done with religion by a public school.

The public schools are necessary for our democracy. "The establishment of a republican government without well-appointed and effective means for the universal education of the people is the most rash and foolhardy experiment ever tried by man," said Horace Mann. Whether the public schools have produced our democracy or the democracy produced the schools, our system of free public schools remains one of America's greatest contributions to the history of the world. The other great contribution of the American Experiment is the concept of a free church within a free state. A society in which both church and state are free and self-determining is a new phenomenon in history. There is no op-

3

position in America today to the *principle* of church-state separation. It seems clear that it is not advisable for these two great areas
of human concern to become intermingled—not advisable for
either one to try to thwart or support the other. How to apply
this principle in the specific situation of the public schools is an
often confusing and difficult question. The purpose of this book
is to provide the means whereby religion may be incorporated
within the public schools in a manner consistent with both the
nature of the schools and with the American idea of a free church
within a free society.

Religion may be practiced or studied. The practice is what
makes religion meaningful. The study is largely an exploration of
the practice. In private life practice and study may be combined,
but in public life they must be kept separate. The public school
must not sponsor the more important practice of religion, but
only the less important study of religion. Though this is less important, it is not *un*important. And a proper study of religion
will make its practice more meaningful. The school may study
what is practiced—but not practice what is studied. The purpose
of this book is to indicate why and how religion may be studied
in the public school.

In its prayer and Bible-reading decisions the U.S. Supreme
Court has ruled against a school-sponsored practice of religion
but not against a school-sponsored study of religion. The difference
between "study" and "practice" is definitive for what the court
has ruled may or may not be done with religion by a public school.
The court ruled—and it is only common sense—that a school may
not sponsor a prayer meeting, or a Mass, or an evangelistic service, or a Communion, or a Bar Mitzvah, or a baptism. These acts
involve practice of religion, which properly belong under the
direction of the individual. But the court also indicated—and it
is equally good sense—that a school ought to sponsor a course
on the history of religion or comparative religion, or a course on
the Bible. These acts involve the study of religion, which properly
belongs under the direction of the school. The purpose of this
book is to consider the responsibility of public education toward
the study of religion.

The confusion over what the court said about prayer and
Bible reading in a public school may be the best thing that could

have happened to religion. It is characteristic of a human being to want just what he is told he cannot have (that was the trouble with Adam and Eve). There is enough human ingenuity in the world so that when told, even mistakenly, that religion cannot be included in public education, man will find a way to include it. The unfortunate thing is that what could be done easily and with harmony may be done awkwardly and with rancor if what the court said is not properly understood. The purpose of this book is neither to condemn nor to applaud the court's decisions, but to understand them, and in terms of that understanding to suggest the many proper ways in which religion in all its dimensions may find its rightful place in public education.

Although the school may not sponsor a practice of religion, the student may. The school must be neutral toward religion; the student does not have to be. The court has ruled against a school prayer, but not against a student prayer. It is just as unconstitutional to stop a student from praying as it is to make him pray. So long as it does not interfere with the rights of others, any individual, including a student, may practice his religion anywhere, even in school. However, in a public school this practice of religion under the direction of the individual is necessarily limited. The purpose of this book is to implement only the study of religion, which is under the direction of the school.

The Supreme Court did not remove religion from the public schools. We did. Uninformed teachers, an unconcerned public, unconscious churchmen—all have had their hand in systematically eliminating all mention of the Bible and religion from significant areas of school life. The church, largely unconscious of the good that could come from the proper use of the Bible and religion in the schools, has withdrawn from public education. The public, apparently unconcerned, has been content to think that there could be no mention of religion in a public school. Teachers, uninformed about the legal uses of Bible and religion, have tended to use them illegally or not at all. It is apparent that our real problem with religion in the school is simply a misunderstanding of the problem itself. Once it is really understood, most of the difficulties dissolve. The purpose of this book is to identify the problem clearly and to make a positive contribution toward its solution.

2 What Did the Court Really Say?

The Procedure of the Courts

THE UNITED STATES SUPREME COURT never tries a case; it only reviews decisions. Each case has only one trial where evidence is submitted to a judge or a jury, which arrives at a decision about it. This is the trial court. Any case may be appealed to other courts where the trial court decision is reviewed. These are appeals courts. An appeals court, up to and including the Supreme Court, never tries a case on the basis of the evidence. There is no jury in the Supreme Court. That court only reviews what happened at the trial court and decides whether the decision was right or wrong. On trial before the Supreme Court is the trial court decision rather than the case in question.

Every problem that comes up for court action is assigned to some particular court for trial or review. Federal courts are assigned the review of any court decision where violation of rights guaranteed by the Constitution is at issue. The cases involving public schools and religion were reviewed by the Supreme Court because those bringing suit claimed a violation of one or more of their Constitutional rights.

No one has a right per se to have his case reviewed by the Supreme Court. That court alone decides which cases it will review. When the Supreme Court refuses to review a case, the decision of the lower court stands. (This does not necessarily mean agreement with that decision, for there may be other, technical reasons for refusing to review.) When the Supreme Court chooses to review a case it can either affirm or reverse the trial court decision. The Supreme Court has both affirmed and reversed various trial court decisions concerning religion in the schools.

The Supreme Court is limited to this function of affirming or reversing a previous decision. When the court comments beyond what is necessary for justifying its affirmation or reversal, those comments, called "dicta," have no legal force. Although without legal force, dicta frequently become the most widely quoted portions of a decision and are often a shadow of things to come.

A Supreme Court decision is not "the law of the land"; it is only a judgment passed on the outcome of a particular trial in a lower court. Any decision of any court applies only to the case under consideration and to no other, no matter how similar the circumstances. This is why some choose to ignore a court decision, claiming, with some legal accuracy, that the decision does not apply to their situation. However, a decision of the Supreme Court on any particular matter indicates how it would probably rule on similar matters. Consequently, conscientious citizens attempt to bring their activities within the range of what they believe the court will allow, although not always technically required to do so.

The Background of the Legal Issues

There is no provision for education in the federal Constitution. Further the Bill of Rights contains the statement: "The powers not delegated to the United States by the Constitution, nor prohibited by it to the states, are reserved by the states respectively, or to the people." Education, therefore, has become the function of state government. However, the federal government—and this was true even before the adoption of the Constitution—has been involved in education in various ways. Though no provision is made for education in the federal Constitution, parts of it have an effect on education. These include the restrictive religious clauses of the First Amendment: "Congress shall make no law respecting an establishment of religion, nor prohibiting the free exercise thereof . . ." At their adoption these clauses applied to the federal government only. It took a Constitutional amendment in the middle of the twentieth century to bring the states and schools under these same restrictions.

Originally, the individual states were free to do as they pleased about religion. It was only the federal government that was prohibited from passing a law "respecting an establishment of religion"; that is, the federal government could make neither a law *requiring* a state-established religion nor—and we have almost forgotten this—a law *prohibiting* a state-established religion. Originally it was considered perfectly proper for a state to have a state religion if it so chose, and the federal government by virtue of the First Amendment could not interfere. At one time in their history, nine of the thirteen original Colonies had state religions. The Congregational Church was established in Massachusetts, Connecticut, and New Hampshire. The Anglican Church was established in New York, Maryland, Virginia, North Carolina, South Carolina, and Georgia. Four of these maintained established churches for more than twenty-five years after the adoption of the First Amendment.

In the early 1800's state-established religions became a problem. By 1833 a case (*Barron* v. *Baltimore*) had made its way to the Supreme Court which involved those who claimed that state-established religions were in violation of the United States Constitution. The Supreme Court, however, refused to extend the restrictions of the religious clauses of the First Amendment to include the states. It required a Constitutional amendment and a series of court decisions to extend the restrictions on the federal government to include state governments as well. The Fourteenth Amendment, adopted in 1868 in the aftermath of the Civil War, says in part: "No state shall make or enforce any law which shall abridge the privileges or immunities of citizens of the United States . . ." Over the years the Supreme Court has been called upon repeatedly to identify the "privileges or immunities" of United State citizens which may not be violated by the states. In a 1940 case (*Cantwell* v. *Connecticut*) the Supreme Court firmly established that the religious clauses of the First Amendment now apply to state governments, and thus to public schools. The stage was set for a series of post-World-War-II cases concerning religion and the public schools.

Cases of Primary Interest

This series of a half-dozen school-religion cases, based on the First Amendment, began with the *Everson* v. *Board of Education* decision (New Jersey 1947). In *Everson* the Supreme Court by a 5–4 vote affirmed a lower court decision that there was nothing in the federal Constitution to prohibit a local community from busing non-public-school students to and from school. The court ruled that the federal Constitution neither required nor prohibited busing non-public-school students. Busing is a decision "reserved by the states respectively, or to the people" (Tenth Amendment). Some states require busing; others prohibit it. Still others permit it. These latter have made no state-wide decision, thus leaving the matter up to local communities. The trend of events since this 1947 bus decision has been such that those opposed to the decision believe it may be reversed to prohibit busing, should the Supreme Court choose to review another bus case now pending in the lower courts. These recent events include: a change of mind on the part of Mr. Justice Douglas, who originally voted with the majority in the close 5–4 decision; large-scale school reorganization, which since 1947 has made busing of students an integral part of education; and recent Supreme Court decisions which have tended to emphasize a separation of church and state. Although the court has had opportunity to review the bus decision, during the last year or two, it has refused to do so.

Within a year of the *Everson* decision the Supreme Court decided the first of two released-time cases. (Released time is the arrangement by which public school pupils are released for part of the school day to attend religious classes of their choice.) The two cases are *McCollum* v. *Board of Education* (Illinois 1948) and *Zorach* v. *Clauson* (New York 1952). In *McCollum* the Supreme Court by an 8–1 vote reversed a lower court decision and ruled that sectarian religious classes were not permissible in the public school. In the furor that followed, every aspect of religion in the school became suspect—an attitude that unfortunately lingers still.

Four years later, in a temporizing and refining mood, the Supreme Court revealed the error of this attitude. In *Zorach* the Court by a 6–3 vote affirmed a lower court decision and ruled that, although sectarian religious classes could not take place on school property, they could take place on school time. A significant difference between *McCollum* and *Zorach* lies in whether the classes take place on school property (*McCollum*) or off school property (*Zorach*). Mr. Justice Black, a dissenter in *Zorach,* said: "Except for the use of the school buildings in Illinois, there is no difference between the systems . . . ." (that is, no difference in kind) between *McCollum* and *Zorach* but only a difference in degree. Mr. Justice Douglas, writing the opinion of the court in *Zorach,* said, "The problem, like many problems in Constitutional law, is one of degree . . . ." For the majority of the court this difference in degree was the determining factor. The problem is how to provide accommodation without coercion—accommodation of those who want religion (a guarantee of their right of free exercise) without coercion of those who do not want religion (a guarantee of their right of nonestablishment). The court, in *Zorach,* struck the balance at the point of allowing religious classes on school time but off school property. Although the released-time decisions have bitter enemies, there is no serious attempt to reverse them as there is with the *Everson* bus decision. The *Zorach* decision legalized and gave a big boost to released-time classes, which had begun years earlier (in Gary, Indiana, in 1914).

After a decade of silence on the school-religion issue, the Supreme Court spoke again in the *Engle* v. *Vitale* decision (New York 1962). This is the famous Regents' prayer case in which a preworded prayer was approved by the New York Board of Regents, the controlling body for education in that state, for voluntary use by the schools. In *Engle* the Supreme Court by a 6–1 vote reversed a lower court decision and ruled that a school may not require pupils to pray. (The 6–1 decision was due to the nonparticipation of Mr. Justice Frankfurter because of his pending retirement and Mr. Justice White because of his recent appointment.) In *Engle* the school had offered the student a choice between a preworded prayer and no prayer. The Supreme Court ruled that such a choice was improper. The entire choice, even to the wording of the prayer, must be left to the individual student. What the court really ruled was that no one may word a prayer for another. It is important to note that the Supreme Court did not say that a student might not pray, but only that the school might not compel the student to pray. It seems that there must be no compulsion, direct or indirect, either to force a student to pray or to prohibit a student from praying (as guaranteed by the nonestablishment clause). But that any student has the right to pray on his initiative is guaranteed by the free-exercise clause. So it is equally unconstitutional to restrain a student from praying or to compel him to pray. There have been various attempts to reverse the *Engle* decision, including Court cases (*Stein* v. *Oshinsky, De Spain* v. *De Kalb*) and Constitutional amendments (proposed by Congressman Frank Becker and Senator Everett Dirksen). Although these attempts have had popular vocal support, they have not yet succeeded and with the passage of time seem even less likely to succeed.

A year after *Engle* the court reinforced its position on prayer and broadened the field to include devotional Bible reading, with one decision covering two similar cases: *Abington* v. *Schempp* (Pennsylvania 1963) and *Murray* v. *Curlett* (Maryland 1963). These two cases came to the Supreme Court with opposite lower court decisions. In *Abington* the Federal District Court in eastern Pennsylvania ruled against required prayer and devotional Bible reading, while in *Murray* the Maryland Court of Appeals ruled in favor of required prayer and devotional Bible reading. The Supreme Court by an 8–1 vote affirmed *Abington* and reversed *Murray* to rule against required prayer and devotional Bible reading in a public school.

The court viewed the aspects of prayer in *Abington* and *Murray* as substantially the same as in *Engle*. In *Abington* and *Murray* the prayer at issue was the Lord's Prayer while in *Engle* the prayer at issue was the Regents' prayer. However, the Supreme Court was not concerned with what prayer was furnished to a student— only with the fact that any prayer at all was furnished. The student must be free to make his own choice. On his own initiative he may choose the Lord's Prayer or the Regents' prayer or any other prayer.

The court viewed the aspects of Bible reading in *Abington* and *Murray* as devotional exercises rather than academic study. And as part of a devotional exercise the court ruled Bible reading to be improper. It did not intend to eliminate all Bible reading, and tried to indicate this in oft-quoted but little-heeded dicta, saying: "It certainly may be said that the Bible is worthy of study for its literary and historic qualities. Nothing we have said here indicates that such study of the Bible or of religion, when presented objectively as part of a secular program of education, may not be effected consistent with the First Amendment."

The Meaning for the Teacher

Stripped to its essentials the legal background indicates that the teacher may expose but must not impose religion. "Expose" here means to convey understanding of a phenomenon, the reasons

Significant Supreme Court Decisions on Cases Involving Religion and the Public Schools

CASE	STATE	DATE	ISSUE	DISPOSITION	VOTE
Everson v. Board of Education	New Jersey	1947	Busing	Affirmed	5–4
McCollum v. Board of Education	Illinois	1948	Released time	Reversed	8–1
Zorach v. Clauson	New York	1952	Released time	Affirmed	6–3
Engel v. Vitale	New York	1962	Prayer	Reversed	6–1
Abington v. Schempp	Pennsylvania	1963	Prayer and Bible reading	Affirmed	8–1
Murray v. Curlett	Maryland	1963	Prayer and Bible reading	Reversed	8–1

Everson—Permits busing of non-public-school pupils.
McCollum—Prohibits sectarian instruction of pupils on school time on school property.
Zorach—Permits sectarian instruction of pupils on school time, but off school property.
Engel—Prohibits required school prayer.
Abington—Prohibits required school prayer and devotional Bible reading.
Murray—Prohibits required school prayer and devotional Bible reading.

for it, the personalities who developed it, and its subsequent influence. "Impose" means to require a commitment to a particular value system.

An analogy may be helpful. In social studies the public school requires students to study history, politics, civics, government, and economics. In any such studies the school seeks to convey to the student an understanding of Republicans and Democrats, but does not require from the student a commitment to either one. Every student should know what Republicans and Democrats are, what they believe, how they came by that belief, and how that belief has affected our history and development. That is exposing; that is education. But no student should be required to *be* either a Republican or a Democrat. That would be imposing; that would be indoctrination.

As with politics, so with religion. Every student should know what the major representative religious bodies are, what they believe, how they came by those beliefs, and how those beliefs have affected our history and development. That is exposing; that is education. But no student should be required, either directly or indirectly, to accept any religious belief or participate in any religious expression. That would be imposing; that would be indoctrination.

Nothing religious is barred from the public school per se. There is no theme, no concept, no idea, no personality, no object, and no book that has been banned from the public school as such. The legality depends on the use. If the use is to expose for understanding, it is legal; if it is to impose for commitment, it is illegal.

BIBLIOGRAPHY

American Association of School Administrators. *Religion in the Public School*. New York: Harper & Row, 1964.

Boles, Donald E. *The Bible, Religion, and the Public Schools*. "Collier Book" No. BS 172. New York: Crowell-Collier, 1963.

Duker, Sam. *The Public Schools and Religion: The Legal Context*. New York: Harper & Row, 1956.

Fellman, David, ed. *The Supreme Court and Education*. "Classics in Education" No. 4. New York: Columbia University Press, 1962.

James, Leonard F. *The Supreme Court in American Life*. Chicago: Scott, Foresman, 1964.

Kauper, Paul G. *Religion and the Constitution*. Baton Rouge, La.: Louisiana State University Press, 1964.

Reutter, E. Edmund. *Schools and the Law*. Dobbs Ferry, N.Y.: Oceana, 1964.

Stokes, Anson Phelps, and Pfeffer, Leo. *Church and State in the United States*. New York: Harper & Row, 1964.

Tussman, Joseph. *The Supreme Court on Church and State*. New York: Oxford University Press, 1962.

3 What Did You Ask?

In this chapter an attempt has been made to answer the questions most commonly asked. There are seventy questions, divided into five categories:

General Questions
1. Why should a public school consider religion at all? The public school, as we have seen, has no choice; it teaches something of religion whether it teaches religion or not. If a school eliminates all consideration of religion it teaches by inference that religion is not an important human concern. The valid question is not whether the school should consider religion, but rather *how* it should consider it. The American Association of School Administrators made this point clearly when they said: "A curriculum which ignored religion would itself have serious religious implications. It would seem to proclaim that religion has not been as real in men's lives as health or politics or economics. By omission it would appear to deny that religion has been and is important in man's history—a denial of the obvious" (*Religion in the Public Schools* [New York: Harper & Row, 1964], p. 56).

The public school should consider religion because the school has chosen, or has been forced, to include in the curriculum everything considered necessary for life. Twentieth-century Americans worship education. Any problem—technical, social, or emotional

15

—is expected to be dealt with by an educational program. If there are too many highway accidents, we need a driver's education course. If the young wife burns the toast, we need home economics courses. When everything important for life is included in the curriculum, the student learns by inference that what is not in the curriculum is not important.

The school should give positive consideration to religion because of the continually greater influence the school exerts on the life of a youngster. When other institutions exerted the dominant influence on the lives of children, the way the public school handled religion was less important than it is today, when the school so controls the life of the student—indeed, of the family as well. Family routine and vacations during the year are largely built around the school schedule; school events and the varying load of homework during the year more and more determine the family's opportunity for recreation or time together. But more importantly, the increasing emphasis on education makes the school far more important than it once was in the student's development of a philosophy of life. Life occupations, life partners, and a basic orientation to life itself are acquired through school activities to a constantly increasing degree.

A public school should consider religion because such consideration is basic to good education. The U.S. Supreme Court, in limiting the practice of religion in the public school, went out of its way to suggest that education is not complete without the study of religion. Historians, men of letters, sociologists, and others who have examined the role of the school in contemporary society are unanimous in their conviction that the proper inclusion of religion in the public school curriculum has not kept pace with the increased influence of the public school. The challenge is there.

2.   Did the court ban the Bible and religion from the public school? No. The court banned an activity, not a book or an area of study. It banned imposing a religious philosophy on a youngster, but did not ban exposing students to religious beliefs or religious literature. Nothing is banned from the public school when it is a legitimate part of an educational program. The court banned the school-sponsored practice of religion, but encouraged a school-sponsored study of religion.

3. Why does the public school have trouble in handling religion?
Every public activity in a pluralistic society has a problem of
adjusting to the different religious convictions of its citizens; the
problem is not unique to the school. In Indiana white crosses
placed at the site of death due to motor vehicle accidents drew
objections from those who opposed placing a religious symbol on
public property. In Florida an evangelist was put on trial because
of the death of a young cripple who was told to put down his
crutches and walk during a healing meeting. In Boston a woman
was brought into court for allowing her five-year-old daughter to
die rather than seek medical attention, because of religious convictions. The LSD cult has asked for immunity similar to that given to
Indians, who are allowed the use of narcotics in ancient Indian religious rituals. After harassing the Amish for decades on the matter
of social security insurance, the federal government finally passed
legislation exempting religious groups from mandatory insurance
payments when it is a matter of religious conviction. Exemption
from union shop regulations is allowable to those who cannot join
mixed groups because of religious conviction. A convicted mur-
derer appealed his death sentence on the ground that his execu-
tion would violate his right to practice his religion, which required
him to make restitution for the sin of murder in this life. Other
areas of conflict include Sunday closing laws, birth control laws,
holy day observances, abortion laws, conscientious objector regulations, and blood transfusions.

We have never been without religious problems, and probably
never will be. As long as we keep living and acting and speaking
it is inevitable that from time to time we do or say something
that runs afoul of the religious convictions of our neighbor. There
is no law that could be passed that would solve the problem.
What we must do is to learn to react to each situation in a balanced way more quickly. We should not have harassed the Old
Order Amish for thirty years before exempting them from social
security. In a free society the problem of adjusting the life of the
social body to the religious convictions of its members is one
of the most pressing human tasks.

**4. Why hasn't the public school had trouble with religion in the
past?** It has. How to handle religion in the public school has been

a much more acute problem in the past than it is today. There
was a time when several religious groups were unable to find a
place in public education and withdrew to build school systems
of their own. There was a time when hill-country disagreements
were solved by shotguns; twenty-two persons were killed in one
instance, in a feud over the version of the Bible to be used in
their public school—and this didn't even solve the problem! There
was a time when the school-religion problem ignited city riots.
One city has in its history a period called the "Bible War." There
was a time when teachers and preachers were tarred and feathered
over the issue of religion in the public school. There have been
periods when young people have been harassed and maligned
in the classroom for their religious convictions. Many a young person has been whipped for not reciting the Lord's Prayer, or prose-
cuted in the courts for refusing to profess certain religious beliefs.

**5.   Why has religion in the public school suddenly become such
a great problem?** Though the problem is an old one, the vehicle
by which it comes to our attention in this generation is new. This
vehicle is the United States Supreme Court. The court became
involved partly because the religious restrictions of the First
Amendment have been extended to include state governments
as well as the federal, and partly because the Supreme Court has
emerged as a more significant branch of government. Urban
renewal was made possible by court rulings. The reapportionment
rulings will change representative government at the state level
in our generation. In the system of checks and balances that constitutes our political structure, emphasis always shifts from one
branch of government to another. There have been times when
the Congress seemed to dominate the scene and almost impeached
a President. At other times the Executive has been a dominant
element and Congressmen complained of having to vote for legislation before there was time to read it.

In a quiet way, because of a number of far-reaching decisions,
the Supreme Court has emerged as a more influential branch of
government in our own day. Several major internal problems
of our country have been vitally affected by those decisions. The
civil rights movement was sparked by the school desegregation
cases of the mid-fifties. Law-enforcement officers have had to

change their methods of apprehension and prosecution as the result of Supreme Court decisions.

The authors of this book neither condemn nor praise these decisions. We cite them here only to note that the problem of religion in the school has been recently activated by the Supreme Court, which thus constitutes a source outside the field of education creating a problem in education. Most problems within the field today, such as those concerned with the new math, sex education, reading innovations, and programmed learning, have been formulated by educators as they conscientiously strive to better the school program. It is understandable that the internal, educator-motivated problems are more easily solved than are external, court-activated ones.

6. Did the Supreme Court decision produce a "Godless" school? That depends on one's concept of God and of the school. The traditional concept of God is one of omnipotence and omnipresence, in which case no combination of men, including the United States Supreme Court, can keep God out of where He is. More pertinent to our discussion, however, is the fact that the concept of the Godless school rests on a fallacy. We have no concern for "Godless" hardware stores or a "Godless" bank. The hardware store, bank, and school, though by no means equivalent, all exist for purposes which can be carried out without adopting a specific theological position.

7. Did the Communists have anything to do with limiting prayer and Bible reading in the public school? Probably not. The individual citizens who brought court suits were loyal Americans who had a different opinion of what should go on in the public school from those who were administering the particular schools with which they were involved. Though it is doubtful that Communists initiated any of the actions that resulted in limiting prayer and Bible reading in the public school, it may be assumed that they supported the limitation. However, to blame the Communists is to take the easy way out. Prayer and Bible reading have been limited to the present extent, and even eliminated in some situations, not because of the court cases or the Communists, but rather because of an uninformed and uninspired citizenry.

8. Should there be a Constitutional amendment to permit prayer and Bible reading in the public schools? There already has been such an amendment—the very first one. The First Amendment assures that there will be no governmental establishment of religion, but also secures the right of an individual to practice his religion as he sees fit. This would include praying and reading the Bible in school. What is needed now is not another Constitutional amendment but administrative rulings that will implement the First Amendment. Recent court decisions have ruled against a school prayer, but not against a student prayer. The court has said the school must not make a student pray, but did not say that the student might not pray at his own initiative. The right *not* to pray is a sacred right and should be protected; but it does not carry with it the right to expect, or force, everyone else not to pray. The right to pray is also a sacred right that needs protection. A way must be found to allow the student to pray who wants to pray, without forcing another student who doesn't want to. That way will be found, not in additional Constitutional amendments, but rather in implementation of the existing amendment.

9. Should a justice be impeached because of the prayer and Bible-reading decision? It depends on whether or not he has committed an impeachable act. A justice cannot be impeached for making a decision over which there is disagreement. If this were true, every justice would be subject to impeachment on every decision, since nothing goes to the Supreme Court unless there is genuine and deep disagreement. Regardless of how any one justice decides, there are many sincere people who have reason to disagree. Nor can a justice be impeached for making a mistake. Many justices have admitted mistakes, and on occasion the court has reversed itself to indicate that the whole court has made a mistake. As long as a justice makes his decision on the basis of what he honestly believes to be right at a given time, he is not subject to impeachment. Incompetence or chicanery would be grounds for impeachment. But the fact is, impeaching Earl Warren or anyone else would hardly solve the problem. There are better things to do about it.

10. Is it true that all forms of crime and violence have increased since the Supreme Court limited prayer and Bible reading in the

public School? If the statistics are correct, yes. However, it is also true that the same categories of crime and violence were on the increase before the Supreme Court limited prayer and Bible reading in the public school. This would indicate that crime and violence have been generally increasing, irrespective of these limitations.

11.   Did the Supreme Court make any mistakes in their decision limiting prayer and Bible reading in the public school? This, of course, is a matter of opinion. But even one of the Supreme Court justices thought the court had made a mistake and so indicated in a dissenting opinion. There are at least four areas in which those studying the court's decision have suggested the possibility of error: (1) in the cases chosen for review, (2) in the clause on which the decisions have been based, (3) in the ambiguous nature of the test, and (4) in a violation of judicial procedure.

First, it has been noted that in the cases the court chose for review it was forced to take a position against prayer and Bible reading in the public school in spite of the fact that it did not intend to ban all religious activity. It has been suggested that better cases could have been chosen, for the purpose of indicating the positive and proper uses of religion and religious material in the schools.

Second, some feel that by basing this decision on the "establishment" clause rather than the "free exercise" clause, the court made the right decision for the wrong reason. Third, some feel that the ambiguous test set down in the Abington decision, though all would agree with its intention, is impractical, in fact impossible, to administer. In part the test says, "There must be a secular legislative purpose and a primary effect that neither advances nor inhibits religion." The test becomes impossible to administer because if the primary effect must be neither to advance nor inhibit religion, then the purpose in order to control the effect, must be either to advance or inhibit religion. But the test indicates that neither the purpose nor the effect must advance or inhibit. As a practical matter the school should control its purpose and produce good education—the effect of that education is up to the individual.

Fourth, some have suggested that the court made a mistake

by going outside the evidence submitted at the trial courts for
the basis of its decisions. Mr. Justice Stewart in a dissenting
opinion in *Abington* said, "It seems to me clear that the records
in both these cases before us are wholly inadequate to support
an informed or responsible decision." In a brief concurring opinion
in this same decision Mr. Justice Douglas said ". . . coercion, if
it be present, has not been shown; so the vices of the present
regime are different." An error in judicial procedure would suggest that the court made a mistake in the way it said what it said,
though not necessarily a mistake in what it said.

**12.   What should a teacher do if the principal will not allow
use of religion or religious literature, including the Bible?** Obey
the principal. A teacher who expects to be obeyed by the students
must in turn obey the principal. If he has been denied the use
of religious material by his principal, he should still strive to be
at least two things: accurate and professional. When a principal
denies a teacher the right to use such materials, he may just possibly be right. It may be that the teacher is using the material
improperly. In fact, traditionally religious material has been used
improperly in the public schools more often than not. Both the
teacher and the principal must understand the difference between
"study" and "practice," the difference between "imposing" and
"exposing," and the difference between "education" and "indoctrination." The use of religious material in the public school must
be part of a genuine program of education rather than an attempt
to bring in religion under some other guise. Any teacher denied
the use of religious material in the classroom should first check
to see that his use is legitimate and accurate. It may be that a
particular use of religious material might be acceptable in a
classroom situation—the responsibility of the teacher—but questionable in terms of the total approach of the school—the responsibility of the principal. Any attempt to change an administrative
decision regarding the use of religious material must be at the
highest professional level. The good school administrator, when
made aware of the difference between a right and a wrong use
of religious material, and when presented with a good use of it
as part of a regular program of education, conducted by a competent teacher, will allow the use of that material in the classroom.

13. What about the teacher who deliberately disparages religion?
That teacher is wrong and unprofessional. Religion should be
neither disparaged nor extolled by the public school teacher. The
scornful treatment of it by a teacher often occurs in classes which
have no direct bearing on religion, and reflects the views of the
teacher. When this happens it is not an issue of religion—it is
just poor teaching and should be recognized as such.

14. What about the teacher who "preaches" to his class? That
teacher, too, is wrong and unprofessional. Religion should be
studied, but not preached by the public school teacher. Again,
the preaching or endorsement of religion often occurs in classes
which have no direct relation to religion, and reflects the views
of the teacher. When this happens, here once more it is not a
religious issue but just poor teaching, and should be seen as such.

**15. Are teachers trained to handle religion and religious ma-
terial?** Teachers are not as yet well trained in this area as they
could be, but neither are they as poorly prepared as some think
they are. Literature teachers are trained to teach literature, of
which the Bible is a part. History teachers are trained to consider
major historical movements, of which religion has been a powerful motivating force. But training or the lack of it cannot, in any
case, be the finally decisive factor in eliminating religious material
from the public schools. At one time teachers were not trained
to handle driver education or teach the new math. They got
trained. Whatever training teachers lack in order to handle the
Bible and religion well should be acquired.

**16. What will the church do if the public school studies the
Bible?** If the public school explores the Bible properly for education, it will give the church greater opportunity to teach for
commitment. The public school is limited in its activities to studying for understanding. Obviously, the church has no such limitation and may teach for either understanding or commitment or
both. But in its limited time with a student it is virtually impossible
for the church to teach adequately in both aspects. The way in
which the public school and the church handle the Bible need
not be in conflict, and if well handled should be complementary.

**17. Should the religious community develop the religious courses
for the public school?** No. It is the public school's responsibility

in its own right to prepare curriculum. The school should not pass the buck to the church. The political science course is not developed by the political parties—neither should the religious course be developed by the religious community.

All churches have never agreed on any one thing before and it would be unrealistic to suppose that they will agree on a course in religion. Though there are many community activities in which a majority of religious groups cooperate, there are also many from which certain groups drop out and still others in which some never participate at all. In voluntary associations any combination of religious communities is acceptable. But in a compulsory situation such as exists in the public school it is incumbent upon the administration of the school to take into consideration the broad spectrum of religious views, whether those views seek representation or not.

The school has the responsibility in its own right to develop curriculum. Duncan Hines does not write the school cooking courses, nor does General Motors set up the driver education course. A public school may use any community resources it feels necessary in developing its courses, but the responsibility for curriculum must lie with the school.

18.   What should be the role of the clergy in regard to religion in the public school? The clergyman has both the right and the responsibility to express what he thinks the school ought to do to those who control the school program. It is primarily through such responsible discussion that adequate programs are ultimately constructed. Community elements, of which the clergy are a part, have a responsibility to tell the school what they want taught, while the school has the function of deciding how to teach it. The clergyman is not out of place in asking the school to teach something of religion, but it is not his role to supervise or determine the teaching.

The producers of automobiles, stoves, typewriters, and a wide variety of other items, as well as many organizations with particular viewpoints are constantly pressuring the school to see that their product or view is represented. There is no objection to the competition these pressures bring about, in fact, it is this competitive situation that best describes our way of life. A strong objection would be raised if one product or idea were to be given preference over another in the school. The clergyman's role is to insist that religion be considered properly in the school but to allow the school to determine the nature of that consideration.

19. What is released time? Released time is the arrangement whereby students who desire to do so may be released for part of the school day to participate in a service involving the practice of religion. The program is not sponsored by the school and must be conducted off school property. Most of the present released-time programs use facilities near the school or classroom trailers parked adjacent to it. In 1952 the U.S. Supreme Court established the legality of the released-time program in the Zorach case.

20. What is shared time? This is an arrangement whereby the student will enroll part time in a public school and part time in a private school. It often means that the student will take math, science, and vocational subjects at the public school while taking literature, history, and social studies at the private school. The legality of shared time has not been firmly established, nor has the custom grown very rapidly—no doubt because of the difficulty of administration and the lack of enthusiastic support from large sections of the religious community.

21. What is dual enrollment? This is the newer and more popular term for shared time.

22. What is the "child benefit" theory? The child-benefit theory suggests that government aid is permissible for items that benefit the child, while not permissible for those that more clearly benefit the school. This theory got its start in 1930 when the Supreme Court in *Cochran* v. *Louisiana Board of Education* permitted the state to purchase textbooks for all its students, including non-public-school students. The reasoning was that the purchase of the textbooks benefited the child rather than the school. The child-benefit theory was given major recognition in 1947 in the *Everson* v. *Board of Education* case, when the U.S. Supreme Court permitted public financing of the transportation of non-public-school students to school. Again the reasoning was that the transportation benefited the child and not the school. In a great measure the aid to education acts of recent years have been built on the child-benefit theory. The federal government is to finance only those items and activities that benefit the child. However, as more items and activities come in question, it becomes more and more difficult to determine at what point benefit to the child becomes a benefit to the institution.

The theory has bitter opponents who are challenging its validity in the courts, and apparently Mr. Justice Douglas is among those who question its legality. In his concurring opinion in *Abington* he noted: "Financing a church either in its strictly religious activities or in its other activities is equally unconstitutional, as I understand the establishment clause. Budgets for one activity may be technically separable from budgets of others. But the institution is an inseparable whole, a living organism, which is strengthened in proselytizing when it is strengthened in any department by contributions form other than its own members."

23.   Is it better to study religion in a separate course or as part of already existing courses? The study of religion or religious literature in a public school may take the form of (1) a special course, (2) a unit within an existing course, or (3) an enrichment activity in any course. Special courses include history of religion, comparative religion, and Biblical literature. Units within existing courses might include a unit on the Reformation in a world history course, a unit on the influence of Colonial religions in a U.S. history course, and a unit on the Bible in the literature course. Enrichment involves the contingent and relevant aspects of religion as they come up every day, in any classroom at any grade level.

It is better to study religion in existing courses, either as a unit within a course or as an aspect of subject under study. Including religion in every subject area and at every grade level is far more important than including it in a specific course at a specific time. The influences of religion and religious literature, both good and bad, should be included at every point in the curriculum where relevant to the subject under study, and to a degree commensurate with the abilities of the student. More and better learning takes place when the elements under study are considered in their relation to each other. Students will have a better understanding of religion and religious literature when these are integrated into the curriculum.

Special courses do have their place for students who have a particular interest in religion. As specialized courses are offered in other fields, so, too, courses in the history of religion or comparative religion or religious literature ought to be considered.

Questions On the Study of Religion

24. Is it possible for a public school to consider a subject as controversial as religion? Different subjects bring forth varying degrees of concerns from different people. While some persons are quite unconcerned about religion, they become deeply involved emotionally with politics or economics. If the public school were to eliminate every subject over which there might be controversy, there would be little left to study. A public school deals best with a controversial subject by not taking sides, but by stating all sides of a question objectively—as seen by their partisans, showing both the strengths and the weaknesses.

25. What religion will the public school teach? The public school will teach no religion, but will study all religions. The public school is not to teach what religion to believe, but what the various religions believe. Obviously, not all religions will be studied to the same degree at the same time. The maturity of the student and the purpose of the curricular unit will determine what elements of what religions are included at any given time. Unfortunately, in the past the public school has all too often taught the student to believe in one or another religious system, or has sought to eliminate religion entirely. Recent decisions of the Supreme Court have forced the school to assume a new position of studying religion without imposing any particular religious system. The court's words were, "One's education is not complete with a study of comparative religion or the history of religion and its relationship to the advancement of civilization."

26. Why should the public schools teach comparative religion when they do not teach comparative anatomy or comparative law? The public school teaches both comparative anatomy and comparative law even at the lowest levels. When the school notes the difference between a giraffe and a squirrel it studies comparative anatomy. When the school notes why the Pilgrims left Europe it considers comparative law. Comparative religion as a college course belongs on the upper level of education, along with comparative anatomy as a college course. But religious differences and similarities when part of a subject under study should be included at every grade level and in every subject area where they naturally appear.

27. To avoid controversy could all religion be taught outside the public school hours? Only if the same is done for other controversial subjects. There is no valid reason to single out religion and say this one area of human concern cannot be considered within school hours. On the matter of teaching for religious commitment the U.S. Supreme Court used the released-time cases to recognize and permit the teaching of commitment on school time, but off school property. On the matter of teaching for religious understanding the court used the prayer and Bible-reading decisions to recognize and indicate that the study of religion may be a proper part of the public school curriculum. A human concern as important as religion has been, and is, in the life of man deserves some "prime time" and ought not to be relegated to the incidental hours of a student's day.

28. When a public school considers religion, does this violate the principle of separation of church and state? That depends on what is or is not being separated. Separation of church and state applies to the control of one over the other, but not to contact between them. The separation is absolute in the area of control: the state must not control the church, nor the church the state. But there is no separation of church and state in the matter of contact. A publicly financed fire department may put out a church fire. The publicly paid policeman may apprehend a criminal or guard traffic as they relate to a religious activity. Publicly financed sewer lines and water mains may be connected to a church. None of these services involves control by either the church or the state over the other. When the public school considers religion in such a way that the church controls the thinking of the students it is a violation of the church-state principle. When it considers religion as an academic subject, there is contact between the two but this does not violate the essential principle of separation.

29. Can a teacher be objective when studying religion in a public school? Perfect objectivity is impossible, unnecessary, and under certain circumstances may not even be desirable. If school subjects were eliminated for lack of a perfectly objective teacher very little if anything would be taught. All that the community

asks, and all that good education requires, is practical objectivity
—that the teacher be as objective as reasonably possible. The
public school teacher can be as objective with religion as he
is with other controversial subjects. By training and inclination
the public school teacher is far more objective than the average
person—at least in the classroom situation. Teachers can be
objective enough to permit the successful study of religion in the
public school.

30. May a teacher give his views on religions? It depends on the
purpose for which those views are given. If the teacher gives his
views in order to persuade the student to accept them, it is illegal
and improper. If he gives his views in order to help the student
understand a religious position, it is both legal and proper. At
the lower grade levels students are more anxious to emulate their
teachers and particular care must be taken not to express personal
opinions in areas where this is inappropriate and unnecessary. At
the upper grade levels the teacher may give his views as an appropriate teaching technique, and also in recognition of the need to
alert the student to his own (the teacher's) bias.

Although the teacher has the same rights of free speech as any
other citizen, he gives up some measure of those rights when he
becomes a teacher. As a teacher and representative of the state,
he does not act in a purely personal capacity in the classroom—
he is speaking for all citizens and not for himself alone. Obviously,
a teacher has greater freedom to express his views during non-
school hours, but even away from school the teacher must be
careful not to use his position as a teacher to influence students
improperly.

**31. To avoid controversy, could a public school teach only
what is common to all religions?** No. Both the similarities and
differences between religions must be considered in any adequate
study. If only what is common to all religions is considered, very
little if anything will be available for study. But more importantly,
religions have made a contribution to human development through
their differences as well as through similarities. If a history course
or political science course were to consider only what is common
to the political parties, the real significance of the subject would
be lost. Religious personalities and religious movements have

made a contribution to the world scene through the way they have differed with each other. Such differences must be understood if there is to be any meaningful study of religion.

32.   When a public school considers religion will it be a "watered down" religion? That depends on whether the school considers religion in terms of a "practice" or a "study." If the school seeks to sponsor a practice of religion, it certainly would have to be "watered down" to whatever is common among those who wish to practice together. History has not been kind to those who have sought a common denominator for the practice of religion. But since the school seeks to sponsor a study of religion the term "watered down" does not apply. In the study of religion, no faith needs to be "watered down." Each faith is explored for what it believes and why. In study no attempt should be made to defend or condemn or alter any belief of any faith.

33.   Will students be embarrassed if religion is studied? No one need be embarrassed. Embarrassment is a personal matter, and people are embarrassed for all kinds of reasons—sometimes for no apparent reason. The same situation may cause one person to be embarrassed and another not. Embarrassment is determined not by an external situation but by an internal attitude. Some students may be embarrassed if religion is studied, but they need not be.

It is incumbent upon the school to control the classroom situation so that factors that might produce discomfort are held to a minimum. But just because someone is embarrassed does not mean that the school is at fault.

34.   Will a study of religion cause a student to lose his faith? It may. Just as a study of any controversial issue may cause a student to change his position on that issue, so a study of religion may cause a student to change. (This may be seen as a loss of faith, depending upon the nature of the change and the perspective of the observer.) An honest, academic study of religion ought not to harm any well grounded faith. The Court has admonished the school to seek to neither advance nor inhibit religion. This means at a minimum that the school should not seek to cause a student to lose or alter his faith. But if in an adequate study a student chooses to alter his faith, this should be viewed as the product of education rather than that of indoctrination. Good education will cause changes. It is only when the education seeks to control the nature of a change that it becomes a biased indoctrination, and thus poor education. Many a father has sent his son away to college with one political persuasion only to have his son return with another. The irate father often accuses the college of deliberately changing the views of his son. Although this is certainly a possibility, more often than not, the son studied the subject and arrived at his own conclusion.

35. Can a teacher adequately describe a belief he does not personally hold? Though a teacher may not be able to describe such a belief perfectly, he ought to be able to do so adequately. If differing views in the many areas of controversy were to be presented only by the adherents of those views it would be impractical, if not impossible, to conduct school. A teacher ought to be able to present all views sympathetically, the way those who hold those views would present them. Admittedly this is difficult, but it is not impossible, and in the last analysis, it seems to be the only practical way to handle controversial issues.

36. Will religion become "just another subject"? One of the dangers in studying religion is that we may give the impression that this study of religion is the whole of religion. This question is really part of a larger question which asks, is the study of religion sufficient? We have argued earlier that it is not. It is really the practice of religion that makes religion significant. In its broadest scope the practice of religion is an integrative philosophy of life that runs through every discipline and every activity. But the public school, as an arm of civil government, is prohibited from advancing this practice of religion. The function of the school is to study about it. Moreover, the study of religion must be done in such a way as not to inhibit its practice.

Treating religion as "just another subject" should not carry with it the implication that religion be degraded, it is merely recognizing the limitations of the public schools. To the extent that religion contains truth, treating as "just another subject" should allow it to rise to whatever its inherent abilities will allow.

Questions On the Study of the Bible

37. What makes the Bible worth studying? The Bible is worthy of study for at least two general reasons: its great influence on our society and its intrinsic value as an outstanding piece of literature. One reason is practical, the other aesthetic. The court may have had both reasons in mind when it stated in *Abington:* "It certainly may be said that the Bible is worthy of study for its literary and historic qualities." Biblically inspired thought and action has been one of the major motivators of human life. The Crusades made the European aware of the world beyond his feudal farm. This helped to make him an explorer, and contributed to the discovery of America. The Biblically inspired concept of the value of the individual to a large extent produced the Reformation, which in its turn spawned the Industrial Revolution. The founding of our country is heavily steeped in Biblical connotations of every sort.

Literature and the arts have been greatly influenced by the Bible, and countless books have been written to indicate the depth and variety of this effect. Through the King James Version the Bible became the greatest single influence on the English language. So small a thing as a postage stamp may show a Biblical background. A leading automobile magazine compares a small foreign import to an American-made model by calling them "David and Goliath." A sports announcer refers to a baseball pitcher who is returning to a field of play where he was disliked, as a young man "for whom no fatted calf has been prepared." Twentieth-century American life has been so saturated with Biblical allusions that they are generally unrecognized as such.

Moreover, the Bible has influenced the basic philosophy of Western civilization. Our founding fathers said in the Declaration of Independence that their right to start a new nation came from God. They went on to say that individual rights also come from God—rights that are then delegated to government in order to conduct an orderly society. The high value of the individual soul, a Biblically inspired concept, serves as the real basis of Western culture. When a man is caught in a mine or a youngster in a well shaft, no effort is spared to rescue him. It would be unthinkable in the West to hear a newscaster say that a youngster could be rescued, but that the machine necessary to do the job costs too much to transport. Whatever the cost, whatever the effort, the protection of the person is the primary concern. This high valuing of the individual derives from the Biblical concept of man's responsibility to God. If a man is personally responsible to God, then the individual is all-important.

Many societies on the contemporary world scene do not share this concept of individual worth. Our failure to comprehend a pattern of life where the person is not ultimately important is responsible for many of our difficulties with other societies. Even within our own society the value set on the individual has caused us problems, as for instance with capital punishment, or abortion laws. If an individual is responsible to God, who has the right to take his life? And when does an individual *become* an individual—at conception or at birth?

Beyond its practical and historical value, study of the Bible is important for its aesthetic content. This great book—this library of many centuries of thought and feeling—contains a tremendous variety of literary expressions: in song, poetry, prose, essay, and many other forms. As literature it is superb in the way it reveals human nature.

Literature deals with what goes on inside a person. It reveals love and hatred and expresses joy and sorrow. The Bible reflects human emotions as they relate man to man and man to God. Human emotion remains much the same in any generation. True literature does not deal with externals. It would be difficult now to find—for instance—a book on how to grease oxcart wheels. Yet oxcart wheel greasing was quite important at one stage of man's history. Men must have known what animal to kill and what part of the animal to prepare and how to prepare it in order to produce the best grease for the purpose. Today our libraries do not house books on this subject. But they do have material on automatic transmissions. A thousand years from now this topic will be as obsolete as the oxcart. Both have been merely part of the means by which man moves from place to place. The means change with the generations, but man remains the same. Being good literature the Bible speaks to man's inner emotions, and so remains relevant for every age.

An old automobile catalog lists a running-board luggage rack.

Forty years ago running boards and luggage racks for them were common. The catalog deals with externals and is outdated in forty years, while the Bible deals in interior problems and values which are never old. As long as man lives on earth, the Bible will be valid and illuminating. Two thousand years ago he traveled in a chariot; today by automobile; two thousand years hence it may be a space ship. The vehicle is of little consequence. Regardless of how he moves about, his inner life is what will always really concern him. Great literature, of which the Bible is a part, reflects and speaks to that inner life.

In a sense literature is a word "mirror." Just as a mirror reflects objects, the writings of man reflect inner experience. Some of the greatest writers have testified that they were not aware of all the implications in their own writing. They put down their words, and reflected their inward emotions without even being conscious of it. As a piece of literature that reflects inner emotions the Bible has no equal.

38. What does it mean to study the Bible "as literature"?
Literary study assumes no dogmatic position on meaning, but rather attempts to explore all possible meanings. It subjects a piece of writing to such questions as: Why was it written? Does the writer accomplish his purpose? What literary forms are used? How does it reveal human nature? What effect has it had? What does it mean to you?

Every piece of literature speaks best when simple questions are asked of it, without preconceived notions about what it "ought" to say. Thus the Biblical Book of Jonah is often associated with the whale. Yet simple study with no preconceived ideas of what it is about reveals that the whale plays a very slight part in it. Why was Jonah written? To inform us that travel by whale belly was popular in the ancient Mediterranean? Was the book set down in order to tell us that swallowing people makes a whale sick?

The Book of Jonah was written to say that the God of the ancient Israelites is the God of the whole world. God wanted the Ninevites saved; Jonah wanted them destroyed. God sent Jonah on a preaching mission; Jonah chose to go elsewhere. But God had His way after all, and Jonah went to the Ninevites. Even while teaching them he still wanted them destroyed, and went up on the hillside to watch what he hoped would be their annihilation. When the Bible is studied as literature the emphasis in a book like Jonah will not lie on the question of whether or not God made use of a remarkable fish, or whether or not a man could live three days in the fish's belly; but on the author's purpose, and how he seeks to accomplish it, and whether in fact he does. Another important line of approach in the study of Jonah as literature is the question of how it reveals human nature. In a literary study of this book the physical question of whether or not a man could survive three days in the interior of a whale is not an issue.

When the Bible is studied as literature, consideration must be given to the literary forms that are used. The Gospels have been accused of being poor history, bad science, and terrible storytelling. But such an analysis disregards literary form. They were not intended to be historical, technological, or mere agreeable narrative. By literary form, the Gospels attempt to propagate a belief and are therefore propaganda. There is nothing wrong or evil in propaganda as such, though the word often carries that connotation. Propaganda as a literary form means simply an attempt to move another person to believe something. That the Gospels are propaganda is attested by the authors themselves. John says, "These are written that ye might believe that Jesus is the Christ" (John 21:31). The study of the Gospels as literature might analyze how the authors use their material to accomplish their purpose.

In any analysis the Gospels cannot be validly criticized for not doing something they did not intend to do. A piece of literature must be viewed in the perspective of its own purpose. If the author of a book states that he is going to show that A is A, it would be a poor reviewer who would criticize it for not showing that B is B. The Gospel of John has been called poor narrative—for being a haphazard collection of unrelated incidents. In terms of narrative the stories of Nicodemus and the Woman at the Well in connected chapters are certainly ineffective. But in terms of John's purpose, to show that Jesus was the Christ, the selection of these stories and their proximity to one another is a stroke of literary genius. By using Nicodemus and the Woman at the Well, John shows that both the highest and lowest in society believed Jesus to be

the Christ. Nicodemus was a cultured, refined religious leader—
the very highest in society. The Woman at the Well was a de-
praved Samaritan prostitute—the very lowest. John does not tell
us all about the people who didn't believe—and there were many
—but rather selects certain of those who did, in order to accomplish his purpose. The Gospels have affected more people over a
longer period of time, and to a greater degree, than any other
piece of literature in recorded human history. The violent objection some have expressed toward them is witness to their
effectiveness. No knowledge of literature can begin to be complete
without a consideration of the Bible.

**39. Should a public school offer a course in the Bible if students
request it?** Not necessarily, though the school should certainly
give it consideration. There are many factors to determine whether
or not a particular course should be taught which have nothing
to do with the nature of the course itself. Available space, quali-
fied teachers, and scheduling problems are among the many
elements that have to be taken into account by the school administrator. Many foreign languages are offered in current curricula, including French, Latin, German, Spanish, and now even
Russian, yet few schools are able to offer all of them. So, too, with
courses in religion or Biblical literature. English literature, American literature, journalism, and drama are among the offerings in
every English department with which a Biblical literature course
would have to compete. (Any course on religion would be com-
peting with courses in the social studies such as World History,
U.S. History, Civics, and Political Science.) Courses on the
Bible should be considered and offered when the above factors
allow.

Any good school system will give adequate considerations to
any request for special courses made by students. The community,
including the students, are the ones to determine what is offered
in the school, while the school is to determine the *how*. There
may be some overlapping. A good school system will help the
community to know best what it wants. And a good community
will support the school system by serving as resources to help
with the *how*.

40. Can the Bible be studied without considering interpretation?
No. One part of the study of literature—and this is especially

true of the Bible—is consideration of the ways in which people have interpreted various passages—including the students themselves. In studying the Bible as literature in a public school, no attempt must be made to impose any particular interpretation upon the class. But, depending on the ability of the students and the purpose of the curricular unit, the responsibility of the school would be to consider major representative interpretations and meanings. The strengths and weaknesses, the origins and effects of differing interpretations are proper subjects of study. In a public school no single interpretation can be imposed upon the student as the "correct one," but all interpretations should be exposed for an understanding of their nature.

In explaining a particular view it is incumbent upon the teacher to present it in a sympathetic manner. He or she must become somewhat of an actor and set forth any interpretation as those who hold it might present it, being careful to avoid either scorn or endorsement. The teacher's responsibility is not to guide the student into acceptance or rejection of any particular view, but to help him understand the range of interpretations.

41. Is the public school the best place to study the Bible? Maybe not. But it is one place. Maybe the best place to study the Bible is within a community of faith. However, it is more important now than ever before that the public school consider the Bible, for the public school has emerged as a dominant influence in contemporary society. It may not be the best place to study the Bible for its theological implications, but it is a good place to study it for historic and literary qualities.

42. What version of the Bible should a public school use? As many as possible, consistent with the abilities of the students and the goals of the curricular unit. There is no version that is banned from the public schools, and no version can be considered best for all purposes. A course with a historical emphasis would probably find a modern translation most useful, while a course with a literary emphasis would more naturally use the King James Version. The latter has been a most influential factor in the development of the English language. Quotations of the Bible, and the many less precise allusions to it, are more likely to be from the King James Version than from any other. Quite apart from theological considerations, this version of the Bible is a master-

piece of the English language. No English literature course, and
certainly no Biblical literature course, would be complete without
significant use of the King James Version.

**43.   May a student be forced to read the Bible in the public
school?** Yes and no. Yes, if the reading is part of an educational
program. No, if it is part of a religious exercise. No student may
be forced to participate in a religious exercise in a public school,
whether it includes reading portions of the Bible or not. It is
not the Bible that has been banned, but a worship service. In
a course where the reading of the Bible is a legitimate part of an
educational program, any student may be required to read any
portion of it. Parts of the Old Testament are logical and natural
reading material in the consideration of ancient history. In a
study of the Middle Ages or the Reformation, to read portions
of the New Testament would certainly be in order. Any study of
poetry would be deficient if it did not consider some of the
great Psalms. Bible reading may be required in a public school
when the purpose of the reading is for understanding as opposed
to commitment.

Because a student does not "believe in" or like the Bible is not
a legitimate reason to excuse him from reading it, when that reading is part of an educational program. Some students may not like
Franklin D. Roosevelt or Herbert Hoover, but that is hardly a
reason to exempt them from reading the history of their adminis-
trations or the writings of the men themselves, if these are pertinent in a modern history course.

**44.   What about those who object to teaching the Bible "as any
other book"?** If treating the Bible as "any other book" carries
with it an atmosphere of disparagement, such teaching is unacceptable. There is no religious issue at stake here; it is just poor
teaching. The public school should neither "degrade" nor "up-
grade" anything. Treating the Bible as "any other book" should
mean an honest study, through which the intrinsic values of the
Bible will be allowed to appear.

There are two kinds of people who are afraid of dealing with
the Bible as with any other book. There are those who believe
it is the inspired word of God, but are afraid it might not seem
so and want to be there to defend it. And there are those who
believe it is *not* the inspired word of God but are afraid it might

seem to be, and want to be there to disparage it. The teaching of the public school should be wise enough and balanced enough to make both forms of defense unnecessary.

45. Should religious literature other than the Bible be studied in the public school? Yes. One of our problems in dealing with other nations is our failure to comprehend their religious systems. A greater consideration of all religious literature in an educational program could easily be justified. Any course in world history or world literature is lacking if it does not give adequate coverage to the religious faiths behind that history and literature. Any religious literature may be studied as a special course where student interest warrants. The determining factor in offering a special course in it has nothing to do with the nature of the material under study, but rather with administrative problems of space, trained teachers, and the value to the total educational program. Other things being equal, religious literature should be studied in proportion to its influence on our society.

Questions On Prayer in the Public School

46. Are prayers banned from the public school? No. The court banned a school prayer, but not a student prayer. The court said the school cannot make the student pray, but did not say that the student could not pray at his own initiative. Within weeks after the 1962 prayer decision, Mr. Justice Clark quoted approvingly the following, "Most commentators suggested that the court outlawed religious observances in the public schools when, in fact, the court did nothing of the kind." The office of the U.S. Attorney General in attempting to interpret court actions to citizens who inquire, has repeatedly made such statements as, "You will note that the decisions in the Engle case in no way restrict the right of individuals to pray." Or, "These decisions do not in any way restrict the right of private individuals or groups to pray, but are aimed at the use of power of government to channel religious observances into prescribed official forms."

47. May a student pray at any time in a public school? Yes and no. It depends on whether the prayer is disruptive to others in the school or hinders the student from satisfactorily completing school assignments.

To the degree that prayer is an inward confession it may go

on at any time concurrent with other activity. Apparently St. Paul had this inward concept of prayer in mind when he suggested that believers pray without ceasing. A man as active as Paul obviously did not mean that he would do nothing else but pray, but rather that the inward communion of prayer would continue regardless of outward activities. Brother Lawrence made a similar observation when he noted that he went about his daily activities in an attitude of prayer. In our time Thomas Kelly has observed that it is possible to order our mental life on more than one level at the same time. While we are meeting the demands of external affairs at one level, we may be at prayer at another level.

This makes possible, at any time, what some consider a very high form of prayer. The decisions of the court apply only to outward manifestations and do not—in fact could not—apply to this type of inner prayer, any more than to a man's conscience.

Student prayer as a visible and audible phenomenon, though not barred from the school, may not be practiced at will. To allow anyone to pray aloud at any time would render the school useless for the accomplishment of its purposes. Even a church finds it necessary to establish orderly ways of conducting its affairs, which involve limiting the outward expression of prayer and setting definite times for it. The school has both the right and the responsibility to limit prayer, but not to eliminate it. The First Amendment guarantees any individual, including a student, the right to pray anywhere, including the school, so long as it does not interfere with the rights of others.

48. Why stop the public school from suggesting prayer when prayer does not harm anyone? Some people have felt that the way schools handled prayer was harmful to their children. Moreover, school prayers are harmful to students when the school and the home have different concepts of prayer, or when the school misuses prayer. In a pluralistic society it is difficult, if not impossible, to have a school prayer in total agreement with the home prayer of all its students. The misuse of school prayer has been attested to by teachers themselves who have admitted using school prayer as a means to quiet students after a recess period. In many cases the school monotonously used the same prayer and Biblical passage to open every school day. Finally, some people do not want their children to acquire the habit of prayer, which they regard as unsound. They have a right to this opinion, which the Constitution is bound to protect—but no right to force it on others.

49. Why haven't efforts to amend the Constitution to permit prayer in the public school been successful? They have. The founding fathers recognized the need for a Constitutional amendment to guarantee the right to pray by enacting the very First Amendment, which guarantees that a citizen's right to practice his religion in any way that he sees fit, including prayer, may not be prohibited by the state.

Since the recent Supreme Court decisions regarding school prayer, several major attempts have been made in Congress to amend the Constitution to permit school prayer. The first was that of Congressman Frank Becker in 1964; others were by Senator Everett Dirksen in subsequent years. Becker, a Roman Catholic, had his amendment referred to the House Judiciary Committee, where he prevailed upon Committee Chairman Emanuel Celler, a Jew, to conduct hearings. Though Celler was an announced foe of the amendment, he permitted lengthy testimony. Becker was not in the power structure of the House and was unable to bring his amendment to the floor for a vote.

In 1966 Senator Everett Dirksen submitted his first amendment, which said in part, "Nothing contained in this Constitution shall prohibit the authority administering any school, school system, educational institution, or other public building supported in whole or part through the expenditure of public funds from providing or permitting the voluntary participation of students or others in prayer. Nothing contained in this article shall authorize any such authority to prescribe the form or content of any prayer."

The Dirksen Amendment was given to the Senate Subcommittee on Constitutional Amendments chaired by Senator Birch Bayh of Indiana. Bayh, like Celler, was unconvinced that another amendment was necessary, but unlike Celler was sympathetic with the purposes of the amendment. As the Committee hearings opened he said, "It seems to me that Senator Dirksen and I have a common goal." But apparently that was all they had in common. As the hearings progressed, Bayh opposed the amendment and countered with a "sense of the Senate" resolution of his own, which said in part, "It is the sense of the Congress that nothing in the Constitution or the Supreme Court decisions relating to religious practices in our public schools prohibit local officials from permitting individual students to engage in silent, voluntary prayer or meditation." Hearings on the Dirksen amendment were about one-third the length of those on the Becker amendment, with many of the same people saying many of the same things.

Dirksen, unlike Becker, is in the power structure of the Senate and was able to bring his amendment to a vote, only to have it defeated 49 for, 37 against, 9 short of the necessary two-thirds majority. Bayh's "sense of the Senate" resolution was also defeated, 33 for, 52 against. As Congress adjourned in the fall of 1966, Bayh's senatorial partner, Vance Hartke, who has introduced prayer legislation of his own, attached a "sense of the Congress" resolution to the Secondary Education Act of 1966 urging schools to permit prayer. The Hartke resolution was tabled on a motion by Majority Leader Mike Mansfield, who contended that it was just not the "proper vehicle" for challenging the Supreme Court.

By the end of 1966 school prayer amendments had stirred both the House and the Senate, only to fail both times. But Senator Dirksen, who attributes the healing of an eye ailment some years ago to prayer, vowed to continue the fight. "This amendment is not going to die," he said. "I'm not going to let it die." When the Senate opened early in 1967, Dirksen's second prayer amendment was submitted as Senate Joint Resolution No. 1. This second amendment, much simpler and more effective than the first, states in part, "Nothing in this Constitution shall abridge the right of persons lawfully assembled, in any public building which is supported in whole or in part through the expenditure of public funds, to participate in non-denominational prayer."

One reason for the failure to get a Constitutional amendment to permit school prayer is the simple fact that there already is such an amendment—the First Amendment, which needs implementation. Another reason for failure is that amending the Constitution is one of the most difficult political actions possible. It was deliberately made so in the Constitution itself, and the difficulty has been reinforced by a tradition of infrequent amendment. But probably the most important reason for the failure of prayer amendments has been their inability to speak to the real nature of the problem, which is the need for administrative action rather than Constitutional change. What is needed is clarification of the Constitution, which comes, however, not through amendment but rather through administrative rulings. On this point Senator Bayh observed, "If every time there was doubt about what the Constitution said or a Supreme Court decision said, we rushed out and amended the Constitution, we would have a volume . . . five foot thick." The measured words of Justice Felix Frankfurter, one of the most colorful and brilliant jurists ever to sit on the Supreme Court, are worthy of note: "Preoccupation by our people with the Constitutionality, instead of the wisdom, of legislation or executive action is preoccupation with a false value." Constitutional amendments have failed because they have sought to solve the problem from the wrong direction.

Proposed Constitutional amendments would not solve the problem of school prayer. The proposed amendments have said that nothing in the Constitution shall be taken to prohibit it providing for prayer. But they did not say that the schools must provide for prayer. Therefore, even if one of them had been enacted, any school official could still effectively deny the opportunity for prayer by simply not providing for it. When Bertram B. Daiker, attorney in the Engle-Vitale prayer case and a supporter of prayer amendments, was asked by Senator Tydings if the Dirksen amendment reversed any of the holdings of the court in the prayer case he replied, "Specifically, no." Republican Senator Roman Hruska, a Unitarian and strong supporter of a prayer amendment, recognized this flaw when he said, "There is nothing in this amendment that says a school board must provide it." In other words, none of the proposed amendments would really have altered the situation.

It is lack of administrative action rather than a Constitutional flaw that frustrates school prayer. There is nothing now in the Constitution that would prohibit persons from praying in a public building or a public park or a public street or any other public place. This would be true whether they were lawfully assembled or not. The prayer offered need not be nondenominational, but could be any prayer a person chose. The right to pray is guaranteed by the First Amendment, which says in part: "Congress shall make no law respecting an establishment of religion, or prohibiting the free exercise thereof." This means that no one can make a student pray—thus "establishing" a religion; but neither can anyone stop a student from praying—thus prohibiting his free exercise. What is needed now is not an alteration or extension or addition to the Constitution, but administrative action that will implement the First Amendment. Dr. Leo Pfeffer, a Jewish Constitutional lawyer, put this most succinctly in testimony before Congress when he said, "If a student felt it was necessary to say a prayer before partaking of bread or milk or cookies and the state says you cannot do that, that would be a violation of the free exercise clause and just as unconstitutional as the Supreme Court says in *Murray* that it is for the teacher to say to the children that you will now say grace."

50. Why permit any prayer in a public school? Compulsory school attendance demands as a consequence of its compulsion that the school permit prayer, if the First Amendment allowing for the free expression of religion is to be obeyed. Wherever attendance is required by government, opportunity for religious expression is provided. The government reasons that any time it forces its citizens to be at a place not of their choosing, it is thereby obligated to provide an opportunity for expression of religion that may otherwise be denied. For this reason the government builds chapels and hires chaplains for the military services and the penitentiaries. Both Mr. Justice Brennan and Mr. Justice Stewart have noted the government's obligation to provide for religious expression in situations of compulsory attendance. In separate opinions in the Abington case Mr. Justice Brennan said, "Hostility, not neutrality, would characterize the refusal to provide chaplains in places of worship for prisoners or soldiers cut off by the state from all civilian opportunities for public communion," while Mr. Justice Stewart said, "A lonely soldier stationed at some faraway outpost could surely complain that a government which did not provide him with the opportunity for pastoral guidance was affirmatively prohibiting the free exercise of his religion."

A soldier and a student have at least one thing in common: they are forced to be at a place not necessarily of their choosing. The difference between the compulsion upon a student and that exercised upon a soldier is one of degree rather than of kind. Because the seriousness of compulsion upon the student is not nearly so great as for the soldier, the remedies need not be so drastic. The school need not provide a chapel or a chaplain. But the compulsory attendance requirement does demand that the school provide some opportunity for prayer consistent with the nature of its business and the rights of all students.

The same compulsory attendance requirement that denies the school the right to prohibit prayer also requires the school to limit prayer. There are students compelled to attend school who want no part of prayer, and their rights, too, need protection. The school must find a way to permit prayer without requiring it.

51. What is voluntary prayer? Voluntary prayer means different things for different people. Unable to understand the reasoning of one witness, Senator Bayh commented that the two of them had different definitions for the word "voluntary." For some the term "voluntary prayer" means a student's own choice of a prayer, while for others it may mean the student's consent to reciting a school-suggested prayer. What must be left for the student's voluntary choice is not mere consent to recite a school-selected prayer, but the nature and selection of the prayer itself.

The prayer decisions limit the source of prayer but not prayer itself. If the school is the source of prayer it is illegal. If the student is the source of prayer it is legal. Only when the student is the source of prayer is the prayer truly voluntary. On the point of the source of prayer, Professor James C. Kirby, Professor of Law at Vanderbilt University said, "It is my opinion from the narrow holdings in these cases dealing with law compelling official forms for religious ceremonies, that that which originates from the individual . . . is not affected. And it is permissible." A further question is whether a group of individuals could originate a genuine voluntary prayer. On this point Dr. Robert V. Moss, President of Lancaster Theological Seminary observes, "The real problem here is corporate voluntary prayer. The moment it becomes corporate, it seems to me, it almost ceases to be voluntary."

The confusion over voluntary prayer could be materially reduced if different words were used to represent the different kinds of meaning for voluntary prayer. The words "spontaneous" and "suggested" may be helpful. Spontaneous prayer is student-initiated, whether preworded or not, and is permissible in the public school. Suggested prayer is school-initiated prayer and is in no

form permissible in the public school. It is not the prayer that
determines whether it is permissible or not, but rather the source
of it—whether it is spontaneous or suggested. Spontaneous prayer
is voluntary; a suggested prayer is not voluntary.

52. How can a public school provide for prayer? A "moment
of meditation" is emerging as one way in which a public school
may provide an opportunity to pray for those who wish to do so
without forcing others to pray who do not wish to. The basic
nature of the moment of meditation is the provision of a limited
time in which the school will neither schedule nor suggest any
activities that would hinder prayer.

Many individual classrooms, schools, and individual school systems observe a moment of meditation. One state has enacted a
state-wide law requiring a moment of meditation, and others are
on the verge of doing so. Early in 1966 Governor John A. Volpe
of Massachusetts signed into law Bill No. 734, which says in part,
"At the commencement of the first class each day in all grades in
all public schools the teacher in charge of the room in which
such class is held shall announce that a period of silence not to
exceed one minute in duration shall be observed for meditation,
and during any such period silence shall be maintained and no
activities engaged in." Before signing the bill Governor Volpe re-
quested and received an official opinion on its legality from the
then Attorney General Edward W. Brooke, now a member of the
U.S. Senate. Mr. Brooke said in part, "It is my opinion that
Senate Bill No. 734 does not conflict with the provisions of the
First Amendment to the Constitution of the United States."

Traditionally the public school has dealt with prayer in one of
four ways. All are inadequate. They are: (1) prayer required
directly, (2) prayer required indirectly, (3) prayer eliminated
directly, and (4) prayer eliminated indirectly. Schools have gone
from one extreme to the other. There was a time when it was
universal to require prayer directly; now it is common to eliminate
it indirectly.

At one time schools enforced their direct requirement of prayer
by administering severe punishment if a student had the audacity
to refuse to pray. The historical record is replete with incidents in
which pupils were physically whipped for not reciting a prayer.
But it is inconceivable today that any public school would di-

rectly require a student to pray. From direct requirement the schools drifted to indirect requirement, by controlling the classroom situation so that psychological pressures made a student feel he had to pray even if he did not want to. With many students the psychological pressure of indirect force is more effective than the physical pain of direct force. But the Supreme Court has ruled that no school may require prayer either directly or indirectly.

In recent years the tendency has been to eliminate prayer. To some extent this has been done directly through board action or administrative decision, either written or unwritten, by which the student is made to understand that no prayer may be made in the school. This direct elimination of prayer is a flagrant violation of both the spirit and the intent of the court decision, as well as of the Constitution itself. Fortunately, direct elimination of prayer is uncommon; but—unfortunately—indirect elimination is very common indeed. Indirect elimination of prayer occurs when, in the classroom situation, the psychological pressures are so great that a student who feels he wants to pray is inhibited from doing so. Indirect elimination occurs automatically when the school does not provide an opportunity. Because the school controls all the student's time, prayer is indirectly eliminated when opportunity for it is not provided. Proposed Constitutional amendments regarding prayer do not solve the basic problem, since they do not require that opportunity for prayer be provided.

Although better ways may be found in the future for the school to provide for prayer, a moment of meditation is one way in which it can do so now.

53. What about those who object to a moment of meditation?
No one is compelled, or could be, to meditate. No one has the right to object to someone else's meditating. A moment of meditation is the school's attempt to refrain from prohibiting the free exercise of religion as required by the First Amendment. The right not to meditate is a sacred right worthy of protection. But the right to meditate is also a sacred right that must be protected.

In a somewhat parallel situation the Supreme Court ruled that a student may not be compelled to give the pledge of allegiance to the flag. But in protecting his right not to give the pledge, the court neither excused him from the class while others give it nor abolished the pledge itself. The right not to give the pledge does not carry with it the right to expect everyone else not to give the pledge. Likewise the right not to meditate does not carry with it the right to expect everyone else not to meditate. More importantly, a moment of meditation gives the student an opportunity to develop sensitiveness to religious experience which he may grow into or encounter in later life.

Those who object to a moment of meditation may have to tolerate it so that the school can maintain a position of neutrality. Professor Paul G. Kauper of the University of Michigan Law School has observed, "There is merit to the argument that if the public schools are indifferent to the religious factor in the life of the nation, they are thereby contributing to an official philosophy of secularism and, therefore, not really neutral in religious matters."

54. Is a moment of meditation legal? Apparently it is. What has not been declared illegal is presumed legal. Although the court has not ruled specifically on the moment of meditation, there has been no serious challenge of its legality. Professor Willard Heckel, Dean of Rutgers University Law School, has said, "I think clearly there is nothing unconstitutional about giving young people the opportunity, the time for silent prayer or meditation." The late Attorney General of the Commonwealth of Pennsylvania, Walter E. Allessandroni, said, ". . . Nor is there any restraint upon unorganized, private, personal prayer. . . ." Congressman Emanuel Celler, a bitter foe of Constitutional prayer amendments and the man principally responsible for the defeat of the Becker Amendment has said, "I say that the teacher could say to the children 'You are now permitted for a period of two minutes to recite to yourselves, if you wish, a prayer.' " In making recommendations to Congress about what could be done in view of the court's decision on prayer in the public school, Professor Paul A. Freund of Harvard University Law School suggested, "The first, closest to the prayer itself, is the brief period of silent reverence or meditation during which each pupil will recite to himself what his heart or his upbringing will prompt."

55. May there be oral prayer during a moment of meditation? At the moment, yes; although as the moment of meditation is used more extensively it may be apparent that oral prayer is too disruptive. And it may depend on how oral it is. Robert Mathews,

Attorney General of Kentucky, has declared, "In our opinion, nothing objectionable would be found in a student, during a period of meditation, voluntarily or spontaneously saying a prayer, silent or vocal." Congressman Emanuel Celler has said of students and prayer that "they could do it out loud or they could do it meditatively." However, the obvious objection to a vocal prayer during a moment of meditation is that any vocal prayer in a sense imposes itself on all its hearers, or at least interferes with their own right to meditate without distraction. Punctiliousness in guarding the right of students not to pray must be matched, surely, by equal care in safeguarding a genuine opportunity for those who want to use it.

56. What should be the teacher's role during a moment of meditation? This depends somewhat on the grade level. At the upper levels no teacher participation would be necessary. At the lower levels the teacher may find it necessary to help the child understand what meditation is. The choice whether to meditate or not is, of course, up to the student. But he has a right to know what meditation is. The role of the teacher during a moment of meditation is to help the youngster to meditate in whatever way he chooses. At the lower levels the teacher helps the student blow his nose, put on his boots, and eat his soup. There is no reason to prohibit the teacher from helping the student with his own prayer.

But just as the music teacher does not sing the song for the student nor the art teacher draw his picture for him, neither should the teacher word the prayer or set the mood for his moment of meditation. The teacher's role is to provide the opportunity and allow the student to find his own meaning in it. Some of the best advice to teachers on the role they should play has come from Dr. Eugene C. Jorgensen, Superintendent of Schools at Portland, Maine, who told his teachers, "If a child feels he should quietly repeat a blessing, or a prayer, before his meal, the teacher or person in charge should see that he has the opportunity."

The role of the teacher is to provide an opportunity for "voluntary prayer," as noted in question 51, without providing a "prayer that is voluntary." This distinction, though confusing, is really the heart of the matter. By "voluntary prayer" is meant prayer in which the student determines what is said, when it is said, where it is said, and how it is said. By "prayer that is voluntary" is meant prayer determined by the state, acting through the school; here the "voluntary" aspect is that the student may choose whether or not to recite it. Repeatedly the Supreme Court has ruled that the second type—"prayer that is voluntary"—is illegal. However, the court has never ruled against the first type, or "voluntary prayer." The role of the teacher is to provide the student an opportunity for "voluntary prayer."

Questions On the Legality of Various Activities

57.   Is it legal for the public school to sponsor a religious service in the classroom if everyone in the community wants it? No. No more than it would be right to drive at sixty miles an hour in a thirty-mile-an-hour speed zone, even if everyone in the community happened at that moment to want it. Some things are proper, or wrong, because of their nature and are not subject to majority vote. Further, because public schools are financed by the state government, and in recent years to a greater degree by the federal government, everyone in the country has a stake in what is taught in every school in the country. As we have seen, though a public school may not sponsor the practice of religion, it may sponsor the study of it. The potential in the study of religion has only begun to be explored.

58.   Is it legal for a public school to be used for religious purposes? Yes, providing they are not school-sponsored and do not occur during school hours. A public school that allows community groups to use its facilities may not discriminate against religious groups because of their religious nature. The school has the right and responsibility to set up rules by which community groups may use public school facilities, but these must be set up and administered without religious discrimination. A church or religious organization might use school facilities on the weekend, after school, or in the evening.

59.   Is it legal to distribute Gideon Bibles? Technically, there is no such thing as a Gideon Bible. What is referred to is usually a King James Version produced by the Gideon organization. A "Gideon Bible" or any other Bible has a valid place in the public school when it is there as part of the educational program. What has been declared illegal by several states and many communities has been the method of distribution, which usually includes presentation of a Bible by a Gideon in a public school classroom on public school time. In places where Gideon distribution has been denied, it is on the basis of the method of distribution and not the book itself.

60. Is it legal for teachers to wear special religious garb in the public school? This question has not been resolved nationally. A citizen who takes a position as a public school teacher, thereby representing the state, must necessarily give up certain of his rights. A public school teacher is not as free to expound his political and religious views in the classroom as in the community. Even in the community, it is inappropriate for him to use his position to influence students unduly. To the degree that religious garb sets an atmosphere that would impose a religious value system on a student, that religious garb would be improper. Where the religious garb would not produce such an atmosphere it may be permissible. For these reasons religious garb may be proper or improper depending upon the grade level or subject area.

61. Is it legal to have Bible clubs in public school? Yes and no. Yes, if it is part of an educational program as opposed to a religious service. Yes, if it is not sponsored by the school and meets outside of school time. No, if it is a religious as opposed to an educational activity and/or is conducted on school time. A Bible club, along with any non-school-sponsored activity, may use public school facilities during non-school hours consistent with school rules and regulations. (See Question 58.)

62. Is it legal to have the phrase "under God" in the pledge to the flag? Yes. The phrase "under God" was added to the pledge of allegiance to the flag in 1954. Without ruling on it directly, the court on one occasion observed that this phrase was merely a recognition of historical fact, and on another occasion refused to review a lower court decision which permitted the phrase.

63. Is it legal to study evolution? Yes. However, because evolution like politics and religion is something over which citizens disagree, it is incumbent upon the school to "expose" the theory of evolution without "imposing" it. The school has the right and the responsibility to study the theory of evolution, considering both its strong and weak points. A good public school curriculum will include other views of the origins of man and the universe, with their strengths and weaknesses.

64.   Is it legal to have special programs at religious seasons such as Christmas, Easter, and Thanksgiving? It depends on the purpose of the program. A program designed to nurture a particular religion would be illegal. A program designed to help students understand the significance of a particular event would be legal. Unfortunately special programs at religious seasons have tended to be worship services. Schools will have to work hard to overcome past tradition and develop proper educational programs if special programs at religious seasons are to be successful.

65.   Is it legal to sing Christmas carols? Yes. No piece of music has been banned from the public schools as such. It is illegal for a public school to sponsor a religious service which would include prayer, Bible reading, or religious music. The religious activity has been banned, but not the religious material as such. If the singing of a Christmas carol is part of a worship service it is illegal. If it is part of a music educational program it is legal.

66.   Is it legal to have nativity scenes on public school property? Yes, but only if they are there as part of an educational program. It would be unthinkable to excuse students who think of themselves as Democrats from drawing pictures of Lincoln. It is assumed that when students draw pictures of Lincoln on his birthday this is done as part of a study of a man who made a major contribution to world history, and not in order to persuade students to join the Republican Party. Schools may use nativity scenes as part of the study of a great life which made a significant contribution to world history, but not as a means to persuade students to a particular religious belief. Unfortunately, schools have used nativity scenes as part of worship services more often than not.

67.   Is it legal to have religious symbols on public school property? Yes. In fact, because religion has so permeated our society it would be difficult to find a public school that did not have religious symbols in one form or another. No religious symbol has been banned from the public school as such. It is just the use of religious symbols and material in worship that has been declared illegal. The public school may not use such symbols as part of a worship service, but any religious symbol has a legitimate place in a public school curriculum when part of the program of education. Every student has a right to know the significance of religious symbols when relevant to the subject under study.

68. Is it legal to have a baccalaureate? It would be difficult if not impossible to have a legal baccalaureate service. Baccalaureate by its very nature is a religious service. And a public school may not sponsor a religious activity. Of course, the baccalaureate services that are not part of the school program are perfectly legal and have not been banned by any court decision.

It is questionable whether it is worth the time and effort to attempt to structure a legal baccalaureate. Religion is not studied through a baccalaureate any more than American history is studied through a Fourth of July parade. If religion is to find its rightful place in the public school curriculum it will have to be something more significant than a half-hour program at the end of a twelve-year experience. Unfortunately, the baccalaureate has become a symbol. A school that drops it is often accused of being "Godless." There is nothing wrong with the baccalaureate as such, except that it is woefully inadequate as a school's recognition of the contribution religion has made to human history.

69. Is it legal to have convocations? Yes and no. Where convocations are designed as worship services, they are illegal. Where convocations are part of an educational program, they are legal. The public schools' use of community resources is becoming increasingly more popular. Depending upon the ability of students and the purposes of the curricular units, any minister may be invited to participate in any school program where the purpose of his participation is for education rather than introduction.

70. Is it legal to transport non-public-school students to and from school? Yes. But not mandatory. In the Everson case in 1947 the Supreme Court by a 5-4 decision ruled that a community may bus non-public-school students. As it stands now, busing of non-public-school students is a matter for the states and local communities to decide for themselves. Several groups are making concerted efforts to force the court to reconsider the bus decision.

In October of 1967 the Supreme Court refused to review a bus case, with only Mr. Justice Douglas voting in favor of review. It is interesting to note that Mr. Justice Douglas, who voted with the majority in the first, 5-4, Everson case which permitted busing non-public-school students, has since publicly changed his mind and would now apparently rule against such busing.

4 WHAT IS GOING ON?

THE STUDY of religion or religious literature in a public school may take the form of (1) a special course, (2) a unit within an existing course, or (3) an enrichment activity in any course. Special courses include History of Religion, Comparative Religions, and Biblical Literature. Units within existing courses include a unit on the Reformation in a world history course, a unit on the influence of colonial religions in a United States history course, and a unit on the Bible in a literature course. Enrichment includes the contingent and relevant aspects of religion as they come up any day in any classroom at any grade level.

Under "Sample Curricular Units" are listed a few representative projects being conducted by school districts or individual teachers. No evaluation is here attempted and inclusion in this list does not necessarily constitute endorsement. Under "Topical Guide" are listed items which may be used by the resourceful teacher. The number preceding each entry in the topical guide refers to the number under which the item appears in the "Resources" or "Bibliography" chapters of this book.

At the end of this chapter is a list of "Relevant Organizations" that either directly or indirectly provide methods or materials that could be useful to the public school teacher.

SAMPLE CURRICULAR UNITS

Claremont, California. A college professor and a high-school teacher have collaborated to produce a senior high-school course titled "The History of World Religions." A detailed study is made of the religions of India, the Orient, and the Bible lands. Mr. Joseph Forcinelli, Claremont High School, Claremont, California. 91711

North Haven, Connecticut. A new course titled "Religion in Culture" is being offered at North Haven High School. The course includes a study of the religious literature of the world and its influence on twentieth-century America. Mr. Charles Church, North Haven High School, 222 Maple Avenue, North Haven, Connecticut. 06473

Deland, Florida. A workbook for a high-school Bible course is available from a long-time teacher of the course. A special guide for the teacher is also available. Miss Amelia H. Fowler, 734 Montreville Avenue, Deland, Florida. 32720

Fort Lauderdale, Florida. The English Department of the Broward County Schools has developed a one-semester course on the literature of the Bible which stresses literary forms. A guidebook titled *The Bible as Literature* is available from the English Department, Broward County Schools, Fort Lauderdale, Florida. 33312

Milton, Florida. A new program is being launched at Milton whereby senior high-school students will receive credit for courses in the Bible taken during school time but off school property. The program is controlled and financed by a private organization set up for that purpose. Mr. J. W. Hunsucker, 218 Pecon St., Milton, Florida. 32570

Tallahassee, Florida. A state committee has been organized and privately funded to develop courses on religion and religious literature for the public schools of Florida. Dr. Robert A. Spivey, Florida State University, Tallahassee, Florida. 32306

Tampa, Florida. A "Biblical History" course is included in the offerings of Tampa High School. The entire Bible is considered in chronological order, stressing literary forms. A syllabus is available. Mr. J. Sydney Barrett, 4409 W. Fligh Avenue, Tampa, Florida. 33614

West Palm Beach, Florida. A community-wide, school-oriented program of value analysis has been developed by an inter-faith group in cooperation with the schools. Project: Value Search, P.O. Box 3224, West Palm Beach, Florida. 33401

Valdosta, Georgia. A Bible course is one of the offerings in the English program at Valdosta. The course stresses content and literary form. Printed material is available. Mrs. Elizabeth D. Hamill, 400 W. Alden Avenue, Valdosta, Georgia. 31601

Chicago, Illinois. Philosophy will be taught in twelve Chicago-area high schools by college professors as part of an experimental program financed by the Carnegie Corporation and administered by the Central States College Association. The program will include a study of ethics, logic, and selfhood as a unit within the social studies or literature course. Through summer-school grants, high-school teachers will be prepared to teach the unit. Dr. Pressley McCoy, Central States College Association, 2530 Crawford Avenue, Evanston, Illinois. 60201

Glen Ellyn, Illinois. A unit on the types of literature found in the Bible has been developed at Glenbard High School. A syllabus is available from the teacher. Mr. Alton Capps, ONO 46 Page St., Winfield, Illinois. 60190

Wheaton, Illinois. A course for teachers on the relationship between religion and public education is offered each summer at Wheaton College. The legal issues, the element of appropriateness, and the programs involving religion and the public schools are analyzed. Director of Summer School, Wheaton College, Wheaton, Illinois. 60187

Wheaton, Illinois. In rewriting the social studies curriculum at Wheaton, religious elements have been included where relevant. Mr. Edward P. Storke, 812 Webster St., Wheaton, Illinois. 60187

Bloomington, Indiana. A junior high unit on select Biblical passages has been prepared by the Indiana University Curriculum Study Center. A book for the teacher entitled *On Teaching the Bible as Literature* is available for $1.45 from the Indiana University Press, Bloomington, Indiana. 47405

Indianapolis, Indiana. A new committee has been organized and is preparing a new study guide for the long-standing "Biblical Literature" course offered in that state. Biblical Literature Committee, P.O. Box 2556, Fort Wayne, Indiana. 46807

Kansas City, Kansas. The Association of Theological Seminaries in the Kansas City Area is cooperating with schools, teachers, and teacher training institutions of that area to produce curricular materials which reflect the influences of religion and to train teachers in the use of these materials. Dr. Paul T. Losh, Central Baptist Theological Seminary, Kansas City, Kansas. 66102

Paducah, Kentucky. A full year course on Biblical history is offered at Paducah High School. Old Testament history and its relationship to secular history is stressed. A course outline is available for $2. Mr. Marvin Montgomery, 2835 Clark Street, Paducah, Kentucky. 42001

Newton, Massachusetts. The Bible is taught as a source book for the humanities in certain senior high English courses at Newton. The unit is the work of Mr. Thayer Warshaw, who reported his activities in the February 1964 issue of the *English Journal*. Material for the unit is now available in printed form titled, *Teaching Aids for Bible Unit*, from the Newton School Foundation, Inc., Newton, Massachusetts. 01355

Chelsea, Michigan. Techniques for integrating Biblical history into a junior high-school world history course have been developed at Chelsea. Mr. George Marshall, 750 Flanders Street, Chelsea, Michigan. 48118

Grand Rapids, Michigan. Financed by the U.S. Office of Education and working in cooperation with a public school system an organization is seeking to determine the role education plays in the development of student values. Curricular and informational material, workshops, and pilot projects are part of the program. Project on Student Values, 3860 Plainfield Road, NE, Grand Rapids, Michigan. 49505

Hudsonville, Michigan. A full year course on Biblical history is offered in a number of Hudsonville area high schools. The courses have a strong historical emphasis. A course outline is available. Mr. Robert W. Serum, Hudsonville High School, Hudsonville, Michigan. 49426

Royal Oak, Michigan. A unique course on comparative religions is offered at Royal Oak High School. The course includes the major religions of the world. An outline is available. Mr. Paul Will, Kimball High School, Royal Oak, Michigan. 48067

Bloomington, Minnesota. A significant unit on the Bible originally intended only for honor students has become part of the regular English program at Bloomington, Minnesota. Mrs. Betty Stainer, Lincoln High School, Bloomington, Minnesota. 55420

Detroit Lakes, Minnesota. A new course titled, "Man's Religious Experience," has been inaugurated at Senior High School. Mr. David L. Bender, Senior High School, Detroit Lakes, Minnesota. 56501

Columbus, Mississippi. A full year course on the Bible is offered at Columbia Senior High. The course is chronologically arranged with a literary emphasis. A course outline is available. Mrs. Evelyn D. Rogers, 624 Eighth Avenue, Columbus, Mississippi. 39701

Lincoln, Nebraska. "Hebrew literature" is the title of a seventh grade unit which considers the literary construction and influence of ancient Hebrew literature. There is both a student packet and a teacher packet available at 30¢ each from the Nebraska Curriculum Development Center, 208 Andrews Hall, University of Nebraska, Lincoln, Nebraska. 68508

Laconia, New Hampshire. A unit on the literature of the Bible is an integral part of the senior high English program at Laconia. Printed material is available. Miss Marie Forsberg, Laconia High School, Laconia, New Hampshire. 03264

Bound Brook, New Jersey. A six-week unit on selected passages from the Old Testament is included in the senior high English program at Bound Brook. The literary forms are stressed. Miss Susan Hill, Bound Brook High School, Bound Brook, New Jersey. 08805

Corning, New York. A new plan has just been inaugurated at Corning whereby students will receive high-school credit for work completed at the church. Mr. Charles H. Chase, 291 East First Street, Corning, New York. 14830

New York, New York. A program for the direct teaching of citizenship values in the elementary grades has been developed. Council for Citizenship Education, 122 E. 42nd Street, New York, N.Y. 10017

Burlington, North Carolina. The Bible Department of the North Carolina Education Association has produced a guide for the study of the Bible titled, "Suggested Five Year Program of Biblical Education for the Public Schools of North Carolina." A copy of the guide is available from the North Carolina Education Association, 111 West Morgan Street, Raleigh, North Carolina 27600. A detailed outline for the course is available from one of the teachers, Miss Mildred Kichline, Burlington High School, Burlington, North Carolina. 27215

Dayton, Ohio. A unique series of student-sponsored devotional programs is in operation at Fairview High School in Dayton. An outline describing the program and the materials used is available for $1.00. Mrs. Miriam Fabian, Fairview High School, Dayton, Ohio. 45400

Kent, Ohio. Kent State University offers two courses concerned with religion in the public school: Ed 661 "Teaching Moral and Spiritual Values in the Public Schools," and Ed 662 "Religion and the Public School." Kent State University, Kent, Ohio. 44240

Massillon, Ohio. A unit on the Bible as literature has been in the senior high-school English program at Massillon for many years. The program was reported on in the November, 1966, issue of the *English Journal.* An outline is available. Mr. R. Paul Hildebrand, 1121 Singing Brook Avenue. NW, Massillon, Ohio. 44646

Enid, Oklahoma. A course in the Bible is included in the senior high-school offerings at Enid. The course has a historical emphasis but includes literature study. A course outline is available. Mr. Stanley Jenkins, Enid High School, Enid, Oklahoma. 73701

Beaverton, Oregon. The English Department at Sunset High School has integrated selected Biblical passages throughout the entire senior high English program. A printed outline is available. Mr. Richard Uyesugi, Sunset High School, Beaverton, Oregon. 97005

Harrisburg, Pennsylvania. The Pennsylvania Humanities Commission has developed six experimental units on the humanities, the last of which is titled "Man's Relation to God." The historical development and the significant contributions of the major world religions are considered. The unit includes a bibliography, suggested resources, and study questions. The unit title for the six parts is "Universal Issues in Human Life," and it is available from the Department of Public Instruction, Commonwealth of Pennsylvania, Harrisburg, Pennsylvania. 17126

Rosemont, Pennsylvania. The Harriton High School has a unit on religion which uses the religious resources of the community. Mr. Donald P. Anderson, 600 N. Ithan Ave., Rosemont, Pennsylvania. 19010

University Park, Pennsylvania. A unit on religious literature is being developed at Penn State. This consists of the Old Testament plus three groups of religious writings coming from it—the New Testament, the rabbinic writings, and the Koran. Material will soon be available. Dr. John R. Whitney, 116 Sackett Bldg., Penn State University, University Park, Pennsylvania. 16802

Columbia, South Carolina. A full year course in the Bible has long been offered in South Carolina high schools. A detailed workbook has been prepared by one of the teachers, Miss Sara Overstreet, Box 3122, Columbia, South Carolina. 29203

Chattanooga, Tennessee. Full-credit courses in the Bible have been offered in Chattanooga public schools since the 1920's by a private organization. The courses are a part of the school program, while the teachers are selected and financed by the organization. Materials for most grade levels are available. Miss Mary Moore, 549 Crest Road, Chattanooga, Tennessee. 37400

Dallas, Texas. In the Dallas high schools credit is given for Bible study conducted on a cooperative basis. The teacher and classroom facilities are provided by religious groups in the community while the textbook and final tests are supplied by the school. The text books for the courses (*Bible Study Course, Old Testament* and *Bible Study Course, New Testament*) are available for $1 each from the Dallas Independent School District, Dallas, Texas. 75204

Swanton, Vermont. A unique combination of public and parochial education is being planned. The public and parochial elements will be combined in one building complex and administrative structure but will be financed and taught separately. Rev. John LaBrake, St. Anne's Academy, Swanton, Vermont. 05488

Richmond, Virginia. A Bible course has long been offered in Virginia high schools. Textbooks and other materials are available. Miss Elizabeth Longwell, 2321 Westwood Avenue, Richmond, Virginia. 23230

Seattle, Washington. A unit on the literature of the Bible in the senior high school has been developed at Seattle. Mr. Douglas Parris, Edmonds High School, Seattle, Washington. 98100

TOPICAL GUIDE

THE "Topical Guide" contains only a sampling of the resources and books that are listed in the last two chapters of this book. The number preceding each entry refers to the number under which the item appears in the last chapters. This guide lists items under twenty arbitrary subject areas which the public school teacher will recognize as pertinent to the school program.

Art   At every grade level and in almost every subject area the significance and themes of the great religious masterpieces are relevant. **Bible** As public schools move to include religious literature more significantly, items related to the Bible will be increasingly more useful. **Christmas** The great emphasis given to the Christmas season in our culture requires that the school have the best materials available in order to respond adequately. **Display** From time to time every teacher has responsibility for the school display cabinets, which on occasion may have a religious emphasis. **Drama** Religious drama has a role to play in the creative-expression programs of the public school. **Field Trip** Every community has religious field-trip possibilities. Many schools take a trip to the nation's capital, where items of religious significance should be noted. **Geography** As study of the nations of the world becomes more popular, the Bible lands assume a more significant position. **Hobby** A "hobby day" at school may find many pupils bringing stamps or coins or other items with religious connotations. The teacher who is aware of those connotations will be able to point them out to the student. **Jesus** As the study of religion and religious literature assumes a more prominent place in the school program, so will religious leaders. **Jewish Holidays** As we become a pluralistic society, it becomes important that we recognize and understand the major religious holidays of all groups. **Language** As foreign languages and the development of the English language are given greater attention in the public school the religious implications will also require consideration. **Literature** The religious influences on literature are overwhelming and need to be brought to the attention of pupils. **Music** Great music owes much to religious themes. **Paul** Because Paul brought Christianity to Europe, from which it spread to the Western Hemisphere, few persons in history have been more influential. **Projects** Both teacher and pupil are looking for new and novel projects. **Psalms** If an English program includes any of the Bible now, it is likely to be selections from the Psalms. The items listed here should be helpful in making the study of the Psalms more meaningful. **Recess** Listed here are religious items that may be used during recess or in other free time. **Religion** As the study of religion assumes a more significant place in the public school the items included here will be increasingly more useful. **Science** The religious implications in science are often neglected and need to be reconsidered. **Social**

Studies Many major world movements have profound religious significance which needs to be brought to the attention of pupils.
Thanksgiving The items listed here will be useful to the teacher who seeks to capture the original spirit of "Thanksgiving."

ART

15 Slide set of famous stained glass windows
30 Film "Michelangelo and His Art"
40 Filmstrip "Modern Art and the Gospel"
59 Filmstrip "Christmas in the Arts"
84 Filmstrip "Symbols of the Church"
87 Filmstrip using art to portray the Reformation
180 Print of Dali's "Christ of St. John"
182 Print of Michelangelo's "Pieta"
184 Special religious issue of periodical
186 "Paintings Depicting the Life of Christ"
190 Puzzle of the "Last Supper"
202 Art exhibit
209 Replica of Michelangelo's "Moses"
210 Mural on life of Jesus
227 Booklet on the witness of the arts
246 A full-color religious art catalog
389 Barbour and Barbour. RELIGIOUS IDEAS FOR ARTS AND CRAFTS
448 Eversole. CHRISTIAN FAITH AND CONTEMPORARY ART
475 Harned. THEOLOGY AND THE ARTS
527 Male. RELIGIOUS ART
531 Maus. THE CHURCH AND THE FINE ARTS
540 Mirsky. HOUSES OF GOD
551 Newton and Neil. 2,000 YEARS OF CHRISTIAN ART
575 Rest. OUR CHRISTIAN SYMBOLS
593 Short. THE GOSPEL ACCORDING TO PEANUTS
765 Kilby. CHRISTIANITY AND AESTHETICS
837 Wright. LET THE CHILDREN PAINT

BIBLE

16 Film on how our Bible came to us (also 43)
54 Filmstrip "Gateway to the Bible"
75 Filmstrip "Bible Cities"
76 Filmstrip on Dead Sea Scrolls
77 Filmstrip on life in Bible times
103, 108 The complete Bible on records
105 Record of 50 favorite chapters
107 Record of the more important Bible people, ideas, and events

119 Record of Bible stories for children (also 125–26)
200 Display of great Bibles of history
217 Notebook inserts on Biblical topics
219 A standardized Bible test
222 "Bible Search Series"
224 Poster on National Bible Week
238 Leaflets on the Bible
241–42 *National Geographic* articles on Palestine
243 *Life* magazine special Bible issue
251 Reprints
395 Barton. THE BOOK NOBODY KNOWS
399 Beegle. GOD'S WORD INTO ENGLISH
415 Cassels. YOUR BIBLE
427 Davies. INVITATION TO THE NEW TESTAMENT
433 Dennett. A GUIDE TO MODERN VERSIONS OF THE NEW TESTAMENT
473 Halley. BIBLE HANDBOOK
502 Keller. THE BIBLE AS HISTORY IN PICTURES
505 Kenyon. THE STORY OF THE BIBLE
581 Sandmel. THE HEBREW SCRIPTURES
621 Watts. OLD TESTAMENT TEACHING
624 Wegner. 6,000 YEARS OF THE BIBLE
815 Arch Books. BIBLE STORIES (for children)

CHRISTMAS

26 Film history of "Silent Night"
27 Film of Christmas customs
55 Filmstrip "The Other Wise Man"
56 Filmstrip "Christmas Songs in Foreign Languages"
58 Filmstrip on arts and crafts projects for specific holidays
59 Filmstrip "Christmas in the Arts"
65 Filmstrip dramatization of poem, "The Night Before Christmas"
66 Filmstrip adaptation of Dickens' "A Christmas Carol"
67 Filmstrip "Christmas with Our World Neighbors"
70 Filmstrip "The Story of Hanukkah and Christmas"
91 Filmstrip "The Story of Hanukkah"
101 Record of Handel's *Messiah*
133 Record "Christmas as It Happened"
135 Record of Christmas songs by Mormon Tabernacle Choir
214 A Christmas-Hanukkah play
215 Play based on Dickens' *Christmas Carol*
229 Book about postage stamps with Christmas significance
251 Reprints
576 Reynolds. CHRIST AND THE CAROLS
818 Dearmer *et al.* OXFORD BOOK OF CAROLS FOR SCHOOLS
835 Sawyer. JOY TO THE WORLD, CHRISTMAS LEGENDS

DISPLAY
170   Model of Gutenberg Press
171–76   Models of Biblical items
177   Elaborate model of Tabernacle
178   A mezzuzah
189   Bible balloons
208   Stereo discs
209   Replica of Michelangelo's "Moses"

DRAMA
118   Record of a characterization of the book of Job
121   Record of a characterization of the book of Job
214   A Christmas-Hanukkah play
215   Simple play based on Dickens' "Christmas Carol"
234   Booklet on the clergy in fiction and drama
235   Booklet on the Bible in fiction and drama
239   The death of Judas as a dramatic reading
383   Bachman and Brown. BETTER PLAYS FOR TODAY'S CHURCHES
398   Baxter. CONTEMPORARY THEATRE AND THE CHRISTIAN FAITH
410   Brown and Heltman. CHORAL READING FROM THE BIBLE
421   Corey. THE BOOK OF JOB
448   Eversole. CHRISTIAN FAITH AND THE CONTEMPORARY ARTS
526   MacLeish. J.B.
537   Merchant. CREED AND DRAMA
579   Rutenborn. THE SIGN OF JONAH
599   Speaight. CHRISTIAN THEATRE

FIELD TRIP
204–207   Field trip possibilities
14   Slide set "Leaders Under God"
33   Film "This is Our Heritage"
136   Record "Sacred Shrines of Washington"
230   Booklet on religious shrines in Washington

GEOGRAPHY
3   Slide set "Geographic Setting of Palestine"
11   Slide set "Temple Area"
74   Filmstrip "Geography of the Holy Land"
75   Filmstrip "Bible Cities"
92   Filmstrip "Israel: The Land and the People"
120   Record of songs about Biblical locations
241–42   *National Geographic* magazine articles on Palestine

251 Reprints
374 Adams. BIBLICAL BACKGROUNDS
388 Baly. THE GEOGRAPHY OF THE BIBLE
702 Kraeling. (RAND McNALLY BIBLE ATLAS)
704 Rowley. STUDENT'S BIBLE ATLAS
705 Stirling. AN ATLAS OF THE LIFE OF CHRIST
717 Anderson. (An atlas of Christianity in the Middle Ages and Reformation)

HOBBY

 35 Film on religious significance of postage stamps
166 "Widow's mite" coin
167 Sample packet of stamps
169 Biblical coins in replica
187 Print of section of Michelangelo's "Creation of Man" used on stamp
229 Booklet *Putting Christmas in Your Stamp Album*
236 Booklet *Moneys of the Bible*
247 Booklet *Religion on Stamps of the United States*
248 Booklet "A History of Religion on Postage Stamps"
251 Reprints
389 Barbour and Barbour. RELIGIOUS IDEAS FOR ARTS AND CRAFTS
779 Mueller. POSTAGE STAMPS AND CHRISTIANITY

JESUS

  6 Slide set "Crossing Palestine Following the Gospels"
 31 Film "Life of Christ in Art"
 82 Filmstrip "The Story of Jesus"
 94 Filmstrip "The Four Gospels"
101 Record of Handel's "Messiah"
127 Record "The Seven Last Words of Christ"
146 Charts on genealogy of Jesus (also 157)
149 Map of Palestine in Jesus' time
185 Contemporary paintings of Jesus
186 Jesus in famous paintings
191 Puzzle of map of Palestine in Jesus' time
210 Mural on life of Jesus
396 Barton. THE MAN NOBODY KNOWS
443 Edersheim. THE LIFE AND TIME OF JESUS THE MESSIAH
589 Shepard. THE CHRIST OF THE GOSPELS
600 Stalker. THE LIFE OF JESUS CHRIST
616 Trueblood. THE HUMOR OF CHRIST
661 Robertson. A HARMONY OF THE GOSPELS
797 Sandmel. WE JEWS AND JESUS

JEWISH HOLIDAYS

70 Filmstrip "The Story of Hanukkah and Christmas"
89–91 Filmstrips about Jewish holidays
132 Record "The Jewish Holiday Album"
140 Record "The Passover Seder Festival"
733 Cohen. A BASIC JEWISH ENCYCLOPEDIA
746 Finkelstein. THE BELIEFS AND PRACTICES OF JUDAISM
752 Goldberg. HOLIDAYS FOR AMERICAN JUDAISM
822 Goldberg. STORIES ABOUT JUDAISM
834 Rubin. A PICTURE DICTIONARY OF JEWISH LIFE

LANGUAGE

16 Film on how our Bible came to us
56 Filmstrip "Christmas Songs in Foreign Languages"
99 Record "Abba Eban Reads from the Psalms"
139 Tape showing language change in the Bible
225 Special Bibles in Braille, foreign languages, etc.
251 Reprints
377 American Bible Society. A READY-REFERENCE HISTORY OF THE ENGLISH BIBLE
445 Elliot. THE LANGUAGE OF THE KING JAMES BIBLE
552 Nida. GOD'S WORD IN MAN'S LANGUAGE

LITERATURE

5 Slide set on Biblical themes
9 Slide set including "Inn of the Good Samaritan"
97 Record "The Holy War"
100 Record of modern songs including an adaptation of Ecclesiastes
115 Record of inspirational meditation themes from popular authors
116 Record of readings from *Paradise Lost*
117 Record of readings from books of Judith and Ruth
118 Record of a dramatization of the Book of Job
121 Record of a dramatization of the Book of Job
123 Record of the Beatitudes
131 Record "The Five Books of Moses"
200 Facsimile pages from historic Bibles
201 Posters about English Bibles
233 A bibliography on the infiuence of Bible on English language
234 Booklet on the clergy in fiction and drama
235 Booklet on the Bible in fiction and drama
257 A checklist of Biblical novels
243 LIFE magazine's special Bible issue
251 Reprints
252 Hawthorne's *The Celestial Railroad*
373 Ackerman. ON TEACHING THE BIBLE AS LITERATURE

401 Belford. RELIGIOUS DIMENSIONS IN LITERATURE (Series)
409 Brooks. THE HIDDEN GOD
416 Chase. THE BIBLE AND THE COMMON READER
426 Davies. A MIRROR OF THE MINISTRY IN MODERN NOVELS
454 Frank and Hogan. OBSCENITY, THE LAW, AND THE ENGLISH TEACHER
456 Frye. SHAKESPEARE AND CHRISTIAN DOCTRINE
457 Fulghum. DICTIONARY OF BIBLICAL ALLUSIONS IN ENGLISH LITERATURE
466 Good. IRONY IN THE OLD TESTAMENT
468 Gordis. THE BOOK OF GOD AND MAN: A STUDY OF JOB
474 Hamilton. IN SEARCH OF CONTEMPORARY MAN
486 Hopper. SPIRITUAL PROBLEMS IN CONTEMPORARY LITERATURE
489 Howse. SPIRITUAL VALUES IN SHAKESPEARE
496 Jellema. CONTEMPORARY WRITERS IN CHRISTIAN PERSPECTIVE (Series)
524 Lynch. CHRIST AND APOLLO
530 May. SYMBOLISM IN RELIGION AND LITERATURE
543 Mosley. PSEUDONYMS OF CHRIST IN THE MODERN NOVEL
546 Murdock. LITERATURE AND THEOLOGY IN COLONIAL NEW ENGLAND
587 Scott. THE CLIMATE OF FAITH IN MODERN LITERATURE
602 Stewart. AMERICAN LITERATURE AND CHRISTIAN DOCTRINE
607 TeSelle. LITERATURE AND THE CHRISTIAN LIFE

MUSIC

26 Film history of "Silent Night"
57 Filmstrip "The Story of Handel's Messiah"
59 Filmstrip on Christmas in art, with musical background
71 Filmstrip "Stories About Our Christmas Carols"
73 Filmstrip "Christmas Songs and Carols"
100 Record of modern songs, including an adaptation of Ecclesiastes
101 Record of Handel's "Messiah"
111 Record of spirituals
112 Record of spirituals by Robert Shaw Chorale
120 Record of songs about Biblical locations
122 Record of songs based on the Psalms
128 Record "The Majesty of Sacred Music"
251 Reprints

576   Reynolds. CHRIST AND THE CAROLS
818   Dearmer *et al.* OXFORD BOOK OF CAROLS FOR SCHOOLS

PAUL
13   Slide "Color Map of Paul's Routes"
51   Filmstrip on Paul's teacher, Hillel
83   Filmstrip "The Story of Paul"
96   Record "A Letter from Paul"
141   Record "Paul Speaks"
150   Map of Paul's journeys
164   Map and chart of Book of Acts
393   Barnes. THE APOSTLE PAUL
419   Conybeare and Howson. THE LIFE AND EPISTLES OF ST. PAUL

PROJECTS
163   Contour map of Palestine for painting
170   Model of Gutenberg Press
171–76   Models of Biblical items
177   Elaborate model of Tabernacle
389   Barbour and Barbour. RELIGIOUS IDEAS FOR ARTS AND CRAFTS

PSALMS
4   Slides illustrating the 23rd Psalm
99   Record "Abba Eban Reads from the Psalms"
104   Record of all the Psalms
106   Record of Psalms of Thanksgiving
122   Record of songs based on the Psalms
129   Record "The Psalms and the Tale of David"
240   Booklet of a Nevada (Basgue) Shepherd's interpretation of 23rd Psalm
251   Reprints
438   Drijvers. THE PSALMS; THEIR STRUCTURE AND MEANING
517   Lewis. REFLECTION ON THE PSALMS

RECESS
189–96   Items for use during nonstudy hours
223   Bible coloring books
226   Lunchroom items
244   Crossword puzzles with Biblical terms
245   Booklet of games with Biblical terms
836   White. THROUGH THE BIBLE WITH FINGER PLAYS
837   Wright. LET THE CHILDREN PAINT

RELIGION

SCIENCE

SOCIAL STUDIES

THANKSGIVING

181 Print of Boughton's famous "Pilgrims Going to Church"
829 Luckhardt. THANKSGIVING FEAST AND FESTIVAL

Relevant Organizations

American Academy of Religion, Wilson College, Chambersburg, Pa. 17201

American Bible Society, 1865 Broadway, New York, N.Y. 10023

American Civil Liberties Union, 156 Fifth Ave., New York, N.Y. 10010

American Jewish Congress, 15 East 84th St., New York, N.Y. 10028

Americans United for Separation of Church and State, 1633 Mass. Ave., N.W., Washington, D.C. 20036

Association of Christian Educators, Box 56, Glen Mills, Pa. 19342

Bible Communications Congress, 1319 F Street NW, Suite 1011, Washington, D.C. 20004

Bible Meditation League, P.O. Box 477, Columbus, Ohio 43200

B'nai B'rith, 1640 Rhode Island Ave., NW, Washington, D.C. 20036

Catholic Biblical Association, Catholic University, Washington, D.C. 20017

Character Research Project, Union College, Schenectady, N.Y. 12308

Child Evangelism Fellowship, Box 1156, Grand Rapids, Mich. 49501

Christian Schools Service, Inc., 10119 Lafayette Ave., Chicago, Ill. 60628

Christian Service Corps, 1501–11th St. NW, Washington, D.C. 20001

Collectors of Religion on Stamps, 1222 Travis Street, LaCrosse, Wis. 54601

Commission on Church and Public Education, 475 Riverside Drive, New York, N.Y. 10027

Conference on Christianity and Literature, 36 Cupsaw Ave., Ringwood, N. J. 07456

Confraternity of Christian Doctrine, 1312 Massachusetts Ave., NW, Washington, D.C. 20005

Constitutional Prayer Foundation, 903 Munsey Bldg., Baltimore, Md. 21202

Council for Citizenship Education, 122 East 42nd St., New York, N.Y. 10017

Council for Religion in Independent Schools, 475 Riverside Drive, New York, N.Y. 10027

Educational Communications Association, 704 National Press Building, Washington, D.C. 20004

Educational Council to Preserve the Nation's Religious Heritage, P.O. Box 5436, Fayetteville, N.C. 28302

Educational Research Council of America, Rockefeller Building, Cleveland, Ohio 44113

Evangelical Theological Society, Wheaton College, Wheaton, Ill. 60187

Fourth R Foundation, 4603 Greenwood, Lincoln, Neb. 68504

Gideons International, 2900 Lebanon Road, Nashville, Tenn. 37214

Inspirational Tape Library, 616 N. Third Street, Phoenix, Ariz. 85004

Institute for Social Studies, Paterson State College, Wayne, N.J. 07473

International Catholic Biblical Society, Derby, N.Y. 14047

International Christian Youth, Collingswood, N.J. 08108

International Society of Bible Collectors, 13800 Biola Ave., LaMirada, Calif. 90638

Journal of Church and State, Box 258, Baylor University, Waco, Texas 76703

Laymen's National Committee, 71 West 23rd St., New York, N.Y. 10010

Michigan Teachers Christian Fellowship, 2123 Hazelwood, Saginaw, Mich. 48601

National Association of Christian Schools, Box 28, Wheaton, Ill. 60188

National Conference of Christians and Jews, 43 W. 57th St., New York, N.Y. 10019

National Educators Fellowship, Box 243, South Pasadena, Calif. 91030

National Student Christian Federation, 475 Riverside Drive, New York, N.Y. 10027

National Union of Christian Schools, 865–28th St., SE, Grand Rapids, Mich. 49508

Pocket Testament League, 49 Honeck St., Englewood, N.J. 07631

Project Prayer, 1717 N. Vine Street, Hollywood, Calif. 90028

Project on Student Values, 3860 Plainfield NE, Grand Rapids, Mich. 49505

Religion in American Life, 184 Fifth Avenue, New York, N.Y. 10010

Religion and the Public Order, Villanova University, Villanova, Pa. 19085

Religious Education Association, 545 W. 111th St., New York, N.Y. 10025

Religious Heritage of America, 2430 Pennsylvania Ave. NW, Washington, D.C. 20037

Religious Instruction Association, Inc., 4001 Fairfield Ave., Fort Wayne, Ind. 46807

Restore School Voluntary Prayer, 910 East Street, Three Rivers, Mich. 49093

Service Center for Teachers of History, 400 A Street SE, Washington, D.C. 20003

Society of Biblical Literature, Garrett Institute, Evanston, Ill. 60201

Society for Religion in Higher Education, 400 Prospect St., New Haven, Conn. 06511

U. S. School Character Guidance Committee, Box 44, Algonquin, Ill. 60102

University Christian Movement, 475 Riverside Drive, Room 758, New York, N.Y. 10027

World Jewish Bible Society Foundation, 69 W. Washington St., Chicago, Ill. 60602

Youth Club Programs, Inc., 2500 McCrady, Pittsburg, Pa. 15235

Youth for the Voluntary Prayer Amendment, 4723 Richmond, Houston, Texas 77027

II AUDIO-VISUAL RESOURCES

5 WHAT MATERIALS ARE AVAILABLE?

THE RESOURCES that follow are adaptable to public school use in the study of religion and religious literature. The key word is "adaptable." None of them is good or bad, legal or illegal, in itself. In the hands of the competent teacher, following accepted guidelines of good education, the resources listed here will be tools for greater teaching efficiency. Obviously not all, nor even the best, resources are listed. An attempt was made to have the list representative of the vast and varied pool of available materials with religious significance. Every good teacher will find many more of his own. The "Topical Guide" at the end of Chapter 4 gives a few suggested uses and combinations of these resources, including books from the Bibliography.

Sources for materials are readily available. The suppliers of the art resources itemized here have complete catalogs of their offerings. The religious section of any record shop contains recordings usable in the classroom. Churches and religious colleges often have areas and exhibits worthy of a field trip. Projected visual aids are frequently available through college departments, denominational offices, church associations, and individual churches. No consideration of audio-visual material would be complete without referring to the AUDIO-VISUAL RESOURCE GUIDE. This book, available in most libraries, gives a full annotation and evaluation for virtually every audio-visual produced. It may be purchased for $3.95 from the Broadcasting and Film Commission, 475 Riverside Drive, New York, N.Y. 10027.

Prices quoted as of date of publication of list. Where an order number is given, this should be used in sending for materials.

Slides

1   Approximately 50 full-color, 2″ x 2″ slides of Michelangelo's work in the Sistine Chapel are available. Included are general scenes and close-ups of the more important works. Write for details.

European Art Color Slide Co., 120 West 70th St., New York, N.Y. 10023

2   "Temple Slides" is a set of 5 slides of a model of the Temple of Jerusalem. The model was on display in the Judaism Pavilion at the World Exhibition in Montreal, Canada, in 1967. $2.25 per set.

Lazar Halberthal, 5344 MacDonald Ave., Montreal, Canada.

3   "Holy Land Tour" is a set of 100 slides that give comprehensive coverage of the life and scenes of the Holy Land. $25.00.

Grason, Inc., 1300 Harmon Place, Minneapolis, Minn. 55403

4   "The Twenty-Third Psalm" is a slide set of 14 world-famous color photographs of life in Palestine to illustrate the Psalms. A manual providing information and commentary on each slide comes with the set. $5.00 per set ($3.50 in filmstrip).

Matson Photo Service, 1428 South Marengo St., Alhambra, Calif. 91803

5   A series of slide sets on Biblical themes is available. Typical titles are: "The Twenty-Third Psalm" (slides $5.00, filmstrip $3.50), "Flowers of Palestine" (slides $4.50, filmstrip $3.00), "Blue Galilee" (slides $14.50, filmstrip $6.50), "Babylon" (slides $3.50), "Ruth the Moabitess" (slides $10.00), and "Life of Jesus of Nazareth" (slides $14.50). A free catalog is available.

Matson Photo Service, 1428 South Marengo St., Alhambra, Calif. 91803

6   "Crossing Palestine Following the Gospels" is an excellent set of 150 slides prepared by a scholarly Belgian monk. The slides follow the life of Christ. A booklet describing the significance of each slide accompanies the set. $30.00 per set postpaid.

Ant. Van Overschelde, Boechout (Antwerpen), Belgium.

7   "Holy Land: Then and Now" is a series of 11 sets covering the entire Bible. Reconstructions, specially prepared maps, and select photos are used. Each set consists of 40 slides with printed narration. $19.95 per set.

Wolfe Worldwide Films, 1657 Sawtelle Blvd., Los Angeles, Calif. 90025

8   Produced for an experimental course in the history of religion at Syracuse University, surveying Buddhism, Hinduism, Jainism, Sikhism, Confucianism, Taoism, and Shintoism, are over 650 slides bearing terms, proper names, and diagrams especially de-

signed for courses in the history of religions. A standard set of 150 slides is available for $35.00.

Center for Instructional Communications, Syracuse University, Syracuse, N.Y. 13210

9 "Wilderness of Judah, Jordan" (JD-119) is a 3-slide set, one slide of which pictures the Inn of the Good Samaritan. 75¢ per set.

Pana-Vue, Box 444, Portland, Ore. 97207

10 "Crafts of Early Christians" (AH-1102). $11.40 per set.

American Library Color Slide Co., Inc., 305 East 45th St., N.Y. 10017

11 "Temple Area" (JD-106) is a 3-slide set picturing the Temple grounds and the Mount of Olives. 75¢ per set.

Pana-Vue, Box 444, Portland, Ore. 97207

12 Maps on slides may be obtained individually from slide sets. From the slide set "Geographic" 3 maps are available: "Map of the Near East," slide No. 1; "Relief Map of Palestine," slide No. 2; and "Cross Section of Palestine Indicating Extreme Levels," slide No. 3. From the set "Bible Prophecies" 2 maps are available: "Map of Palestine," slide No. 1 and "Relief Map of Jerusalem," slide No. 24. 50¢ per slide. Order by slide set title and slide number.

Matson Photo Service, 1428 South Marengo St., Alhambra, Calif. 91803

13 "Color Map of Paul's Routes" (T 93). 50¢.

Matson Photo Service, 1428 South Marengo St., Alhambra, Calif. 91803

14 "Leaders Under God" is a set of 40 colored slides of the great religious shrines in the nation's capital, many of them associated intimately with memories of our Presidents and other leaders who have shaped our heritage. $20.00 (includes guidebook).

Educational Communication Association, 143 North Meridian St., Indianapolis, Ind. 46204

15 "The Jerusalem Windows" is a set of 30 slides of the stained glass windows of the twelve tribes designed by Marc Chagall. A booklet accompanying the set describes each window and its symbolism. $37.50.

Sandak, Inc., 4 East 48th St., New York, N.Y. 10017

See also Nos. 531 and 800 in the Bibliography.

Films

16 *Our Bible: How It Came to Us* (18901) is a documentary motion picture which traces the history and development of the Bible from the first century A.D. up to the present time. It shows the Scriptures in use in Palestine in the time of Jesus and how

the letters of Paul and the Gospels were written and used in the church. It provides information on the translation of the Bible into Latin, the spoken languages of Europe, and finally English. Rental is $22.50.

American Bible Society, P.O. Box 100, Ansonia Station, New York, N.Y. 10023

17 "Historic Rome" (3804) is an 8mm color film well suited for background information to New Testament study. $16.00 per print.

Communication Films, 870 Monterey Pass Road, Monterey Park, Calif. 91754

18 "The Giant Buddhas of Afghanistan" (3016) is an 8mm color film appropriate to accompany a study of Buddhism or the Orient. $16.00 per print.

Communication Films, 870 Monterey Pass Road, Monterey Park, Calif. 91754

19 *The Great Religions* is a film series on three world religions: Hinduism, Buddhism, and Islam. The holy river Ganges, the contemplative monk, and the pilgrimage to Mecca are the visible manifestations of worship vividly recorded on film. The sequences are sympathetic in approach, objective in analysis. The camera dramatizes the meaning and significance of each faith in terms of its place in the life of the believer. Available by purchase or rental.

McGraw-Hill, Inc., 330 West 42nd St., New York, N.Y. 10036

20 *The Stones Cry Out* is the filmed record of a pioneer archaeological expedition revealing sites of ancient and Biblical significance. It is a 42-minute full-color print. $12.50 rental fee.

Moody Institute of Science, 12000 East Washington Blvd., Whittier, Calif. 90606

21 *The Holy Roman Empire* describes how an enormous section of western Europe was united under the idea of a single Christian government. Costumed reenactments with dialogue dramatize the divisions of power and the conflict between popes and emperors, as well as the factors that led to the eventual decay of the Empire. $150.00. Available from film rental libraries.

Coronet Instructional Films, 65 E. South Water St., Chicago, Ill. 60601

22 *Christianity in World History* uses historic sites in Italy, the Holy Land, and Turkey to provide the setting for a study of Christianity as a political, cultural, and moral movement. Analyzing the rapid growth from its beginnings under the Roman Empire to the schism between the churches of East and West in 1054 A.D., this film stresses the role of Christianity as a powerful force in the emergence of modern Europe. $150.00. Available from film rental libraries.

Coronet Instructional Films, 65 E. South Water St., Chicago, Ill. 60601

23 *The Holy Land: Background for History and Religion* uses the geography, history, and literature of ancient Palestine to present scenes where important Biblical events took place. $120.00. Available from film rental libraries.

Coronet Instructional Films, 65 E. South Water St., Chicago, Ill. 60601

24 *The Buddhist World* uses scenes from India, Thailand, Japan, and Tibet to review the origins of Buddhism through the life, work, and philosophy of Gautama Buddha. Presented are the major tenets of Buddhist belief and the influence of Buddhism on countries where it is practiced. $120.00. Available from film rental libraries.

Coronet Instructional Films, 65 E. South Water St., Chicago, Ill. 60601

25 *The Hindu World* is an historical and cultural survey of Hinduism set against a background of ancient temples, statues, and scenes of Hindu religious rites. The film stresses the various mental and physical disciplines called "yoga," through which Hindus seek eternal union with Brahma, the universal spirit of God. Also treated are the caste system and reincarnation. $120.00. Available from film rental libraries.

Coronet Instructional Films, 65 E. South Water St., Chicago, Ill. 60601

26 *Silent Night: Story of the Christmas Carol* was filmed in Austria and presents the history of the most inspiring of all Christmas carols. We see how a poem on the beauty of the Christmas season was later set to music, and how it traveled from the small, remote villages of the Alps to become the universal symbol of the Christmas spirit. $150.00. Available from film rental libraries.

Coronet Instructional Films, 65 E. South Water St., Chicago, Ill. 60601

27 *Christmas Customs Near and Far* relates the origins of many of our Christmas customs. Children of German, Swedish, Mexican, Italian, and Chinese descent enact typical Christmas celebrations of those countries. $150.00. Available from film rental libraries.

Coronet Instructional Films, 65 E. South Water St., Chicago, Ill. 60601

28 *Life in Ancient Rome: The Family* was filmed in Rome to portray the activities of a family on a typical day in ancient Rome. $120.00 Available from film rental libraries.

Coronet Instructional Films, 65 E. South Water St., Chicago, Ill. 60601

29 *William Penn and the Quakers* portrays the Quaker struggle for

religious freedom and its effect on Pennsylvania. $120.00. Available from film rental libraries.

Coronet Instructional Films, 65 E. South Water St., Chicago, Ill. 60601

30 *Michelangelo and His Art* uses photographs and analysis to study such works as the "David," "Pieta," and "Moses," the figures of the Medici Chapel, and the "Deposition." $180.00. Available from film rental libraries.

Coronet Instructional Films, 65 E. South Water St., Chicago, Ill. 60601

31 *The Life of Christ in Art* uses paintings from seven centuries of religious art to depict significant events in the life of Christ. Paintings are accompanied by Biblical quotations. (Protestant film uses Revised Standard Version, Catholic film uses Confraternity Version) $240.00. Available from film rental libraries.

Coronet Instructional Films, 65 E. South Water St., Chicago, Ill. 60601

32 *The Reformation* explains the Reformation in terms of the church, the cultural rebirth brought about by the Renaissance, the emergence of national states, and new interpretations of the Scriptures. Such figures as Calvin, Zwingli, and Knox are recognized, while the film devotes special attention to Martin Luther and the Protestant Reformation in Germany. $150.00. Available from film rental libraries.

Coronet Instructional Films, 65 E. South Water St., Chicago, Ill. 60601

33 *This Is Our Heritage* is a 20-minute, 16mm color film featuring two young people touring America's religious shrines in Washington, D.C. They see the original historic freedom documents and visit the places of worship of our nation's leaders of all faiths, past and present. This is a documentary with musical background, filmed on location. $200.00 purchase. $15.00 rental. (An accompanying guidebook is available for $1.00.)

Educational Communication Association, 143 North Meridian St., Indianapolis, Ind. 46204

34 *The Book and the Idol* is a 15-minute, 16mm color film using dramatic portrayal of archaeological artifacts to trace the emergence of monotheism in the Judeo-Christian heritage and its conflict with paganism in early civilization in Israel. The film displays many ancient and revered holy objects. $125.00. It may be borrowed for a nominal service charge from the ADL regional office nearest you. Write for full information.

Anti-Defamation League, 315 Lexington Ave., New York, N.Y. 10016

35 *A Stamp is Born* is a unique and beautiful 14-minute, 16mm film on the creation of postage stamps in Israel. By utilization of postage stamps as mirrors of various aspects of life in Israel,

the sequence covers Israel's archaeological sites, its landscapes, and its historic landmarks. $85.00. The film may be borrowed for a nominal service charge from the ADL regional office nearest you. Write for full information.

Anti-Defamation League, 315 Lexington Ave., New York, N.Y. 10016

36   *The Wilderness of Zin* is a 22-minute, 16mm dramatic film story showing how the Bible is used by the eminent archaeologist Dr. Nelson Glueck to discover water resources and open travel routes in Israel's barren Negev. $135.00. The film may be borrowed for a nominal service charge from the ADL regional office nearest you. Write for full information.

Anti-Defamation League, 315 Lexington Ave., New York, N.Y. 10016

37   *Archeology and the Living New Testament* is a 30-minute color film picturing the areas made famous by the Dead Sea Scrolls, sites significant to the New Testament story, and areas known to Paul, Philip, and other early Christians. $12.00 rental.

Film Services, 3419 W. Magnolia Ave., Burbank, Calif. 91505

Filmstrips

38   "The Story of the Christian Church" is a 54-frame filmstrip which presents church history in five divisions—the Early Church, the Medieval Period, Pre-Reformation, Protestant Movement, and the Last Century. $3.50.

United Church Press, 1505 Race Street, Philadelphia, Pa. 19102

39   "Daily Life in Old Testament Times" is a set of 3 filmstrips giving a panorama of life in the Old Testament by three major periods—Nomad World, Village Life, and City World. Stories are presented of three different families as they react in these three worlds. $15.00 per set.

United Church Press, 1505 Race Street, Philadelphia, Pa. 19102

40   "Modern Art and the Gospel" is a 76-frame color filmstrip that uses the work of many artists to reveal the dehumanization of man through technological, cultural, and social changes of history. The work of famous artists is shown to reveal man's emotions. Complete with record, script, and guide. $15.00.

American Baptist Literature, Valley Forge, Pa. 19481

41   "The Bible and the Presidents" (19002) is a series of 4 filmstrips pointing up the impact of Bible on the lives of some of our greatest Presidents—Washington, Jefferson, Lincoln, and Theodore Roosevelt. Each strip consists of approximately 55 frames and comes with both script and record. $25.00 per set. (Available individually at $9.00 per strip.)

American Bible Society, P.O. Box 100, Ansonia Station, New York, N.Y. 10023

42 "Saga of the Bible" (19001) is a filmstrip which portrays many important events in the development of the Bible and its influence on the history of America. The strip contains 60 frames and comes with both script and record. $6.50 per set.

American Bible Society, P.O. Box 100, Ansonia Station, New York, N.Y. 10023

43 "How Our Bible Came to Us" (19009) is a set of 4 filmstrips prepared from specially selected full-color paintings and photographs based on scenes from the award-winning film, "Our Bible: How it Came to Us." Set of 4 strips with a total of 159 frames, each strip with an accompanying 33-rpm record, script, and teacher's guide. $15 per set.

American Bible Society, P.O. Box 100, Ansonia Station, New York, N.Y. 10023

44 "The Tabernacle as Described in the Bible" (506430) is a filmstrip based on drawings and photographs of scenes in the world-famous model of the Tabernacle in Amsterdam's Museum for Biblical Antiquities. This unusual filmstrip illuminates many customs of the Hebrews during Biblical times and traces development of worship and sacrifice in the Tabernacle. $7.50 includes guidebook.

Union of American Hebrew Congregations, 838 Fifth Ave., New York, N.Y. 10021

45 "Great Stories From the Old Testament" (9060) and "Great Stories from the New Testament" (9070) are two sets of 8 filmstrips each. $48.00 per set includes teacher's guide and reading script.

Encyclopedia Britannica, 425 N. Michigan Ave., Chicago, Ill. 60611

46 "Great Stories from the Book of Acts" (9140) is a 6-set series of filmstrips covering events in the lives of Stephen, Philip, Peter, and Paul. $36.00 per series.

Encyclopedia Britannica, 425 N. Michigan Ave., Chicago, Ill. 60611

47 "The Holy Mass" (8760) is a filmstrip depicting the significance of the acts of the Mass. $6.00 per strip.

Encyclopedia Britannica, 425 N. Michigan Ave., Chicago, Ill. 60611

48 "Early History of the Church" (9250) is an 8-set series of strips covering church history from Jesus' time to the imprisonment of Paul. Comes with reading script booklet. $48.00 per series.

Encyclopedia Britannica, 425 N. Michigan Ave., Chicago, Ill. 60611

49 "Thanksgiving Day" (7840) is a filmstrip giving the historical events behind this national holiday. $6.00 per strip.

Encyclopedia Britannica, 425 N. Michigan Ave., Chicago, Ill. 60611

50 "Ancient Rome" (10860) is a series of 5 filmstrips spanning the panorama of daily life in ancient Rome. Individual titles are (1) "Great Accomplishments of the Roman Empire"; (2) "Julius Caesar: Politician and Dictator"; (3) Living in Ancient Rome"; (4) "Two Boys in Ancient Rome"; and (5) "Architecture of Rome." $6.00 per strip, $30.00 per set of 5.

Encyclopedia Britannica, 425 N. Michigan Ave., Chicago, Ill. 60611

51 "Hillel: Teacher of Love" (506400) is a filmstrip on the life and work of the great Hillel of Jerusalem. $7.50 includes guidebook.

Union of American Hebrew Congregations, 838 Fifth Ave., New York, N.Y. 10021

52 "The Early Christians" shows Peter and Paul and the progress of the Christians and their church. The filmstrip is one in a 5-part series titled, "Rome: The Eternal City." $6.00 per strip, $25.00 per series.

Life Filmstrip, Time & Life Bldg., Rockefeller Center, New York, N.Y. 10020

53 "World's Great Religions" is a 6-part series with guidebook. Individual titles are: (1) "Hinduism," (2) "Buddhism," (3) "Confucianism and Taoism," (4) "Islam," (5) "Judaism," and (6) "Christianity." $30.00 per series, $6.00 per individual title.

Life Filmstrip, Time & Life Bldg., Rockefeller Center, New York, N.Y. 10020

54 *Gateway to the Bible* is a series of 54 color filmstrips with 27 accompanying records covering the entire Bible. The total cost with metal file cabinet is $315.00. Items are available separately. One record with two accompanying filmstrips is $13.50. Write for descriptive catalog.

Eye Gate House, Inc., 146 Archer Ave., Jamaica, New York, N.Y. 11435

55 "The Other Wise Man" (850–11R) is the story of the fourth wise man. When the three wise men left him behind he spent a lifetime searching for Jesus. He finally found and recognized him even though he had never seen His face before. This adaptation of Henry Van Dyke's famous tale is narrated by Franklin McCormick. The strip comes with record and guidebook. $8.50 per set.

Society for Visual Education, Inc., 1345 Diversey Parkway, Chicago, Ill. 60614

56 "Christmas Songs in Foreign Languages" (847-SR) is a set of 4 filmstrips in French, German, Spanish, and Latin presenting both carols traditional to the country and songs that have well-known English versions. As the lyrics appear on the screen the recorded carol is sung with organ accompaniment. $23.50 per

set includes record and guidbook. (Individual titles available at $8.00 per title.)

Society for Visual Education, Inc., 1345 Diversey Parkway, Chicago, Ill. 60614

57 "The Story of Handel's *Messiah*" (860-5R) portrays the dramatic story of Handel's life and the inspiration, composition, and premiere performance of this masterwork of religious music. A study of the music and the Scriptures on which it is based. $12.50 per set includes record and teacher's guide.

Society for Visual Education, Inc., 1345 Diversey Parkway, Chicago, Ill. 60614

58 "Holiday Art Activities" (656–S) is a set of 6 filmstrips illustrating arts and crafts projects. Photographs of children at work encourage students to express their own creativity. The individual titles are: (1) "Thanksgiving," (2) "Christmas," (3) "St. Valentine's Day," (4) "Easter," (5) "Mother's Day," and (6) "Halloween." $27.00 per set of 6, $5.00 per individual title.

Society for Visual Education, Inc. 1345 Diversey Parkway, Chicago, Ill. 60614

59 "Christmas in the Arts" (C729–2R) is a portrayal of 43 artistic masterpieces in full color. Included are Angelico's "Annunciation," Van Eyck's "Annunciation," and Rembrandt's "Visitation." The accompanying record features music from Handel's *Messiah* and Bach's "Magnificat." $10.00 per set includes record and guidebook.

Society for Visual Education, Inc., 1345 Diversey Parkway, Chicago, Ill. 60614

60 "Why We Have Thanksgiving" (247–1) traces thanksgiving celebrations in Old Testament feasts and Greek festivals, as well as other thanksgiving customs. The Pilgrim celebration and holiday we know today is pictured. $6.00 per filmstrip.

Society for Visual Education, Inc., 1345 Diversey Parkway, Chicago, Ill. 60614

61 "The Story of Thanksgiving" (246–1) relates the story of the Pilgrims' landing and their first year in America. The first Thanksgiving is reenacted. $5.00 per filmstrip.

Society for Visual Education, Inc. 1345 Diversey Parkway, Chicago, Ill. 60614

62 "Mary's Pilgrim Thanksgiving" (860–7) is a documentary based on the first Thanksgiving as recorded in William Bradford's HISTORY OF PLYMOUTH PLANTATION. $6.00 per filmstrip.

Society for Visual Education, Inc., 1345 Diversey Parkway, Chicago, Ill. 60614

63 "Squanto and the First Thanksgiving" (860–15R) dramatizes the friendship between the Pilgrims and the Indians through the authentic story of Squanto, a brave who had much to do with

the Pilgrims' success in establishing Plymouth colony. $9.00 includes records and guidebook.

Society for Visual Education, Inc., 1345 Diversey Parkway, Chicago, Ill. 60614

64 "How We Got Our Easter Customs" and "Easter Around the World" (862–SR) are two filmstrips showing the historical development of Easter customs and current Easter customs around the world. $13.50 includes record and guidebook.

Society for Visual Education, Inc., 1345 Diversey Parkway, Chicago, Ill. 60614

65 "The Night Before Christmas" (860–20R) is a filmstrip presentation of Clement Clarke Moore's much-loved Christmas poem. $6.50 with record and guidebook.

Society for Visual Education, Inc., 1345 Diversey Parkway, Chicago, Ill. 60614

66 "A Christmas Carol" (850–6R). This filmstrip is an adaptation of Dickens' unforgettable Christmas fantasy. $10.50 with record and guidebook.

Society for Visual Education, Inc., 1345 Diversey Parkway, Chicago, Ill. 60614

67 "Christmas with Our World Neighbors" (848–SAE) is a 4-set series featuring photos and musical background, recorded on the scene, of Christmas celebrations in Germany, Mexico, England, and Norway. Comes with records and teacher's guide. $27.00 per series. (Individual titles available at $9.00 per title.)

Society for Visual Education, Inc., 1345 Diversey Parkway, Chicago, Ill. 60614

68 "How We Got Our Christmas Customs" (860–3R) relates the origin of hymns and carols, the crèche, the Christmas tree, decorations, gifts, St. Nicholas, Santa Claus, and the Christmas card. The various customs are related to the true meaning of Christmas. $10.00 per set includes record.

Society for Visual Education, Inc., 1345 Diversey Parkway, Chicago, Ill. 60614

69 "Christmas Around the World" (D 850–19R) shows how Christmas is celebrated around the world and gives glimpses of unusual customs in the United States. $10.00 per set includes record.

Society for Visual Education, Inc., 1345 Diversey Parkway, Chicago, Ill. 60614

70 "The Story of Hanukkah and Christmas" (860–28R). Two boys, Bernie and Bill, a Jew and a Christian, celebrate the holidays of their respective faiths. Bernie lights the Menorah and sings Hanukkah songs while Bill decorates the tree and sings carols. The historical background and meaningful traditions of each faith are authentically traced. $10.00 per set includes record and guidebook.

Society for Visual Education, Inc., 1345 Diversey Parkway, Chicago, Ill. 60614

71 "Stories About Our Christmas Carols" (K–11) relates the development of hymns and carols using 4 Christmas songs: "Away in a Manger," "We Three Kings of Orient Are," "O Come, All Ye Faithful," and "Silent Night, Holy Night." $10.00 includes record and guidebook.

Family Films, 5823 Santa Monica Blvd., Hollywood, Calif. 90038

72 "Stories About Our Christmas Traditions" (K–10) uses a typical family setting to relate the origin and meaning of the crèche, Christmas tree, holly, mistletoe, poinsettias, gifts, St. Nicholas, the yule log, and other traditions. $10.00 includes record and guidebook.

Family Films, 5823 Santa Monica Blvd., Hollywood, Calif. 90038

73 "Christmas Songs and Carols" (64–B) gives words and music for favorite Christmas songs, including "God Rest You Merry, Gentlemen," "Good King Wenceslas," "While Shepherds Watched Their Flocks," and "Angels We Have Heard on High." $10.00 includes record and guidebook.

Family Films, 5823 Santa Monica Blvd., Hollywood, Calif. 90038

74 "Geography of the Holy Land" (K28) visualizes the 4 natural geographic sections of Palestine: Coastal Plains, Central Mountains, Jordan Valley, and Trans-Jordan Plateau. Each section is described photographically from north to south and the distinctive features of each are explained. $9.00 includes record and guidebook.

Family Films, 5823 Santa Monica Blvd., Hollywood, Calif. 90038

75 "Bible Cities" (25B) shows the remains and reconstruction of Biblical cities, including Dothan, Jericho, Hebron, Shechem, Megiddo, and Jerusalem. $10.00 includes record and guidebook.

Family Films, 5823 Santa Monica Blvd., Hollywood, Calif. 90038

76 "Bible Scrolls" (25A) tells the fascinating story of the discovery of the Dead Sea Scrolls and interesting facts about the Essenes, who copied and hid them. $10.00 includes record and guidebook.

Family Films, 5823 Santa Monica Blvd., Hollywood, Calif. 90038

77 "Old Testament Life and Times" (K82) is a set of 4 strips covering (1) "Nomad Life," (2) "City Life," (3) "Military and Political Life," and (4) "Religious Life." The items considered include tent life, the invasion of Canaan, the findings of archaeology, and religious festivals. $29.70 includes record and guidebook. (Individual titles available at $10.00 each.)

Family Films, 5823 Santa Monica Blvd., Hollywood, Calif. 90038

78 "Religions of Our World Neighbors" (K104) is a set of 4 filmstrips covering (1) "Buddhism," (2) "Hinduism," (3) "Shintoism," and (4) "Islam." The items covered include the new Buddhist lay movement, a Hindu wedding and funeral, a purification ceremony, and a muezzin chant. $29.70 includes record and guidebook. (Individual titles available at $10.00 each.)

Family Films, 5823 Santa Monica Blvd., Hollywood, Calif. 90038

79 "The Story of the Pilgrims" (369–SAR) is a set of 2 filmstrips using documents, prints, paintings, and dramatizations to depict the reasons that caused the Pilgrims to leave England, stay eleven years in Holland, and finally voyage to the New World. Included in the presentation are the religious persecutions in England, the "Separatists," the "Mayflower Compact," and the First Thanksgiving. $14.50 per set includes record and guidebook.

Society for Visual Education, Inc., 1345 Diversey Parkway, Chicago, Ill. 60614

80 "The Middle Ages" (381–S) is a set of 4 filmstrips, each of which contains significant references to the influence of religion on the history of the period. The Crusades and the prominence of the medieval church are features. The individual titles are: (1) "Migrations of Medieval People"; (2) "Feudalism"; (3) "The Medieval Church"; and (4) "Medieval Towns and Cities." $21.60 per set. $6.00 per individual title.

Society for Visual Education, Inc., 1345 Diversey Parkway, Chicago, Ill. 60614

81 "The World Believes" (809S) is a set of 6 filmstrips relating the historical background, major beliefs, practices, and particular heritage of (1) Judaism, (2) Protestantism, (3) Catholicism, (4) Islam, (5) Buddhism, and (6) Hinduism. $30.00 includes guidebook. (Individual titles available at $6.00 each.)

Society for Visual Education, Inc., 1345 Diversey Parkway, Chicago, Ill. 60614

82 *The Story of Jesus* is composed of 24 filmstrips divided into 4 parts, covering the entire life of Jesus. $40.50 per part includes record and guidebook.

Cathedral Films, 2921 W. Alameda Ave., Burbank, Calif. 91505

83 *The Story of Paul* is composed of 12 filmstrips divided into 2 parts covering the entire life of Paul. $49.90 per part includes record, guidebook, and map set.

Cathedral Films, 2921 W. Alameda Ave., Burbank, Calif. 91505

84 "Symbols of the Church" is composed of 6 filmstrips covering

the symbols of (1) faith, (2) the Cross, (3) the lost, (4) the House of God, (5) the Old Testament, and (6) the New Testament. $33.75 per set includes record and guidebook.

Cathedral Films, 2921 W. Alameda Ave., Burbank, Calif. 91505

85   *The Old Testament Scriptures* is a set of 14 filmstrips in 4 parts covering the Old Testament characters Abraham, Jacob, Joseph, Moses, Joshua, Gideon, Ruth, Samuel, David, Solomon, and Elijah in dramatic presentation. $97.50 per set includes records.

Concordia Publishing House, 3558 South Jefferson Ave., St. Louis, Mo. 63118

86   "The Reformation" gives the personalities and events of the Reformation. $22.00 (may be rented for $1.50).

Visual Education Service, 409 Prospect St., New Haven, Conn. 06511

87   "The Protestant Reformation" uses paintings of the great masters to portray the Reformation. $6.00.

Visual Education Service, 409 Prospect St., New Haven, Conn. 06511

88   "One God: The Ways We Worship Him" is a 100-frame filmstrip with record depicting the major religious forms of the Jewish, Protestant, and Catholic faiths. This is based on a book of the same title by Florence Mary Fitch. $10.00.

Association Films, Inc., 347 Madison Ave., New York, N.Y. 10017

89   "The Story of Purim" is a 49-frame, black-and-white filmstrip which conveys the gaiety of this holiday through scenes in the synagogue and home. $3.50.

Anti-Defamation League, 315 Lexington Ave., New York, N.Y. 10016

90   "The Story of Passover" is a 52-frame, black-and-white filmstrip portraying the warmth of this holiday by photographs of a family conducting the Passover Seder. $3.50.

Anti-Defamation League, 315 Lexington Ave., New York, N.Y. 10016

91   "The Story of Hanukkah" is a 31-frame, black-and-white filmstrip picture of this holiday, showing its historical background, customs, observances, and association with modern-day Israel. $3.50.

Anti-Defamation League, 315 Lexington Ave., New York, N.Y. 10016

92   "Israel: The Land and the People" is a set of 7 filmstrips of 49 frames each concerned primarily with topography, industry, commerce, and the adjustments of thousands of new citizens to the state of Israel. $6.00 per filmstrip.

Anti-Defamation League, 315 Lexington Ave., New York, N.Y. 10016

93   "Roots of Religious Freedom" is a 41-frame color filmstrip that

shows the part played by religious groups in our colonization and traces the growth of religious freedom. $6.00.

Jam Handy Organization, 2821 E. Grand Blvd., Detroit, Mich. 48211

94 "The Four Gospels" is a set of 4 filmstrips which consider the arrangement of the material presented in each Gospel, relate Jesus to Old Testament promises, and analyze significant words. Each filmstrip comes with record and guide. $29.70 per set ($10.00 per strip).

Family Films, 5823 Santa Monica Blvd., Hollywood, Calif. 90038

Records

95 "The Stories of Ethel Barrett" is a multivolume set of 12", 33-rpm recordings of Ethel Barrett retelling favorite Bible stories. $4.98 each.

Pathway Press, 922 Montgomery Ave., Cleveland, Tenn. 37311

96 "A Letter From Paul" (No. 1331) is a 12", 33-rpm recording of Alice McIntire reading several of St. Paul's letters (New Testament books) in the natural conversational simplicity of a letter being read aloud to an intimate family circle. Passages from all of Paul's Epistles are blended to flow as one inspired letter. $4.98.

Pathway Press, 922 Montgomery Ave., Cleveland, Tenn. 37311

97 "The Holy War" (No. 2031) is a set of two 12", 33-rpm recordings of Ethel Barrett's dramatic readings of John Bunyan's classic, with orchestral background. $7.96.

Pathway Press, 922 Montgomery Ave., Cleveland, Tenn. 37311

98 "The Inaugural Addresses of Eisenhower and Kennedy" (No. 827) is a 12", 33-rpm recording of these recent inaugurals, which contain Biblical allusions. $5.95.

Spoken Arts, Inc., 95 Valley Road, New Rochelle, N.Y. 10804

99 "Abba Eban Reads from the Psalms" (No. 757) is a 12", 33-rpm recording of one of Israel's most prominent statesmen reading selected portions in both English and Hebrew. $5.95.

Spoken Arts, Inc., 95 Valley Road, New Rochelle, N.Y. 10804

100 "Turn! Turn! Turn!" (CL-2454) is a 12", 33-rpm recording by the Byrds, a popular singing group. Their first selection, from which the album takes its name, is a modern rendition of the famous "There is a time to . . ." portion of Ecclesiastes.

Columbia Records, Terre Haute, Ind. 47808

101 Handel's *Messiah* is the single title of this classic work in a record set composed of three 12" 33-rpm records. $8.50 mono, $9.50 stereo.

Reader's Digest, Pleasantville, N.Y. 10570

102   "The Battle for the Mind" and "Life on Other Planets" are two
        sides of one tape dealing with LSD and the population ex-
        plosion in terms of the Bible. $5.95.
            Bible Voice, P.O. Box 3521, Van Nuys, Calif. 91405
103   "The Complete Bible" is a set of fifty-two 12", 16-rpm records
        covering the entire Bible in the King James Version. $117.95.
            Bible Voice, P.O. Box 3521, Van Nuys, Calif. 91405
104   "The Psalms" is a set of five 12", 16-rpm records including every
        Psalm in the King James Version. $11.95.
            Bible Voice, P.O. Box 3521, Van Nuys, Calif. 91405
105   "50 Favorite Chapters of the Holy Bible" (13741) is a set of
        two 16-rpm records from the Revised Standard Version. $1.00
        per set.
            American Bible Society, P.O. Box 100, Ansonia Station, New
        York, N.Y. 10023
106   "Thanksgiving" (13750) is a 16-rpm record of 24 selected
        Psalms of Thanksgiving from the King James Version. 35¢
        per record.
            American Bible Society, P.O. Box 100, Ansonia Station, New
        York, N.Y. 10023
107   "The Bible Story" (12100) is a set of six 16-rpm records
        selected from the Revised Standard Version, telling about the
        more important people, ideas, and events. $2.70 per set.
            American Bible Society, P.O. Box 100, Ansonia Station, New
        York, N.Y. 10023
108   "The Talking Bible" is a set of sixty-seven 16-rpm records
        covering the entire Bible. Available in King James or Revised
        Standard Version. 45¢ per record. $30.15 complete set.
            American Bible Society, P.O. Box 100, Ansonia Station, New
        York, N.Y. 10023
109   "Star Over Bethlehem" is a 7", 33-rmp record combining orig-
        inal drama and song. The dramatization vividly captures the
        mood of the first Christmas. $1.10.
            Christ in Christmas Activities, P.O. Box 3545, Milwaukee,
        Wis. 53206
110   The Inspirational Tape Library maintains an extensive collec-
        tion of tapes available on a rental basis. Write for free catalog.
            Inspirational Tape Library, Box 788, Phoenix, Ariz. 85001
111   "Spirituals" (No. T818) is a 12", 33-rpm recording by Ten-
        nessee Ernie Ford including such selections as "Noah Found
        Grace in the Eyes of the Lord," "Wayfarin' Pilgrim," and
        others. $2.99.
            Capitol Records, Capitol Towers, Hollywood, Calif. 90028
112   "Deep River and Other Spirituals" (No. LSC–2247) is a 12",
        33-rpm recording by the Robert Shaw Chorale including such
        selections as "Didn't My Lord Deliver Daniel?," "There Is a
        Balm in Gilead," "Dry Bones," and others.
            RCA Victor Mail Order Service, P.O. Box 1979, Indianapolis,
        Ind. 46206

113 "What Wondrous Love" (LSC–2403) is a 12″, 33-rpm recording of the Robert Shaw Chorale in a selection of religious songs.
RCA Victor Mail Order Service, P.O. Box 1979, Indianapolis, Ind. 46206

114 "I'll Walk with God" (N. LM–2607) is a 12″, 33-rpm recording of Mario Lanza in a selection of songs of devotion and love.
RCA Victor Mail Order Service, P.O. Box 1979, Indianapolis, Ind. 46206

115 "Meditations for the Modern Classroom" (No. TC–1222) is a 12″, 33-rpm recording of inspirational reading from the works of Emerson, Sandburg, Lincoln, Frost, Stevenson, and others. Selections have been picked for their interest and liveliness as well as stress on character-building, moral and spiritual values, and good citizenship. $5.95.
Caedmon Records, 505 Eighth Ave., New York, N.Y. 10018

116 "Paradise Lost" (No. TC–2008) is a set of two 12″, 33-rpm recordings of Anthony Quayle's dramatic reading of selections from John Milton's classic. $11.90.
Caedmon Records, 505 Eighth Ave., New York, N.Y. 10018

117 "Books of Judith and Ruth" (No. TX 1052) is a 12″, 33-rpm recording of Judith Anderson reading Judith and Claire Bloom reading Ruth. $5.95.
Caedmon Records, 505 Eighth Ave., New York, N.Y. 10018

118 "Job" (No. TC 1076) is a 12″, 33-rpm recording of Herbert Marshall and a cast of 8 reading the Book of Job in shortened form with the "he saids" omitted in order to underscore the grandeur and poetry of the dialogue. $5.95.
Caedmon Records, 505 Eighth Ave., New York, N.Y. 10018

119 "Bible Stories for Children" (No. J. 3258) is a 12″, 33-rpm recording of Claude Rains reading "Noah and the Ark," "Moses in the Bulrushes," "Joseph and the Coat of Many Colors," and "The Story of Jesus." $1.18.
Capitol Records, Capitol Towers, Hollywood, Calif. 90028

120 "The Holy Land" (No. LSP 2189) is a 12″, 33-rpm recording by George Beverly Shea. Twelve songs are selected to give a "musical tour" of the Holy Land. Titles include "Zion Stands with Hills Surrounded," "Go Down, Moses," "On Jordan's Stormy Banks," and "Joshua Fit de Battle of Jericho." $4.95.
RCA Victor Mail Order Service, P.O. Box 1979, Indianapolis, Ind. 46206

121 "The Book of Job" (No. 3292) is a 12″, 33-rpm recording of the dramatization of the story of Job by the Everyman Players. This presentation of Job is given annually each summer at Pine Mountain State Park, Pineville, Kentucky and has been presented in theaters around the world. $4.98.
Word Records, Waco, Tex. 76703

122 "Songs from the Psalms" (No. W–4023) is a 12", 33-rpm recording of the Lutheran Hour Choir singing a selection of songs based on Psalms. $4.98.
Word Records, Waco, Tex. 76703

123 "The Beatitudes" (No. 6120) is a 12", 33-rpm recording of William Barclay reading. Dr. Barclay is a Scottish translator of the New Testament, scholar, and teacher. $4.98.
Word Records, Waco, Tex. 76703

124 "Old Testament Heroes" (HiFi W–3299, stereo WST–8299) is a 12", 33-rpm recording for children by Dick Anthony and Aunt Theresa. The stories of Gideon, Joseph, Shadrach, Sampson, and Samuel are dramatically presented, with sound effects. $4.98.
Word Records, Waco, Tex. 76703

125 "A Child's Look at the Bible" (No. 3159) is a 12", 33-rpm record of Mary Francis O'Connor reading 12 selected stories, mostly from the New Testament. $1.98.
Word Records, Waco, Tex. 76703

126 "Great Stories from the Bible" (No. 3029) is a 12", 33-rpm record of Wendell Loveless reading 12 selected stories. $1.98.
Word Records, Waco, Tex. 76703

127 "The Seven Last Words of Christ" (No. 4002) is a 12", 33-rpm featuring the Oratoria Singers with full accompaniment. $4.98.
Word Records, Waco, Tex. 76703

128 "The Majesty of Sacred Music" (No. 9027) is a 12", 33-rpm recording by the Stockholm Concert Orchestra of excerpts from 10 religious masterworks by the world's greatest composers. $4.98.
Word Records, Waco, Tex. 76703

129 "The Psalms and the Tale of David" (No. TC 1053) is a 12", 33-rpm recording of Judith Anderson reading the major Psalms and the Saul, Goliath, and Bathsheba episodes from the Old Testament. $5.95.
Caedmon Records, 505 Eighth Ave., New York, N.Y. 10018

130 "Genesis: The Creation and Noah" (No. TC 1096) is a 12", 33-rpm recording of Judith Anderson reading selections from Genesis. $5.95.
Caedmon Records, 505 Eighth Ave., New York, N.Y. 10018

131 "The Five Books of Moses" (No. JRS–9060) is a set of two 12", 33-rpm recordings featuring the inspired reading of Charlton Heston.
Vanguard Recording Society, 154 West 14th St., New York, N.Y. 10011

132 "The Jewish Holiday Album" (No. LN 24172) is a 12", 33-rpm recording with a booklet which explains major Jewish holidays in word and song. $3.00.
Citadel Records, 545 Fifth Ave., New York, N.Y. 10017

133 "Christmas as It Happened" is a 12", 33-rpm recording presenting the events connected with the birth of Jesus in modern radio broadcasting style. Spot reports, interviews, and even "advertising" are woven into an interesting account. $3.00.
Mennonite Broadcasts, Box 472, Harrisonburg, Va. 22801

134 "The Greatest Week in History" is a 12", 33-rpm recording presenting the events of the last week of the life of Jesus in modern radio broadcasting style. Spot reports, interviews, and even "advertising" are woven into an interesting account. Originally produced for the broadcasting industry, the recording is now available to the public. $3.00.
Mennonite Broadcasts, Box 472, Harrisonburg, Va. 22801

135 "The Spirit of Christmas" (ML 5423) is a 12", 33-rpm recording by the Mormon Tabernacle Choir featuring 18 Christmas songs.
Columbia Records, Terre Haute, Ind. 47808

136 "Sacred Shrines of Washington" is a 12", 33-rpm recording describing in words and music the great religious shrines in the nation's capital and the statesmen associated with them. Especially prepared for young people and visitors to Washington. $3.65. (A related leaflet, booklet, and film are also available.)
Educational Communication Association, 143 North Meridian Street, Indianapolis, Ind. 46204

137 "Negro Blues and Hollers" is a 12", 33-rpm recording by a variety of artists edited by Marshall W. Stearns. $5.40. (Make checks payable to Chief, Music Division, Library of Congress.)
Recording Laboratory, Music Division, Library of Congress, Washington, D.C. 20540

138 "Afro-American Spirituals, Work Songs, and Ballads" is a 33-rpm recording by a variety of artists edited by Alan Lomax. Titles include "Handwriting on the Wall," "The New Buryin' Ground," and "Run, Old Jeremiah." $5.40. (Make checks payable to Chief, Music Division, Library of Congress.)
Recording Laboratory, Music Division, Library of Congress, Washington, D.C. 20540

139 "Readings from the Bible in Old, Middle, and Modern English" is a tape recording of select Biblical passages to illustrate language change. $3.00.
Euclid English Demonstration Center, 1520 Chardon Road, Euclid, Ohio 44117

140 "The Passover Seder Festival" (HiFi ML–5736, stereo MS 6336) is a 12", 33-rpm recording by Richard Tucker. Through song, music, and narration this presentation captures the Exodus experience.
Columbia Records, Terre Haute, Ind. 47808

141 "Paul Speaks" is a 12", 33-rpm recording of a dramatic reading of passages from Romans and II Corinthians from the

contemporary language of LIVING LETTERS (see no. 648).
$3.98.

    Tyndale House, Box 80, Wheaton, Ill. 60187

142   "Grady Wilson Reads Living Letters" is the title of an 8-record series of 16-rpm recordings featuring the popular radio personality reading St. Paul's New Testament letters in contemporary language. $9.95 per set.

    Tyndale House, Box 80, Wheaton, Ill. 60187.

Maps and Charts

143   "Student's Map of Palestine" (6–G–0127) is a 22" x 24" map which shows where fifty of the most interesting Bible incidents took place. All important locations are alphabetically listed on the margin. Lithographed in full color. 95¢.

    Union Gospel Press, P.O. Box 6059, Cleveland, Ohio. 44101

144   "Plastic Relief Map of New Testament World" (2674) is a 15" x 27" white plastic raised relief map. $3.25.

    Standard Publishing Co., 8121 Hamilton Ave., Cincinnati, Ohio. 45231

145   "Plastic Relief Map of Palestine" (2675) is a 15" x 27" white plastic raised relief map. $3.25.

    Standard Publishing Co., 8121 Hamilton Ave., Cincinnati, Ohio. 45231

146   "Genealogy of Jesus Christ" (6–G–035) is a 20" x 17" cloth chart. Biblical references from which the information was obtained are listed. $1.00.

    Union Gospel Press, P.O. Box 6059, Cleveland, Ohio. 44101

147   "The Ten Commandments" are available on cloth in two sizes. Small, 18" x 26" for 50¢ and large, 32" x 55" for $1.50.

    A. H. Eilers Co., 1124 Pine, St. Louis, Mo. 63101

148   "Church History Denominational Chart" by Elgin S. Moyer is a comprehensive chart showing the origin in time of virtually every denomination and the relationship between denominations. 35¢.

    Moody Catalog Service, 820 N. La Salle Street, Chicago, Ill. 60610

149   "Palestine in the Time of Jesus" is a 37" x 49" full-color map showing the cities, roads, countries, and provinces as they were in Jesus' time. Available in folded form for $1.00 (no. 85–3629). Available unfolded in laminated, washable material with steel rods top and bottom for $4.95 (no. 85–4917).

    Cicero Press, 2301 Roosevelt Road, Broadview, Ill. 60153

150   "Paul's Journeys" is a 37" x 49" Rand McNally map showing 4 journeys, each in a different color or symbol. Available in folded form for $1.00 (no. 85–3630). Available in laminated, washable material with steel rods top and bottom for $4.95 (no. 85–4917).

Cicero Press, 2301 Roosevelt Road, Broadview, Ill. 60153

151 "The Histomap of Religion" (85–3492) is a Rand McNally chart which lists the origins, development, and influence of religious concepts side by side for comparison. $1.50.

Cicero Press, 2301 Roosevelt Road, Broadview, Ill. 60153

152 "Biblical History and Culture" is a set of four 3′ x 2′ full-color panels of maps, archaeological objects, original drawings, and graphs which outline the political, religious, and cultural history of the Bible regions from 2000 B.C. to the time of Christ. $10.00 per set.

United Church Press, 1505 Race Street, Philadelphia, Pa. 19102

153 "Christian History and Culture" is a set of four 3′ x 2′ full-color panels which trace the path of Christianity through its 2,000 years since Christ. The set includes a comprehensive book that explains each picture and symbol and their relationship. $10.00 includes charts and book.

United Church Press, 1505 Race Street, Philadelphia, Pa. 19102

154 "Bible Charts." Old Testament Patriarchs and Judges (50¢), "Old Testament Kings and Prophets" (50¢), "Babylonian Captivity" ($1.00), "Between the Testaments" (50¢), and "New Testament Chronology" (50¢).

Bible Charts, Box 677, Winona Lake, Ind. 46590

155 "Chronological Chart of Old Testament History" by Guy P. Duffield is a 40″ chart listing in parallel columns 13 major divisions of the Old Testament and the principal characters in each division. 40¢.

B. N. Robertson Printers, 591 Glendale Blvd., Los Angeles, Calif. 90026

156 "Bible Chart by Owen Klooster" is an 18½″ x 31″ four-color map of the Bible world. The map-chart includes a historical outline and index. 75¢.

Earl R. Peck, P.O. Box 169, Dayton, Tenn. 37321

157 "The Chosen Family of God" is a 25″ x 50″ comprehensive chart depicting the Biblical characters and their relationships from Adam to Jesus.

W. A. Thomas Chart Co., Box 86, Griffith, Ind. 46319

158 "Maps of Bible Lands" is a set of eight 42″ x 31″ five-color wall maps based on the OXFORD BIBLE ATLAS. Special plastic paper makes it possible to write on the maps and wash with damp cloth. Titles include: "The Ancient Near East Before the Exodus," No. 492; "The Exodus," No. 493; "Palestine in Old Testament Times," No. 494; "The Ancient Near East in the Time of the Persian Empire," No. 496; "Palestine in New Testament Times," No. 497; "The Background of the New Testament: Rome and the East," No. 498, and "The Cradle

of Christianity: The Eastern Mediterranean," No. 499. The
complete set comes with tripod stand and charthead. $27.50 per
set. $4.50 per map.

Abingdon Press, 201 Eighth Ave. South, Nashville, Tenn.
37203

159   "Bible Maps and Charts No. 2" (2625) is a set of 6 maps and
2 charts, each 19″ x 24″ in full color. The items cover the
Exodus through the Divided Kingdom. $2.50.

Standard Publishing Co., 8121 Hamilton Ave., Cincinnati,
Ohio. 45231

160   "Bible Maps and Charts No. 1" (2626) is a set of 6 maps and
2 charts, each 19″ x 24″ in full color. The items cover all
of Bible history. $2.50.

Standard Publishing Co., 8121 Hamilton Ave., Cincinnati,
Ohio. 45231

161   "Bible Maps and Charts" (8–9676) is a set of 8 maps and 10
charts, each 17″ x 22″, covering Bible history and geography.
$3.95.

Scripture Press, 1825 College Ave., Wheaton, Ill. 60187

162   The "World Civilization Time Line and Date Chart" (1430)
is a 5½′ five-color chart covering history, science, literature,
music, art, and religion. $2.75.

Charles E. Merrill Books, Inc., 1300 Alum Creek Drive,
Columbus, Ohio. 43216

163   "Contour Map of Palestine" is a 3′ x 5′ three-dimensional map
of Palestine, 4 inches thick, cast in plastic. $14.75.

Liturgical Press, Collegeville, Minn. 56321

164   "Acts Map and Chart" (2668) is a set which includes a map
of Paul's journeys printed lightly so they may be emphasized as
study proceeds and a chronological chart of events including
contemporary rulers. $2.50.

Standard Publishing Company, 8121 Hamilton Ave., Cincinnati, Ohio. 45231

165   "Training for Service Maps and Charts" (2600) is a set of
three 18″ x 25″ maps and six charts. Subjects considered include
the Biblical world, events and persons in the Old Testament, the
origin and meanings of various feasts, the life of Christ, versions
of the English Bible, a full-color picture of Solomon's Temple,
and a Tabernacle with furniture to cut out and assemble. $3.50.

Standard Publishing Company, 8121 Hamilton Ave., Cincinnati, Ohio. 45231

Models and Objects

166   The "widow's mite" is the name of a series of small coins in
use in Palestine 2,000 years ago. Crude but authentic ancient
"widow's mites," just as they are unearthed in Israel, are
now available. $6.50 each.

New England Coin Company, 217 E. Fayette Street, Syracuse, N.Y. 13202

167 "Religious Stamps" is a sample packet of postage stamps with religious significance. Included are stamps bearing religious symbols, portraits of religious leaders, and Bible themes. A number of commemoratives have been issued honoring religious organizations and religious holidays. $2.00 per packet.

West Coast Hobby Shop, 9920 California Ave., South Gate, Calif. 90280

168 This is a 12" x 20" color print of a model of the Temple of Jerusalem. The model was on display in the Judaism Pavilion at the World Exhibition in Montreal, Canada 1967. $2.25 per print.

Lazar Halberthal, 5344 MacDonald Ave., Montreal, Canada.

169 Biblical coins are reproduced in every detail except for the metallic content. Set No. 1 covers the period from 37 B.C. to 40 A.D. and includes coins of Herod the Great, the widow's mite, a lepton of Pontius Pilate, Herod Antipas, shekel of Tyre, tribute penny, and stater of Antioch. Set No. 2 covers the period 66–135 A.D. $8.95 per set.

Museum Coins, P.O. Box 206, Flushing, New York, N.Y. 11352

170 "Gutenberg—Famous Inventors Series No. 3100" is a 10" working model of the original Gutenberg Press upon which the first book, the Bible, was printed. The model comes complete with ink, rollers, and plates so that it will actually print a miniature page. $3.95.

The Lionel Corp., Hoffman Place, Hillside, N.J. 07205

171 "Noah's Ark" is a 24" x 4" x 3" scale model of the Ark. The die-cut model comes with stand-up figures and storybook. $1.50.

Scripture Press, 1825 College Ave., Wheaton, Ill. 60187

172 "Palestinian House" (7–3763) is a 5" x 5" x 3" three-dimensional cut-out, paste-up model of a typical house. 50¢.

Scripture Press, 1825 College Ave., Wheaton, Ill. 60187

173 "Patriarchal Tent" (7–3760) is a 7" x 7" x 2" three-dimensional cutout, paste-up model of a typical Old Testament tent. 50¢

Scripture Press, 1825 College Ave., Wheaton, Ill. 60187

174 "Synagogue" (7–3762) is a 4" x 6" x 3" three-dimensional cutout, paste-up model of a typical first-century synagogue. 50¢

Scripture Press, 1825 College Ave., Wheaton, Ill. 60187

175 "Temple of Solomon" (7–3764) is a 9" x 15" x 5" three-dimensional cutout paste-up model of the Temple of Solomon. $1.40.

Scripture Press, 1825 College Ave., Wheaton, Ill. 60187

176 "Tabernacle" (7–3761) is a 6" x 12" x 2" three-dimensional cutout, paste-up model of the Tabernacle. 50¢

Scripture Press, 1825 College Ave., Wheaton, Ill. 60187

75025

177   "The Tabernacle" is an elaborate wooden model in kit form of the Tabernacle and its contents. $13.10.
      Skybook Associates, 382 Chancellor Ave., Newark, N.J. 07112
178   "Mezzuzah" (M97) is a 3-inch item with the symbols of the Ten Commandments. $2.25.
      Bloch Publishing Co., 31 West 31st St., New York, N.Y. 10001

Art

179   "Bible Teaching Pictures" is a series of four sets of 18 pictures per set designed to help in telling the Bible story. The set titles are: "The Creation to Moses' Farewell" (8–7280), "Crossing the Jordan to Queen Esther" (8–7281), "The Birth of Christ to the Good Samaritan" (8–7282), and "Jesus Visits Mary and Martha to the Ascension" (8–7283). $3.25 per set. Order by title and set number.
      Scripture Press, 1825 College Ave., Wheaton, Ill. 60187
180   "Christ of St. John" by Dali is available in a 10″ x 16″ full-color print. $3.00.
      Artext Prints, Inc., Westport, Conn. 06880
181   "Pilgrims Going to Church" by Boughton is available in a 14″ x 22″ full-color print. $3.00.
      Artext Prints, Inc., Westport, Conn. 06880
182   "Pieta" by Michelangelo is available in a 20″ x 14″ sharp black-and-white print. $1.50.
      Artext Prints, Inc., Westport, Conn. 06880
183   "100 Pictures on the Life of Christ" is a series of 5½″ x 8″ half-tone reproductions covering every phase of the life of Christ. $3.00.
      Perry Pictures, Inc., Malden, Mass. 02148
184   The special issue of the February, 1966 INTERNATIONAL JOURNAL OF RELIGIOUS EDUCATION on "Contemporary Art and Christian Education" is still available. Profusely illustrated, the issue contains several penetrating articles on the relation between contemporary art and religious themes. 75¢ per issue. Order by title.
      International Journal of Religious Education, Box 303, New York, N.Y. 10027
185   A set of 4 contemporary religious art paintings in full color is a special insert in the September 2, 1966 issue of CHRISTIANITY TODAY. The issue also contains an article by the artist, Gordon Kelley. 25¢ per issue.
      Christianity Today, 1014 Washington Building, Washington, D.C. 20005
186   "Paintings Depicting the Life of Christ" is an 11″ x 14″ port-

folio containing 15 color reproductions of famous paintings from the life of Christ. Included are "The Rest on the Flight to Egypt" by Gerard David, "The Return of the Prodigal Son" by Murillo, and "The Descent from the Cross" by Rembrandt. A booklet of Biblical passages related to the paintings is included. (Specify either King James or Douay Version.) The above materials are produced by and available from the National Gallery of Art. A special booklet giving the background of each painter and painting has been prepared by Educational Communication Association. Both booklets and all 15 color prints have been assembled as one packet. $5.00. Order by title of portfolio.

Faith Media, Inc., P.O. Box 114, Indianapolis, Ind. 46206

187 "Creation of Man" by Michelangelo from the central panel of the Sistine Chapel is available in two sizes. A portion of this painting appeared on the U.S. postage stamp commemorating the International Geophysical Year (Scott Stamp No. A 554). $18.00 for large size, 46" x 21½", and $7.00 for small size, 11⅛" x 5⅛".

International Art Publishing Co., 243 W. Congress St., Detroit, Mich. 48226

188 A set of thirteen 22" x 14", full-color mounted portraits of Christ and the twelve apostles is available. $14.30 per set.

Church Extension Service, Golden, Colo. 80401

Games

189 "Bible Story Balloons" (8–5038) is a package of 5 balloons with pictures of Bible events. 25¢ per set.

Scripture Press, 1825 College Ave., Wheaton, Ill. 60187

190 "The Last Supper Puzzle" (8–5932) is made up of over 1,000 pieces which when assembled render a 26½" x 19" reproduction of the famous painting by Leonardo da Vinci. $1.29.

Scripture Press, 1825 College Ave., Wheaton, Ill. 60187

191 "With Jesus in Palestine" (T 2688) is a 4-color, 21-piece puzzle of a map of Palestine. 39¢.

Warner Press, P.O. Box 2499, Anderson, Ind. 46011

192 "Life of Jesus" (T 6610) is a set of 4 puzzles of from 12 to 15 pieces each. Titles include: "Wise Men," "Zacchaeus," "Entry into Jerusalem," and "The Boy Who Shared." $1.25 per set.

Warner Press, P.O. Box 2499, Anderson, Ind. 46011

193 A set of pencils with Biblical topics is available. Titles include: Old Testament Books (No. V 1187), New Testament Books (No. V 1188), the Lord's Prayer (No. V 1150), the Ten Commandments (No. V 1155), the Golden Rule (No. V 1156), the Beatitudes (No. V 1157), and the 23rd Psalm (No. V 1159). 5¢ each. Order by title and number.

Warner Press, P.O. Box 2499, Anderson, Ind. 46011

194   "Old Testament" (T 6612) is a set of 4 puzzles of from 12 to 15 pieces each. Titles include: "Noah Built the Ark," "Family Worshipping God," "David the Shepherd," and "Jacob and his Coat." $1.25 per set.
      Warner Press, P.O. Box 2499, Anderson, Ind. 46011
195   "Bible Puzzle Chest" (T 3847) is a set of two checker-type games featuring Christian symbols and Christian mottoes. $1.25.
      Warner Press, P.O. Box 2499, Anderson, Ind. 46011
196   "Quiz Word Bible Game" (10929) is a game similar to Password but using words with Biblical connotations. Designed for 2 to 8 players. $1.00.
      Zondervan Publishing Co., 1415 Lake Drive SE, Grand Rapids, Mich. 49506

Displays

197   "American Way of Life" is a 9" x 14" poster presenting a graphic illustration of our rights—all are shown to be based on on a fundamental belief in God. Complimentary copy to teachers. (15¢ per copy.)
      Freedoms Foundation, Valley Forge, Pa. 19481
198   Four free loan exhibits are available from the American Bible Society. (1) "Bibles Around the World," containing sixteen 9" x 12" color posters each showing a passage of Scripture in a different language, with a picture of the people who speak it (No. 18001). (2) Facsimile pages of eleven historic Bibles (No. 18002). (3) "Scripture Translation," an assortment of 20 Scripture publications in different languages, with information about the translations and languages (No. 18003). (4) "History of the English Bible," including 16 color posters on the development of the English Bible (No. 18004).
      American Bible Society, P.O. Box 100, Ansonia Station, New York, N.Y. 10023
199   "Great Thoughts" is a set of 108 sayings succinctly worded on sturdy 6" x 8" cards. Subjects covered include ethics, morals, character development, spiritual concerns, and the Bible. A plexiglass frame makes cards adaptable for desk use. $2.58 per set postpaid.
      National Educators Fellowship, Box 243, South Pasadena, Calif. 91030
200   "Great Bibles of History" (16565) is a portfolio of twenty-four of 8½" x 11" facsimile pages from historic Bibles. Historical annotations and informative pictorial material is included. $1.00 per set.
      American Bible Society, P.O. Box 100, Ansonia Station, New York, N.Y. 10023
201   "Picture Posters of the History of the English Bible" (15019)

is a set of sixteen 9″ x 12″ full-color reproductions of key scenes. A teacher's guide comes with the set. $1.25 per set.

American Bible Society, P.O. Box 100, Ansonia Station, New York, N.Y. 10023

202 "Great Art for Christian Education" is an exhibit consisting of 60 color reproductions of masterpieces of religious art. The exhibit has been in circulation since 1959. The fee is $20.00 plus shipping costs to the next exhibitor. It is usually reserved for a year in advance. Write for information.

Miss Ann Yeargin, 475 Riverside Drive, Room 710, New York, N.Y. 10027

203 A 2½″ x 3½″ attractive decal bearing the words "One Nation Under God" from the pledge to the flag is available. The red lettering is on a white map of the United States placed on a blue background with white stars. 20¢ per decal.

Christ in Christmas Activities, P.O. Box 6663, Milwaukee, Wis. 53216

Field Trips

204 Among religious art centers of particular value to teachers are:
Christian Art Gallery, 1801 West Greenleaf Ave., Chicago, Ill. 60626
Contemporary Christian Art Gallery, 1060–A Lexington Ave., New York, N.Y. 10021
Religious Art Center, Interstate Trust Building, Denver, Colo. 80200
Center for Contemporary Religious Art, 161 Newbury Street, Boston, Mass. 02116

205 The Oriental Institute of the University of Chicago is the world's only major research enterprise concerned exclusively with the study of the origin and historical development of the great civilizations of the Near East. Many of the Institute's 70,000 objects are on display in its museum. A brochure describing the Institute program will be sent on request. Free guided tours are available.

The Oriental Institute, 1155 East 58th St., Chicago, Ill. 60637

206 "The Star of Bethlehem" is an annual presentation in the Adler Planetarium, Chicago, Ill. During the hour-long performance audiences are taken to the Holy Land via the Planetarium instrument to view the skies as they appeared at the time of the birth of Christ. The Planetarium lecturer discusses the various astronomical phenomena which possibly took place and speculates as to which of these occurrences might have been the star.

Chicago Park District, 425 East 14th Blvd., Chicago, Ill. 60605

207 "Sacred Shrines of Washington" is a handy map and guide listing 26 places of worship and national monuments in Washington, D.C. $2.00 per 500.

Educational Communication Association, 143 North Meridian St., Indianapolis, Ind. 46204.

Miscellaneous

208 The popular modern stereoscopic viewer and picture discs by Sawyer include a series of religiously oriented disc sets. Each set includes 21 pictures on 3 discs plus a descriptive booklet. The titles include "Birth of Jesus" (B–875), "The Easter Story" (B–880), "Jesus Teaches Forgiveness" (B–877), "Miracles of Jesus" (B–878), "Parables of Jesus" (B–876), "Bible Heroes" (B–852), "A Christmas Carol" (B–380), "The Littlest Angel" (B–381), "The Night Before Christmas" (B–382), and "The Christmas Story" (B–383). $1.25 per title.

Individual disc titles include "The Wilderness of Judea," "The River Jordan," "Gethsemane to Calvary," "The Samaritan" "Old Jerusalem," and "Bethlehem." 45¢ per title.

The stereo viewers available include the Standard Viewer (2014), $1.75; the Lighted Viewer (2026), $3.95; and the Focusing Viewer (2011), $6.95. The first uses natural light, while the latter two use standard batteries or transformer (92052). $2.95.

Sawyer's, Inc., P.O. Box 444, Portland, Ore. 97207

209 "Moses" (ST–100) is an 8¼" replica in caststone on a marble base of Michelangelo's famous sculpture. $13.25.

Bookshelf of America, Inc., 627 Broadway, New York, N.Y. 10012

210 "Life of Christ Mural" is a packet of ten 12" x 16" ready-to-paint panels depicting important scenes and events in the life of Jesus.

Standard Publishing Co., 8121 Hamilton Ave., Cincinnati, Ohio. 45231

211 "Tabernacle in the Wilderness" is a 14" x 22" picture poster of the Tabernacle surrounded by the yard and tribal encampment. The plain line picture on heavy bristol paper is suitable for coloring or painting. 30¢

A. H. Eilers Company, 1124 Pine, St. Louis, Mo. 63101

212 The Christian Hall of Fame is a conservative Protestant project to honor outstanding leaders of the past. Portraits of those selected are hung in specially prepared rooms. Free guided tours are available. A book of full-color reproductions with descriptive materials is planned.

Christian Hall of Fame, 515 Whipple Ave. NW, Canton, Ohio. 44708

213 The "Interdenominational Religious Unit" is a 4-part series of overhead color transparencies covering the life of Christ and the Bible world. Printed originals (2057) $4.00, printed spirit masters (800–3) $18.00, and prepared color transparencies (2557) $120.00. Order by number.

Visual Products Division, Box 3100, St. Paul, Minn. 55101

214 "A Christmas-Hanukkah Program" permits your school to put on a dramatic presentation of the interrelationship between the the birth of Christ and God's careful preservation of the Jewish nation as His chosen People throughout the Old Testament. Complete stage directions for this simple yet beautiful and moving program are supplied. The booklet is valuable in itself for information on Hanukkah. $125.

Our Sunday Visitor, Huntington, Ind. 46750

215 *A Christmas Carol* is a simple play based on the classic dramatization of Dickens by Martha B. King. The production requires 10 women, 11 men, and 5 children. A unit set allows screens to suggest different backgrounds. $1.00 per book. $15.00 royalty per performance.

The Anchorage Press, Anchorage, Ky. 40223

216 Free Christian novels are available for the classroom library or reading table. The books are arranged in sets by grade level. Teachers write to Mr. A. J. Abuhl.

Moody Literature, 820 N. LaSalle, Chicago, Ill. 60610

217 "Studygraphs" are one-page cardboard, plastic-coated notebook inserts on various religious themes. Titles include: "The Pentateuch," "Old Testament Survey," "New Testament Survey," "Pauline Epistles," "Bible Doctrine I," "Bible Doctrine II," "The Life of Christ," "Church History," "History of Missions," "History of Christian Education," "Survey of Major Cults," and "World Religions." 89¢ per "Studygraph." Order by title.

Moody Catalog Service, 820 N. LaSalle, Chicago, Ill. 60610

218 The popular Eureka gummed seals include several religious sets. "Thanksgiving" (No. 85570) includes Pilgrim man, Pilgrim woman, Mayflower, etc. "Christmas Religious" (No. 95532) includes Mary and Joseph, manger, Wise Men, etc. "Old Testament" (No. 85514) includes Noah's Ark, Moses, Daniel, Joseph, etc. "New Testament" (No. 85515) includes Head of Christ, Gethsemane, the Loaves and Fishes, etc. "Easter Religious" (No. 85510) includes the tomb, Mary, the cross, Bible, etc. 19¢ per set.

Cicero Press, 2301 Roosevelt Road, Broadview, Ill. 60153

219 "The Standardized Bible Test" measures Bible knowledge at the high-school level. It is a genuine standardized test. A percentile chart is supplied. Manual (10¢), Test booklet (12¢), Answer Sheets (03¢), Scoring Stencil (40¢).

Bible Tests, P.O. Box 22008, Phoenix, Ariz. 85028

220   "Our Heritage Book Covers" is a set of high-quality, full plastic book covers with inspirational messages such as quotations from the Psalms, the Ten Commandments, the Golden Rule, and prayers and statements of famous leaders. $1.00 for sample set.

   Our Heritage Book Covers, 52–22nd Ave., Paterson, N.J. 07513

221   "Perspective" and "Truly Educated" are the titles of two full-color book covers with campus scenes and inspirational messages geared to students. 25¢ each (write for quanity prices).

   Collegiate Conversationals, Oradel, N.J. 07649

222   "Bible Search Series" is a set of 12 cards each of which makes a dramatic comparison between an item in the Bible and its modern counterpart. Under the caption "Is This in the Bible?" the comparisons are made in the style of Ripley's "Believe It or Not." Bible references are used in each case. Titles include, "The Southpaw," "Dieting," "Artificial Respiration," "Forest Fires," etc.

   Berg Enterprises, P.O. Box 66066, Portland, Ore. 97266

223   "Bible Coloring Books" is a series of 8 books, divided into two parts—Part 1 for the lower grades and Part 2 for the middle grades. Part 1 provides big coloring spaces for vigorous drawing and a short-story line with each picture. Titles include: "Noah's Ark" (62 C 1088), "Miracles of Jesus" (62 C 1089), "Heroes of the Bible" (62 C 1090), and "Christmas" (62 C 1091). Part 2 provides more detailed drawings and brief story description with Bible reference for each picture. Titles include: "Old Testament 1" (62 C 1084), "Old Testament 2" (62 C 1085), "New Testament 1" (62 C 1086), and "New Testament 2" (62 C 1087). 25¢ per coloring book. Order by title and number.

   Cicero Press, 2301 Roosevelt Road, Broadview, Ill. 60153

224   "National Bible Week" is an annual event sponsored by the Laymen's National Committee. Free posters and other promotional material is available.

   Laymen's National Committee, 156 Fifth Ave., New York, N.Y. 10010

225   Foreign language, Braille, and large-type Bibles are available from the American Bible Society. Write for catalog.

   American Bible Society, 1865 Broadway, New York, N.Y. 10023

226   The following lunchtable items are available:

   "Table Placemat" (14″ x 10″) is printed on absorbent, highly embossed paper bearing the words "God's work must truly be our own" from John F. Kennedy's inaugural address and picturing a dozen people in different occupations. $1.25 per 150.

"Table Napkins" (13" x 13") matches the table placemat above. The napkin has line drawings of several houses of worship of various faiths and bears the words "Worship This Week." $1.00 per 150.

Religion in American Life, 184 Fifth Ave., New York, N.Y. 10010

Booklets

227 *Manual for Witness Through the Arts* shows that the gospel is evident in literature, drama, painting, films, music, television, and other art mediums. There are several useful bibliographies. 75¢. Order by title.

American Baptist Literature, Valley Forge, Pa. 19481

228 *The Air Force Academy Cadet Chapel* is a beautiful full-color booklet which describes in words and pictures the chapels and art work in the Academy Chapel. $1.00 per copy.

Air Force Academy Chapel, Colorado Springs, Colo. 80900

229 *Putting Christmas in Your Stamp Album* is a 24-page booklet which gives a picture, description, and background of postage stamps around the world that have been issued to commemorate Christmas. 50¢ per booklet.

American Philatelic Society, P.O. Box 800, State College, Pa. 16801

230 *A Guide to Religious Shrines in the Nation's Capital* is a 50-page booklet which gives a picture and brief description of the major religious buildings and works of art in and around Washington, D.C. An accompanying record and film are also available. $1.00 per booklet.

Educational Communications Association, 143 North Meridian St., Indianapolis, Ind. 46204

231 *The Prayer Room in the Capitol* is a booklet which describes in word and picture the history and physical make-up of the prayer room in the United States Capitol Building. The room itself is reserved for the exclusive use of Senators and Representatives. The booklet is published by the U.S. Government Printing Office and is available free of charge from your Senator or Representative.

232 *The Star of Bethlehem* is a booklet produced by Adler Planetarium which considers various astronomical phenomena that could have produced the "Star of Bethlehem." 10¢ per copy.

Chicago Park District, 425 East 14th Blvd., Chicago, Ill. 60605

233 *A Bibliography of the Influence of the Bible on English Literature* is a listing with notes of select works on the subject. The chapter titles are: "General Works," "Types of Literature," "Biblical Subjects," "Individual Authors," and "Religious Aspects of Modern Literature." 50¢

Library, Fuller Theological Seminary, Pasadena, Calif. 91101

234 *The Clergy in Fiction and Drama* (Newsletter Vol. 34, No. 6) is a bibliography of selected works which contain significant references to the clergy. 50¢.

Extension Library, University of Tennessee, Knoxville, Tenn. 37916

236 *Moneys of the Bible* (9092) is a 61-page booklet which pictures, describes, and gives the scriptural references for virtually every coin mentioned in the Bible. $1.25.

A. E. Bebee, 4514 N. 30th Street, Omaha, Nebr. 68111

237 *The Biblical Novel Checklist* is a listing of genuine Biblical novels as distinguished from religious books. An interesting and informative essay on the Biblical novel is included. $1.00.

Dr. Arnold D. Ehlert, 13800 Biola Ave., La Mirada, Calif. 90638

238 Leaflets.

A variety of leaflets are available from the American Bible Society for 2¢ each or $1.00 per 100 of one kind. Some typical titles are listed below. Write for complete catalog.

"How to Read the Bible," (No. 16210)
"Getting More Out of Your Bible," (No. 16206)
"Where to Look in the Bible," (No. 16202)
"Forty Favorite Chapters," (No. 16208)
"Wisdom from the Bible," (No. 16215)
"Men and Women of the Bible," (No. 16211)
"Songs, Prayers, and Benedictions of the Bible," (No. 16217)
"Stories of the Bible," (No. 16214)
"Poetry of the Bible," (No. 16213)
"Young People Turn to the Bible," (No. 16216)

American Bible Society, P.O. Box 100, Ansonia Station, New York, N.Y. 10023

239 *The Death of Judas* is a dramatic reading of Judas' own reactions to his life and betrayal. A sympathetic presentation in modern idiom adapted from the French by Marie Ponsot. 25¢ per copy.

National Council of Catholic Men, 405 Lexington Ave., New York, N.Y. 10017

240 *The Basque Sheepherder and the Shepherd Psalm* is an interpretation of the Twenty-third Psalm by a Nevada shepherd. Each phrase of the Psalm is analyzed from a shepherd's point of view. 25¢.

Wool Growers' Association, 600 Crandall Building, Salt Lake City, Utah. 84100

241 Three articles on the Bible lands appeared in the December, 1964 issue of the NATIONAL GEOGRAPHIC (Vol. 126, No. 6). They are: "Holy Land, My Country" by King Hussein of Jordan, "The Other Side of Jordan" by NATIONAL GEO-

GRAPHIC staff writer Luis Marden, and "Jerusalem, My Home" by Bertha Spafford Vester, an American who has spent her life helping the unfortunate in Israel. $1.50 per copy.

National Geographic Society, Washington, D.C. 20036

242 An article on the Bible lands by Melville Bell Grosvenor, chairman of the board of the National Geographic Society, appears in the October, 1967 issue of NATIONAL GEOGRAPHIC (Vol. 132, No. 4). Entitled "Journey into the Living World of the Bible," it introduces the public to the Society's book on the Bible, EVERYDAY LIFE IN BIBLE TIMES. $1.00.

National Geographic Society, Washington, D.C. 20036

243 A special double issue of LIFE magazine tells the Bible story in word and pictures. $1.00. Order the December 25, 1964 issue (Vol. 57, No. 26).

Life Bible Issue, Time and Life Building, Chicago, Ill. 60611

244 *Bible Crostic Puzzles* (10813 P) is a book of crossword puzzles that use Biblical terms. 50¢.

Zondervan Publishing Co., 1415 Lake Drive SE, Grand Rapids, Mich. 49506

245 *500 Games for Boys and Girls* (9844 P) is a 96-page book listing puzzles, oral games, and Bible games. $1.50.

Zondervan Publishing Co., 1415 Lake Drive SE, Grand Rapids, Mich. 49506

246 *Religious Art Catalog* contains high-quality, full-color reproductions of the world's great religious art. Many countries, artists, and approaches are represented. $2.25.

New York Graphic Society, Greenwich, Conn. 06831

247 *Religion on Stamps of the United States* (Handbook No. 3) gives a picture and description of virtually every U.S. stamp with religious significance. $2.00.

Collectors of Religion on Stamps, 409 Darrow Street, Albion, Mich. 49224

248 *A History of Religion on Postage Stamps* (Topical Handbook No. 36) gives the religious and historical background for virtually every stamp ever issued anywhere in the world with religious significance. Illustrated and indexed. $4.00 for 2 vols.

American Topical Association, 3306 North 50th St., Milwaukee, Wis. 53216

249 *American Religious History* (No. 65) is a well-written presentation of books on the subject especially prepared for teachers by the American Historical Society. 50¢

Service Center for Teachers of History, 400 A Street SE, Washington, D.C. 20003

250 *Asian Religions* (No. 55) is a well-written presentation of books on the subject especially prepared for teachers by the American Historical Society. 50¢

Service Center for Teachers of History, 400 A Street SE, Washington, D.C. 20003

251   Reprints of a wide variety of articles useful to students and teachers in the study of religion and religious literature are available upon request.

Religious Instruction Association, 4001 Fairfield Ave., Fort Wayne, Ind. 46807

252   *The Celestial Railroad* by Nathaniel Hawthorne is a witty and sometimes sarcastic parody on PILGRIM'S PROGRESS. It is recognized as an outstanding representative piece of American literature and included in many English curricula. The October, 1965 issue of THE ENGLISH JOURNAL carried an article for teachers by Mr. Clifford A. Wood titled, "Teaching Hawthorne's 'Celestial Railroad.' "

In *The Celestial Railroad* Hawthorne is rebelling against the Transcendentalists and Unitarians—against those who claim that the road to Heaven is wide, easy, and open to all without obligation to anyone. The Evangelist is replaced by Mr. Smoothitaway. Wicket Gate is replaced by a railroad station. There is a bridge over the Slough of Despond, and a tunnel through Hill Difficulty. No longer does Pilgrim trudge the road of life under his burden. He now sits in a railroad car with a porter handling the luggage. The Precious Scroll is replaced by a lengthy railroad ticket. Copies of both Mr. Wood's areicle and *The Celestial Railroad* are available in quantity.

Religious Instruction Association, 4001 Fairfield Ave., Fort Wayne, Ind. 46807

6 WHAT BOOKS ARE AVAILABLE?

THE PURPOSE of this bibliography is to place before the teacher a representative list of books which will be helpful in including the Bible and religion significantly and properly in the curriculum, where it belongs. This list is not exhaustive. Some may know of other books that should have been included. This is good. Some may wonder why certain books were included at all. The answer would be that it seemed to us that in some way each of these could help the teacher, in one situation or another, in the proper handling of religion. If the listing stimulates further compilations and annotations, we will be happy, if it stimulates the study of religion in education, we will have fulfilled our aim.

The division into separate subject areas seemed logical to us, though it was hard at times to decide in what category a particular book belonged. There are some double listings. The following four divisions are used:

A *Theoretical, Practical, and Legal.* Books on "how to . . ." handling religion in the schools.

B *Literature, the Bible, and the Arts.* Books useful in full courses or for units in these areas.

C *Social Studies, Religion, and Philosophy.* Books useful in both full courses and units.

D *Children, Youth, and Elementary School.* Books usable by the student.

There are separate sections under division *B* for versions of the Bible, commentaries, and dictionaries for those interested in a detailed survey. Various study editions of the different versions are also listed, in lower-case italics.

A section of periodicals we have found useful has been appended

111

to the bibliography. The annotations on the content of books are designed to be largely factual and objective. We have not attempted to label them acceptable or unacceptable for the public schools. Identical material may be considered legal or illegal according to *how* it is used. At times the reader will certainly detect evidence of our personal enthusiasm for a book, or occasionally our despair. Not all the books have received adequate treatment, and for this we are sorry. We felt it better to include them thus incompletely rather than leave them out altogether. We look forward to a time when each book may receive the treatment it deserves.

Several other bibliographies seem to deserve mention here.

Politella, Joseph. RELIGION IN EDUCATION: AN ANNO-TATED BIBLIOGRAPHY (Oneonta, N.Y.: American Association of Colleges for Teacher Education [11 Elm St.], 1956). 90 pp. This is a very useful compilation of books that certainly deserves to be brought up to date. It is divided into seven sections and includes books on the general problem, religion and the humanities, the social studies, the natural sciences, professional education, and religion connected with the study of values.

Little, Lawrence C. RELIGION AND PUBLIC EDUCATION: A BIBLIOGRAPHY. Pittsburgh, Pa.: University of Pittsburgh, 1966. 200 pp.
This compilation contains "nearly 400 books and pamphlets by individuals and educational agencies; over 200 formal pronouncements and reports issued by religious bodies and public-school systems; over 250 doctoral dissertations and more than 350 masters' and B.D. theses . . . and over 2000 articles . . ." arranged according to these categories, not according to subjects.

Thomas, Walter L. A COMPREHENSIVE BIBLIOGRAPHY ON THE VALUE CONCEPT. Grand Rapids, Mich.: Project on Student Values (3860 Plainfield Blvd., N.E.), 1967, 44 pp.
This is intended to be an exhaustive listing of the serious literature on values and value education, including books and articles. For an explanation on the whole project see the "Grand Rapids, Michigan" entry under Sample Curricular Units.

Drouin, Brother Edmund. THE SCHOOL QUESTION: A BIBLI-OGRAPHY . . . Washington, D.C.: Catholic University of America, 1963.
The material for this book is divided according to type of literature and then further divided by subjects. Within the limits set for himself (1940–60), the author presents a comprehensive listing of the

literature that pertains to religion in public education. This was originally done as a master's thesis and an updating is planned.

Anti-Defamation League of B'nai B'rith. A BIBLIOGRAPHY ON JUDAISM AND JEWISH-CHRISTIAN RELATIONS. New York: B'nai B'rith (315 Lexington Ave.—10016), 1966.
This contains just under 300 books, mostly by Jewish authors, that deal with many different aspects of Judaism today. There are brief annotations for each book.

Religious Paperback Guild. PAPERBACK CATALOG. New York: Religious Paperback Guild (627 Broadway—10012).
This organization publishes a free comprehensive list of popular paperbacks and offers prompt mail order service.

It is hoped that these compilations, as well as the present effort, may be of help to teachers as they seek to handle the comprehensive subject of religion in the schools.

BIBLIOGRAPHY

Section A: Books Dealing with

Theoretical, Practical, and Legal Aspects of Religion and the Schools

301 American Association of School Administrators. RELIGION IN THE PUBLIC SCHOOLS. New York: Harper & Row, 1964. 68 pp. 85¢. Paperback.

The first two chapters of this special report present the historical and legal background. The middle chapter sets up a constructive philosophical framework on how to handle religion. The last two chapters make specific suggestions on how to handle religion in extracurricular and curricular activities respectively. This is one of the finest brief treatments of the subject available.

302 American Council of Education. FUNCTION OF THE PUBLIC SCHOOLS IN DEALING WITH RELIGION. Washington D.C.: American Council of Education, 1953. 145 pp. $2.00.

A very informative report on the exploratory study made by the committee on religion and education. Included are illustrations of current practices in schools and colleges, opinions of various leaders, a section on the education of teachers, and an 18-page bibliography.

303 Bailey, Thomas D. A GUIDE: TEACHING MORAL AND SPIRITUAL VALUES IN FLORIDA SCHOOLS. Bulletin 14 of the Tallahassee, Fla., State Department of Education. 1962. 86 pp. Paperback.

This bulletin is designed to serve as an aid to school faculties as they work together with community members to study and implement their own programs for developing moral and spiritual values. It attempts to define the schools' role in relation to that of the church and the synagogue.

304 Baldwin, A. Graham, *et al.* COMMITMENT AND THE

114

SCHOOL COMMUNITY. Greenwich, Conn.: Seabury Press, 1960. 118 pp. No index.

The proceedings of a conference on religion in education held in 1959 under the auspices of the Council for Religion in Independent Schools.

305 Bedsole, Adolph. THE SUPREME COURT DECISION ON BIBLE READING AND PRAYER, Grand Rapids, Mich.: Baker Book House, 1964. 55 pp. Paperback. No index.

The subtitle of the book is "America's Black-Letter Day." It is an interpretation of the court decisions by one who radically disagrees with both their premise and their conclusion.

306 Beggs, David W., and McQuigg, R. Bruce. AMERICA'S SCHOOLS AND CHURCHES: PARTNERS IN CONFLICT. Bloomington, Ind.: Indiana University Press, 1965. 241 pp. $5.95. No index.

An anthology of speeches and statements on school-religion problems.

307 Blanchard, Paul. RELIGION AND THE SCHOOLS. Boston: Beacon Press, 1963. 265 pp. $4.95. Index. Bibliography.

The author investigates aid to church schools on the basis of a consideration of the Engle case and its logic. There is an appendix on important church-state cases.

308 Boles, Donald E. THE BIBLE, RELIGION, AND THE PUBLIC SCHOOLS. New York. Collier Press, 1962. 320 pp. $1.50, paperback. Extensive index. Bibliography.

A detailed treatment of over 60 court cases dealing with religion and the public schools. Boles concentrates on the practice of devotional Bible reading, to which he is opposed (p. 253 f.). He manages to present both sides of the issue and thus provides excellent background reading for this whole area of religion in the school. A limitation of the book comes from its being written before the Abington case (and most of it before the Engle case), but the author's presentation is entirely in harmony with these rulings. This has become a sort of classic in this field.

309 Boles, H. Leo. MANUAL FOR TEACHER: A HANDBOOK OF PRACTICAL SUGGESTIONS AND HELPS FOR TEACHERS. Nashville, Tenn.: Gospel Advocate Co., 1963.

The author suggests methods for teaching the Bible. Many tables and charts included.

310 Brameld, Theodore, and Elam, Stanley, eds. VALUES IN AMERICAN EDUCATION. Bloomington, Ind.: Phi Delta Kappa, 1964. 180 pp. $4.95. No index.

A report of a symposium featuring major papers and their discussion.

311 Brown, Nicholas C., ed. THE STUDY OF RELIGION IN THE

PUBLIC SCHOOLS. Washington, D.C.: American Council on Education, 1958. $2.50. 229 pp. Paperback.

This conference report, containing the major papers and discussions, wrestles with the problem of the proper relationship between religion and education, and how much and at what level religious matter should be introduced into the curriculum of the public schools. American history is considered in detail.

312   Brubacher, John Seller. MODERN PHILOSOPHIES OF EDUCATION. New York: McGraw-Hill Book Co., 1950. $7.50. 373 pp.

The section titled "Religious and Moral Education" will be of special interest to those concerned with the philosophy of education. This well-known educator deals here with spiritual values, secularism, humanistic religious education, and supernatural religious education.

313   Burstein, Abraham. LAWS CONCERNING RELIGION IN THE UNITED STATES. Dobbs Ferry, N.Y.: Oceana Publications, 1966. 91 pp. $3.00 Index. Short bibliography. Paperback.

A brief account of the general law and 4 Supreme Court cases.

314   Committee on Religion and Education. THE FUNCTION OF THE PUBLIC SCHOOLS IN DEALING WITH RELIGION. Washington, D.C.: American Council on Education, 1953. 145 pp. No index. Bibliography. $2.00.

Deals with the whole gamut of education from elementary school to college, both public and private. After consideration of the scope of the problem, the committee makes the recommendation of " . . . a factual study of religion as the best approach to a solution. . . ." It suggests that much experimentation is needed to ascertain the desirability and feasibility of such a project. An appendix includes summaries of a questionnaire.

315   CONTROVERSIAL ISSUES IN THE CLASSROOM. Washington, D.C.: National Education Association, 1961. 30 pp. 50¢, paperback.

This "how to" book gives seven brief guidelines for handling controversial issues and then surveys current practices and policies. Religious education is the first issue referred to.

316   Costanzo, Joseph F. THIS NATION UNDER GOD. New York: Herder & Herder, 1964. 448 pp. $7.50. Short index. Imprimatur.

Subtitle, "Church, State and the Schools in America." Part I deals with religious liberty in education and traces the history of their relationship; also deals with the matter of prayer. Part II focuses on federal aid to education, which seems to be the author's major burden. Included is a table of legal cases.

317   Cox, Alva I. and Isbell, Janet. AUDIO-VISUAL RESOURCE

GUIDE, 7th ed. New York: Division of Christian Education, National Council of Churches (yearly), 1965. $3.95, ca. 515 pp.

The chief catalog of materials usable in teaching religion.

318 Dierenfield, Richard B. RELIGION IN AMERICAN PUBLIC SCHOOLS. Washington, D.C.: Public Affairs Press, 1962. 115 pp. No index.

The results of a national survey which covers the field: religion and law, curriculum, noncurriculum, released time, etc.

319 Douglas, William O. THE BIBLE AND THE SCHOOLS. Boston: Little, Brown & Co., 1966. 65 pp. $3.75. Bibliography.

A discussion by a Supreme Court Justice who voted with the majority in the prayer and Bible-reading cases. Contains an annotated bibliography.

320 Drinan, Robert F. RELIGION, THE COURTS, and PUBLIC POLICY. New York: McGraw-Hill Book Co., 1963. 261 pp. $5.95. Bibliography. Index. Imprimatur.

The author endeavors to cover the whole field from moral and spiritual values, released time, and Bible reading to aid to education, busing, etc. Includes annotated bibliography of ten selected books.

321 Duker, Sam. THE PUBLIC SCHOOLS AND RELIGION: THE LEGAL CONTEXT. New York: Harper & Row, 1966. 238 pp. $2.75. Index. Paperback.

Excerpts and discusses key court cases in an effort to make them understandable to the interested layman. Includes a table of court cases.

322 Fellman, David, ed. THE SUPREME COURT AND EDUCATION. New York: Columbia University Press, 1960, 1962. 131 pp. $2.50. No index.

A compilation of excerpts from court decisions with an introduction and notes. Also available in paperback.

323 Freund, Paul A., and Ulich, Robert. RELIGION AND THE PUBLIC SCHOOLS. Cambridge, Mass.: Harvard University Press, 1965. 54 pp. $2.00. No index.

Freund discusses the legal issue, Ulich the educational. Both discussions were originally given as lectures.

324 Friedlander, Anna Fay. THE SHARED TIME STRATEGY. St. Louis: Concordia Publishing House, 1966. 87 pp. $3.25. No index. Bibliography.

A discussion of the use of shared time to aid religious education. Contains some interesting charts.

325 Frommer, Arthur, ed. THE BIBLE AND THE PUBLIC SCHOOLS. New York: Pocket Books, 1963. 190 pp. $1.25, paperback.

After reviewing the history of the problem and other church-state issues, the author takes up the Abington case and discusses the alternatives available to the court. He reprints the testi-

mony at the trial court and the total opinion of the Supreme
Court.

326   Fuller, Edmund, ed. THE CHRISTIAN IDEA OF EDUCA-
TION. New Haven: Yale University Press, 1967. 265 pp. $1.75,
paperback.
    Tries to present a Christian philosophy of general education.
Comprises papers and discussion from a conference at Kent
School in Connecticut.

327   Gaebelein, Frank E. CHRISTIAN EDUCATION IN A DE-
MOCRACY. New York: Oxford University Press, 1951. 305
pp. $4.50. Index.
    Report of a committee of the National Association of Evan-
gelicals, including a chapter on the public schools. Although
negative in tone, it makes some good observations about the
whole scope of education.

328   Giannella, Donald A., ed. RELIGION AND THE PUBLIC
ORDER. Chicago: University of Chicago Press, 3 vols. 1964,
1965, 1966. Vols. 1 & 2 $6.00 ea., Vol. 3 $6.95.
    An annual review of church and state, and of religion, law,
and society. Consists of an anthology of significant articles
which report the developments of the past year with editorial
comment. Written in a scholarly and responsible fashion.

329   Gibbs, James E., et al. DUAL ENROLLMENT IN PUBLIC
AND NONPUBLIC SCHOOLS. Washington, D.C.: U.S. Gov-
ernment Printing Office, 1965. 83 pp. 50¢, paperback. Index.
Bibliography.
    Case studies of nine communities which are experimenting
with dual enrollment. Conducted under the auspices of the
U.S. Department of Health, Education and Welfare.

330   Gilbert, Arthur. A CATALOG OF CHURCH-STATE PROB-
LEMS. New York: National Conference of Christians and Jews,
(43 West 57th Street—10019), n.d. 6 pp. pamphlet. Single
copies free.
    A listing of issues on which religious groups differ in the
public order, with some effort at sociological analysis. May be
ordered at the above address or at the NCCJ office nearest you.

331   Hansel, Robert R. FREE TO BE CHRISTIAN IN HIGH
SCHOOL. New York: Seabury Press, 1967. 78 pp. 95¢.
    Written for teens as part of a Christian education curriculum.
Through essays and "problem situations," advises the Christian
teen-ager on how to use his free time, study opportunities, social
life, etc., in a constructive manner. Nearly one third of the
text is given over to "how to use this book"—a discussion guide
and resource list. Designed for use with a high-school youth
group.

332   Henry, Virgil. THE PLACE OF RELIGION IN THE PUBLIC
SCHOOLS. New York: Harper & Brothers, 1950. 164 pp. $2.50.

Intended as a handbook to guide communities, this book contains suggestions for studying religion in literature, social studies, the physical and biological sciences, and in music, art, and drama; also for assembly programing.

333 Huegli, Albert G. CHURCH AND STATE UNDER GOD. St. Louis: Concordia Publishing House, 1964. 516 pp. $8.00. Index.
An anthology.

334 Jacobson, Philip. RELIGION IN PUBLIC EDUCATION. New York: American Jewish Committee (165 East 56th St.— 10022), 1963. 44 pp. 75¢, paperback.
An attractive and useful guide to discussion on such topics as value education, prayer, released time, teaching religion, etc. Tries to bring in both sides of the issues.

335 Kauper, Paul G. RELIGION AND THE CONSTITUTION. Baton Rouge, La.: Louisiana State University Press, 1964. 137 pp. $1.50, paperback. Bibliography.
Includes a table of significant cases.

336 Keller, James. ALL GOD'S CHILDREN: WHAT YOUR SCHOOLS CAN DO FOR THEM. New York: Christopher Books, 1953. 270 pp. 35¢, paperback. Imprimatur. No index.
A practical book on how to teach religious concepts in secular subjects. Keller provides both a rationale and a means for such teaching. Section IV gives excerpts from presidential addresses, state constitutions, etc., that refer to God. Also available from Hanover House, Garden City, N.Y.

337 Kik, J. Marcellus. CHURCH AND STATE: THE STORY OF TWO KINGDOMS. New York: Thomas Nelson & Sons, 1963.
This book fulfills in a commendable fashion its purpose "to give an historical survey of the relationship between Church and State, beginning with the advent of Christ and brought up to the present day." Also attempts an interpretation of present-day trends in the last two chapters; here it does not succeed quite so well.

338 LeBar, Lois E. EDUCATION THAT IS CHRISTIAN. Westwood, N.J.: Fleming H. Revell, 1958. 252 pp. $4.50. No index. Bibliography.
Presents a philosophy of teaching drawn from the Bible and Christian philosophy. Intended primarily for church schools, but provides useful study for all Christian teachers.

339 Little, Lawrence C. RELIGION IN THE SOCIAL STUDIES. New York: National Conference of Christians and Jews (43 West 57th St.—10019), 1966. 122 pp. 75 cents. Paperback.
Reports on a study of the Pittsburgh school system financed by the Ford Foundation. Gives background material as well as a philosophy for including religion and contains a good set of teacher guidelines and a selected bibliography.

340 Loder, James E. RELIGION AND THE PUBLIC SCHOOLS.

New York: Association Press, 1965. 125 pp. 75¢, paperback. No index.

Presents a constructive policy for the place of religion in public education without overlooking the difficulties involved. Philosophical in tone, persuasive in logic.

341 Lowry, Charles Wesley. TO PRAY OR NOT TO PRAY. Washington, D.C.: University Press of Washington, D.C., 1963. 250 pp. Library ed. $5.00, student ed. $2.75. Bibliography. No index.

Subtitled "A Handbook for Study of Recent Supreme Court Decisions and the American Church-State Doctrine," this book takes the position that the court erred in *Engle* and argues from the "founding fathers" for a different decision. Reprints substantial sections of the court's opinions.

342 Marnell, William H. THE FIRST AMENDMENT. New York: Doubleday & Co., 1964. 247 pp. $4.50 Index. Bibliography.

Subtitled "The History of Religious Freedom in America," this is an historical survey of church-state separation from the Middle Ages to the present. Also available in paperback.

343 Mayer, Herbert C., and Towne, Ruth F. THE GOOD AMERICAN PROGRAM. New York: Council for Citizenship Education (122 East 42nd St.—10017), 1964. 62 pp. $2.00. Spiral bound.

This book is designed to facilitate the handling of moral and spiritual values in the classroom. Contains an annotated bibliography of material useful in teaching values.

344 McCollum, Vashti Cromwell. ONE WOMAN'S FIGHT. Boston: Beacon Press, 1951. 221 pp. $3.00.

The "autobiography" of the woman who led the court case against the Champaign, Illinois schools to remove religious indoctrination classes. Basic reading for anyone interested in the details of the case.

345 McDowell, John B. and Powell, Theodore RELIGION AND EDUCATION. New York: National Conference of Christians and Jews (43 West 57th Street—10019), n.d. 49 pp. 35¢.

A dialogue between a Catholic superintendent of schools and a state Department of Education official.

346 McGrath, John J. CHURCH AND STATE IN AMERICAN LAW. Milwaukee: Bruce Publishing Co., 1962. 414 pp. $7.00. Index.

Contains a supplement dealing with cases which came up shortly after it was printed, also a table of important cases.

347 McLean, Milton D. ed. RELIGIOUS STUDIES IN PUBLIC UNIVERSITIES. Carbondale, Ill.: Southern Illinois Universities, 1967. 266 pp. Paperback.

Part I is a collection of papers on the study of religion in public universities, Part II an overview of courses and programs in religion.

348   Michaelsen, Robert. THE STUDY OF RELIGION IN AMERI-
      CAN UNIVERSITIES. New Haven, Conn.: Society for Re-
      ligion in Higher Education (400 Prospect St., New Haven,
      Conn. 06511), 1965. 164 pp. Paperback.
         An examination of ten case studies of universities which
      study religion.

349   Michaelsen, Robert. THE SCHOLARLY STUDY OF RELI-
      GION IN THE COLLEGE OR UNIVERSITY. New Haven,
      Conn.: Society for Religion in Higher Education, n.d. 34 pp.
      Paperback.
         A suggestion as to how to go about studying religion in col-
      lege is presented by the former director of the School of Reli-
      gion at Iowa State University.

350   Murray, Albert Victor. EDUCATION INTO RELIGION. New
      York: Harper & Brothers, 1952.
         Attempts to provide insight into the problem of religion
      and the schools by looking at the religious development of
      English boarding-school children.

351   Murray, John Courtney. WE HOLD THESE TRUTHS. New
      York: Doubleday & Co., 1964. 317 pp. $1.25, paperback. No
      index. Imprimatur.
         The subtitle of this book is "Catholic Reflections on the
      American Proposition."

352   Niblett, W. R. CHRISTIAN EDUCATION IN A SECULAR
      SOCIETY. New York: Oxford University Press, 1960. 136 pp.
      $2.00.
         Deals with the ways in which secular school subjects can
      prepare the ground for a Christian education.

353   Nielsen, Niels C. GOD IN EDUCATION. New York: Sheed
      & Ward, 1966. 245 pp. $4.95. Index.
         A series of essays concerning the study of religion in public
      education, by one who believes that the schools must take an
      active part.

354   Phenix, Philip H. EDUCATION AND THE WORSHIP OF
      GOD. Philadelphia: Westminster Press, 1966. 192 pp. $4.50.
      Index.
         A series of seven essays, the middle five of which consider the
      relation of various disciplines to God (language, science, art,
      ethics, and history). The first and last essays, more general,
      deal with the question of ultimate meanings. Phenix suggests
      that everyone worships his "god" whenever he is concerned
      about ultimate purposes. Thus one may worship even in secular
      studies. The author is Professor of Philosophy and Education
      at Columbia Teachers College.

355   RELIGION AND THE PUBLIC SCHOOLS. Paterson, N.J.:
      Department of Social Sciences, Paterson State College, 1965.
      56 pp. $2.00. Mimeographed.
         Here are the proceedings of the college's seventh annual

institute for social studies teachers. It includes a review of opportunities for teaching about religion in American history, world history, and elsewhere in the social studies curricula.

356   RELIGION IN THE PUBLIC SCHOOLS. Symposium. New York: Religious Education Association (545 West 111th St.— 10025). 1964. 36 pp. 35¢.

A reprint of articles representing nineteen responses to the Supreme Court's invitation to study the Bible objectively in the public schools. From *Religious Education*.

357   RELIGIOUS FREEDOM IN AMERICA: CHANGING MEANINGS IN THE PAST AND PRESENT. Symposium. New York: National Conference of Christians and Jews, 1963. 75 pp. Paperback.

Articles by John Tracy Ellis, Franklin H. Littell, Bertram W. Korn, Edward Duff, and Sidney Hook, giving Catholic, Protestant, and Jewish opinion on religious freedom in America. A reprint from *Cross Currents* for Winter, 1963.

358   Reutter, E. Edmund. SCHOOLS AND THE LAW. Dobbs Ferry, N.Y.: Oceana Publications, 1964. 112 pp. $3.00. Index. Paperback.

Deals with the whole context of the school-law problem: the place of the federal government, local boards, responsibility for pupils, transportation, paying for the schools, and so forth. In the last chapter the author endeavors to show emerging judicial trends.

359   Rice, Charles E. THE SUPREME COURT AND PUBLIC PRAYER. New York: Fordham University Press, 1964. 202 pp. $5.00. Index.

Subtitled "The Need for Restraint."

360   Sebaly, A. L., ed. TEACHER EDUCATION AND RELIGION. Oneonta, N.Y.: American Association of Colleges for Teacher Education, 1959. 292 pp. Index.

Sebaly here gives us an anthology. A bibliography is included with each chapter.

361   Senate Subcommittee on Constitutional Amendments. HEARINGS ON SJR 148: RELATING TO PRAYER IN PUBLIC SCHOOLS. Washington, D.C.: U.S. Government Printing Office, 1966. 884 pp. $3.00, paperback.

A complete transcript of the hearings, with much divergent testimony on Dirksen's proposed prayer amendment. Includes a huge fold-out map of religion in America in 1950, a series of maps and charts relating to religious practices and the schools, and much informative testimony before the committee.

362   Smith, Elwyn A. CHURCH-STATE RELATIONS IN ECUMENICAL PERSPECTIVE. Pittsburgh: Duquesne University Press, 1966.

Here is an anthology on the relationship between church and state by Catholics, Jews, and Protestants.

363   Stedman, Murray S. RELIGION AND POLITICS IN AMER-
       ICA. New York: Harcourt, Brace & World, 1964. 168 pp.
       $2.95, paperback. Index. Bibliography.

364   Stokes, Anson Phelps, and Pfeffer, Leo. CHURCH AND
       STATE IN THE UNITED STATES. New York: Harper &
       Row, 1964. 660 pp. $12.50. Index. Major bibliography.
           The foundations of separation, the early establishment in
       America, and the present situation are dealt with in detail in
       this major work on church-state relations. A condensation by
       Pfeffer of a classic 3-volume work by Stokes.

365   Stoops, John A. RELIGIOUS VALUES IN EDUCATION.
       Danvill, Ill.: Interstate Printers and Publishers, 1967. 161 pp.
       $4.95. Index.
           Shows that we cannot have education that is not permeated
       with religious values of one kind or another—theistic, scientific,
       pantheistic, or atheistic. Also explores how these various philoso-
       phies appear in public school curriculum, with traditional theism
       coming out on the short end. Originally designed for teachers
       in graduate study of the philosophical foundations of education.

366   Stroup, Herbert. CHURCH AND STATE IN CONFRONTA-
       TION. New York: Seabury Press, 1967. $6.95.
           Gives a sociological description and analysis of the nature
       of church and state from a wide historical perspective.

367   Tead, Ordway. THE RELATION OF RELIGION TO EDU-
       CATION. Hazen Pamphlet No. 9. Haddam, Conn.: Edward
       W. Hazen Foundation, n.d.
           One of the best pamphlets on religion in education that this
       theologically liberal-oriented foundation has produced.

368   Tussman, Joseph, ed. THE SUPREME COURT ON CHURCH
       AND STATE. New York: Oxford University Press, 1962. 305
       pp. $1.95, paperback. No. index.
           Compiled to make the work of the Supreme Court more
       easily available for a variety of educational purposes. Reprints 29
       U.S. Supreme Court cases, most of them in full, including all
       important cases on church and state, and nearly all those dealing
       with religion up to 1962. Does not include *Engle* or *Abington*.

369   Wainwright, J. A. SCHOOL AND CHURCH: PARTNERS
       IN CHRISTIAN EDUCATION. New York: Oxford University
       Press, 1963. 107 pp. $1.20, paperback.
           Wainwright gives some suggestions for common action by
       church and school within the framework of the education acts
       in Britain.

370   Warshaw, Thayer. WE'RE STUDYING THE BIBLE IN
       OUR HIGH SCHOOL. New York: National Conference of
       Christians and Jews (43 West 57th St.—10019). A pamphlet.
       Single copies free.
           This is a reprint from *Liberty* magazine, presenting some
       ideas for Bible study in the public school.

371 Wilder, Amos N., ed. LIBERAL LEARNING AND RELIGION. New York: Harper & Brothers, 1951. 338 pp. $3.75.

This professor at Harvard Divinity School has given his book the subtitle: "A Vital Discussion of Major Issues Confronting the Universities Where There Is Serious Concern for Religion."

372 Wolterstorff, Nicholas. RELIGION AND THE SCHOOLS. Grand Rapids, Mich.: Wm. B. Eerdmans, 1965. 45 pp. 65¢, paperback.

Deals with the nature of society and public and private schools. He argues in Part I that a Christian commitment to life dictates a pluralistic society, where each man is free to choose his own position; in Part III, that private schools are the only solution. For he tries to show (Part II) that the public school cannot please at the same time those who believe religion must be part of the education process and those who believe it cannot be.

Section B: Books Dealing with

Literature, The Bible, and the Arts

373 Ackerman, James S. ON TEACHING THE BIBLE AS LITERATURE. Bloomington, Ind.: Indiana University Press, 1967. 121 pp. $1.45, paperback. No index. Selected bibliography.

This book is part of the English Curriculum Study Series and has the subtitle "A Guide to Selected Biblical Narratives for Secondary Schools." Part I contains a brief sketch of Israel's history to the time of David. Part II discusses the history and development of the texts of the Bible themselves. Part III contains sample questions and teacher's notes—this would be the most helpful part to the classroom teacher, although the author is a little dogmatic about his particular interpretations.

374 Adams, J. M. BIBLICAL BACKGROUNDS. Nashville, Tenn.: Broadman Press, 1934. $6.50.

This old classic, which gives geographical background to aid in the study of the Bible, has been recently revised.

375 Ahern, Barnabas M., (gen. ed.) NEW TESTAMENT READING GUIDE. Collegeville, Minn.: Liturgical Press, n.d. Imprimatur.

This is a series of 14 small booklets on the New Testament to aid the general reader. They sell for 35¢ each.

376 Allen, Irene. A SHORT INTRODUCTION TO THE OLD TESTAMENT: A GRADED COURSE FOR MIDDLE FORMS. New York: Oxford University Press, 1963. 193 pp. $1.20.

The book is illustrated and contains maps.

377 A READY-REFERENCE HISTORY OF THE ENGLISH BIBLE. New York, 1965. 43 pp. 25¢, paperback. Bibliography.

This handy booklet traces the development of the English Bible from Wycliffe to modern translations (NEB). It devotes a page or two to each translation, with comparison charts of verses taken from each. It also gives a brief bibliographical description of first editions. A chronology of the English Bible from 1484–1629 is another helpful feature.

378 Anderson, Bernhard W. UNDERSTANDING THE OLD TESTAMENT. Englewood Cliffs, N.J.: Prentice-Hall, 1957, 1966. 586 pp. $8.75. Index. Bibliography.

Gives historical background for biblical study, including information on ancient histories of the areas in and around the Holy Land.

379 Anderson, Bernhard W. THE UNFOLDING DRAMA OF THE BIBLE. New York: Association Press, 1957. 75¢, paperback.

This guide is intended mainly for discussion groups and endeavors to show the "major scenes" of the Bible. Provocative questions are appended to each section to facilitate discussion.

380 Andrews, H. T. AN INTRODUCTION TO THE APOCRYPHAL BOOKS. Grand Rapids, Mich.: Baker Book House, 1964. 140 pp. $2.95. Index. Select bibliography.

Deals with the Apocryphal book of both the Old and the New Testament.

381 Archer, Gleason L. A SURVEY OF OLD TESTAMENT INTRODUCTION. Chicago: Moody Press, 1964. 500 pp. $6.95. Bibliography. Subject index. Scripture index.

A systematic study of Old Testament backgrounds. Part I is a general introduction and deals with higher and lower criticism, Hebrew manuscripts, the documentary theory, canon, etc. Part II is a special introduction and treats each book of the Old Testament as to its background, outline, theories of composition, and problems. This is a major work by a conservative scholar who tries to deal fairly with differing representative views. It was prepared as a text for college and seminary students.

382 Asimov, Isaac. WORDS FROM THE EXODUS. Boston: Houghton Mifflin Co., 1963. $3.25.

A useful and easily read book that traces words in the Book of Exodus to their origin.

383 Bachman, John W., and Brown, E. Martin. BETTER PLAYS FOR TODAY'S CHURCHES. New York: Association Press, 1964. 474 pp. $8.95.

This book contains twelve plays on modern society, Christmas, the Passion, and Old Testament themes.

384 Baird, William. THE CORINTHIAN CHURCH—A BIBLICAL APPROACH TO URBAN CULTURE. New York: Abingdon Press, 1964. 224 pp. $4.95. General index. Scripture index.

A practical book relating the Bible to modern problems. Once a selection for the Religious Book Club.

385   Baker, Archibald G., ed. A SHORT HISTORY OF CHRISTIANITY. Chicago: University of Chicago Press, 1940. 280 pp. $1.50, paperback. Index. Bibliography.

386   Baldwin, Robert Chester, and McPeek. James A. S. INTRODUCTION TO PHILOSOPHY THROUGH LITERATURE. New York: Ronald Press, 1950. 595 pp. $7.00.

387   Ballou, Robert, ed. THE BIBLE OF THE WORLD. New York: Viking Press, 1967. 1415 pp. Text edition $10.00. Other $7.25. Glossary. Index. Bibliography.

This book contains substantial excerpts from the Hindu, Buddhist, Confucianist, Taoist, Zoroastrian, Jewish, Christian, and Muslim holy books. One does not have to agree with the editor's premise that these are all "streams to God" to find this a very valuable book. The author has tried to give the "essential" Scripture of each religion.

388   Barbour, Russell and Ruth. RELIGIOUS IDEAS FOR ARTS
(389) AND CRAFTS. Philadelphia: Christian Education Press, 1959. 95 pp. $2.75. Index. Bibliography.

The purpose here is to "stimulate craft workers and leaders in the field of religion to make use of religious ideas in art and craft work." Suitable craft projects are suggested, with symbols giving instructions to craft leaders for carrying them out. Covers both group and individual work. 50 pages of designs included.

390   Barclay, William. ed. THE GOSPEL OF MARK. Philadelphia: Westminster Press, 1956. $2.50.

This commentary on the Book of Mark is for the average reader and comments on Mark in paragraph fashion. Contains background material as well.

391   Barclay, William. THE MAKING OF THE BIBLE, New York: Abingdon Press, 1961. 100 pp. $1.00.

This book about the origin of the Bible is also an introduction to a series of commentaries.

392   Barclay, William. THE MIND OF JESUS. New York: Harper & Row, 1960. 340 pp. $5.00. Index.

393   Barnes, Albert. THE APOSTLE PAUL. Grand Rapids, Mich.: Baker Book House, 1950. 496 pp.

Gives good insight into scenes and incidents in the life of the Apostle Paul. The author begins with his early training and traces his whole career. A separate chapter is devoted to each of the several cities in which Paul visited, and to each of the individuals and groups before whom he appeared prior to his voyage to Rome. The closing chapters consider his trial in Rome and his death.

394   Barth, Christoph. INTRODUCTION TO THE PSALMS. New

York: Charles Scribner's Sons, 1966. 86 pp. $1.95, paperback. Scripture index. General index. Short bibliography.

This is a scholarly monograph about the Psalms.

395   Barton, Bruce. THE BOOK NOBODY KNOWS. New York: Bobbs-Merrill Co., 1959. 190 pp. $1.35, paperback.

A classic that explains the Bible in popular language. This is a book about the Bible by an advertising executive.

396   Barton, Bruce. THE MAN NOBODY KNOWS. New York: Bobbs-Merrill Co., 1952. $1.35, paperback.

In this classic, Barton examines the character of Jesus as a man. He shows him enjoying life and shaping an organization that is to win the world. He attempts to help us visualize Jesus as a real person.

397   Bassage, Harold. GOD AND HIS PEOPLE. New York: Seabury Press, 1966. 210 pp. $4.95. Index.

A selection of Bible stories from the Old Testament, using the King James Version text and arranged in verse form.

398   Baxter, Kay M. CONTEMPORARY THEATRE AND THE CHRISTIAN FAITH. Nashville, Tenn.: Abingdon Press, 1964. 112 pp. $2.75. Index.

The stated aim of this book is "to observe the points at which the secondary 'new' theater can illuminate some of the problems which Christians face in understanding and communicating their faith."

399   Beegle, Dewey M. GOD'S WORD INTO ENGLISH. Grand Rapids, Mich.: Wm. B. Eerdman, 1960. 230 pp. $2.25, paperback. Scripture index. General index.

By reviewing the highlights of transmission of the English Bible and comparing how translations past and present have dealt with difficult problems, the author seeks to enable the modern reader to understand the message of the Bible. An 8-page section of photographs of old versions and languages is informative.

400   Beek, M. A. A CONCISE HISTORY OF ISRAEL. New York: Harper & Row, 1963. 224 pp. $4.95. Scripture index. Author index.

Covers the history of Israel from the call of Abraham to the revolt of Bar Kochba.

401   Belford, Lee A., gen. ed. RELIGIOUS DIMENSIONS IN LITERATURE. The Seabury Reading Program. New York: Seabury Press, 1967. 85 cents.

A series of booklets which examine the religious dimensions of both contemporary and classical works. Representative titles include THE SPIRE, and GALILEO; future titles include THE PLAGUE, WAITING FOR GODOT, TILL WE HAVE FACES, and others.

402   Benson, Clarence H. OLD TESTAMENT SURVEY: POETRY

AND PROPHECY. Wheaton, Ill.: Evangelical Teacher Training Association, 1963. 96 pp. $1.50. Spiral bound.

Part of the teacher training series described under No. 586. Covers Job through Malachi.

403   BIBLE STUDY COURSE. Dallas, Tex.: Dallas Independent School District, 1960. Approx. 100 pp. each. $1.00. Bibliography. No index.

These two student guides, the Old and New Testaments attempt to avoid controversial issues by emphasizing study of the Bible itself. Questions are given as a guide to student reading.

404   Blaiklock, E. M. THE CENTURY OF THE NEW TESTAMENT. Chicago: Inter-Varsity Press, 1962. 158 pp. $1.25, paperback. Short bibliography. General index. Scripture index.

By thorough knowledge of both the New Testament and other histories of the Mediterranean world, the author enlivens the circumstances surrounding the birth and death of Jesus and the establishment of the church. He places New Testament events squarely in their historical place in the first century. Separate chapters discuss Rome, the emperors, Greeks and Jews, the Herods, the procurators, the rebellion, the Flavians, and the end of the century. Helpful appendices include a chart of the emperors, a chart of the Herod family, a year-by-year chronology of the century, and a discussion of the date of Jesus' birth. An informal and fast-moving book.

405   Bouquet, A. C. EVERYDAY LIFE IN NEW TESTAMENT TIMES. New York: Charles Scribner's Sons, 1953. 236 pp. $4.50. Index.

A history of the life of common people in the Mediterranean world in the first century, amply illustrated with many authentic pictures and drawings. How people lived, in what kinds of houses, what they did to make a living and or for recreation how they carried on their business and their worship—these are only a few of the questions answered by this intriguing book.

406   Bowie, Walter Russell. THE STORY OF THE BIBLE. Nashville, Tenn.: Abingdon Press, 1934. $4.95.

The Biblical story is retold from Genesis to Revelation for both the young and the mature, in the light of present knowledge.

407   Bratton, Fred G. A HISTORY OF THE BIBLE: AN INTRODUCTION TO THE HISTORICAL METHOD. Boston: Beacon Press, 1959. 382 pp. $4.95. ($2.45 paperback.) Major bibliography. Index.

The full story of the origin and development of the Bible as a human document, explaining how it was written, how the separate books were gathered into the canon, how this was translated into English, and how men have read the Bible ever since. By a liberal Christian with a somewhat unsystematic theology. Does a good job of relating archaeology to the Bible and includes a chronology of Bible literature. Designed both for the general reader and as a text in Biblical literature. The author states his purpose as being "to review the main lines of Biblical study and make the reader conscious of the chief critical problems."

408 Bright, John. THE AUTHORITY OF THE OLD TESTAMENT. Nashville, Tenn.: Abingdon Press, 1967. 272 pp. $5.50. Index. Comprehensive bibliography.

Addressed primarily to theological students and ministers, but of some interest to the general reader.

409 Brooks, Cleanth. THE HIDDEN GOD. New Haven: Yale University Press, 1963. 136 pp. $1.45, paperback.

Subtitled "Studies in Hemingway, Faulkner, Yeats, Eliot and Warren," the book studies these authors and their "theological implications."

410 Brown, Helen A., and Heltman, Harry J. CHORAL READINGS FROM THE BIBLE. Philadelphia: Westminster Press, 1955. 63 pp. $1.00. Topical index.

Old and New Testament Scripture passages are arranged into "parts" for dramatic reading (selections from the Revised Standard Version).

411 Browne, Lewis. THE GRAPHIC BIBLE. New York: The Macmillan Co., 1939. A collection of maps & charts.

412 Bruce, F. F. THE NEW TESTAMENT DOCUMENTS: ARE THEY RELIABLE? Chicago: Inter-Varsity Press, 1965. $1.25.

Historical evidence is scrutinized for the reliability, and thus the truth, of the New Testament Scriptures.

413 Bunyan, John. THE PILGRIM'S PROGRESS. New York: Simon & Schuster, 1957. 308 pp. 45¢, paperback.

A reprint of the classic allegory about the Christian life.

414 Burke, Carl F. GOD IS FOR REAL, MAN. New York: Association Press, 1966. 128 pp. $1.75, paperback.

The chaplain of the Erie County Jail in Buffalo, N.Y. here presents an interpretation of Bible passages and stories as told by some of the juvenile delinquents he has worked with: "The Lord is my shepherd" becomes "The Lord is like my probation officer." The "Parable of the Lost Sheep" becomes the "Story of the Lost Heap."

415 Cassels, Louis. YOUR BIBLE. New York: Doubleday & Co., 1967. 220 pp. $4.95. Index.

The author begins with portions of the New Testament (Luke) and works back into parts of the Old Testament. He suggests passages to be studied with special care, to be read for background, or to be skipped. Designed to facilitate an informed reading of the Bible for those not familiar with it.

416 Chase, Mary Ellen. THE BIBLE AND THE COMMON

READER. New York: The Macmillan Co., 1962. 381 pp. $1.45, paperback.

Here a literature teacher has written, for those unfamiliar with the Bible, one of the most popular "Bible as literature" books around. The introduction covers 86 pages and discusses what the Bible is and how it came to us. The Old Testament section in 189 pages covers early stories ("legends"), great leaders, the tragedy of Saul, biography of David, stormy times of the kings, prophecy, fiction (Ruth, Jonah, Esther), Job, poetry, proverbs, Ecclesiastes, and Daniel. The Apocrypha are covered in 10 pages and the New Testament in 56 pages. Luke, Paul's letters, and the Book of Revelation are considered.

417   Chase, Mary Ellen. LIFE AND LANGUAGE IN THE OLD TESTAMENT. New York: W. W. Norton & Co., 1955. $1.45, paperback.

A discussion of the background of the Hebrew people, their philosophy, attitudes, and search for God.

418   Chase, Mary Ellen. THE PROPHETS FOR THE COMMON READER. New York: W. W. Norton & Co., 1963. 183 pp. $4.50. No index.

A popular English professor here considers Amos, Hosea, Isaiah, Micah, and Jeremiah.

419   Conybeare, W. J., and Howson, J. S. THE LIFE AND EPISTLES OF ST. PAUL. Grand Rapids, Mich.: Wm. B. Eerdmans, 1964. 850 pp. $5.50.

An old classic, also available in other editions, including paperback.

420   Corbett, J. Elliott. THE PROPHETS ON MAIN STREET. Richmond, Va.: John Knox Press, 1965. $2.00. 155 pp. paperback.

A very imaginative rendition of sections of Amos, Isaiah, Jonah, and Jeremiah, using modern people and nations and dealing with present-day social problems. The parallels are often striking, though not always accurate.

421   Corey, Orlin. THE BOOK OF JOB. Anchorage, Ky.: Children's Theater Press, 1960. 73 pp.

Job as a religious drama, arranged from the King James Version.

422   Corswant, W. A DICTIONARY OF LIFE IN BIBLE TIMES. New York: Oxford University Press, 1960. 330 pp. $6.50. Illustrated.

Information on the personal, social, and religious life of the Israelites and early Christians.

423   Cunningham, James F. THE LIFE OF JESUS. Huntington, Ind.: Our Sunday Visitor. 200 pp. n.d. Imprimatur.

424   Daniel-Rops, Henri. DAILY LIFE IN THE TIME OF JESUS.

New York: New American Library, 1962. 448 pp. 95¢, paperback. Index. Bibliography. Imprimatur.

Background material for a study of the Gospels, written by a Catholic scholar who has distinguished himself in this field, but writes understandably for the layman. This translation from the French is a reconstruction of Biblical Palestine and the day-to-day life and customs of its people.

425 Daniel-Rops, Henri. WHAT IS THE BIBLE? New York: Guild Press, 1958. 211 pp. 85¢, paperback. Imprimatur.

This translation from the French presents a Catholic look at the Bible, with background, introduction, and survey material.

426 Davies, Horton. A MIRROR OF THE MINISTRY IN MODERN NOVELS. New York: Oxford University Press, 1959. $4.25.

Novels by Hawthorne, Lewis, Maugham and others are examined for their spiritual relevance.

427 Davies, W. D. INVITATION TO THE NEW TESTAMENT: A GUIDE TO ITS MAIN WITNESSES. New York: Doubleday & Co., 1966. 540 pp. $6.95. Index. Bibliography.

Written for the nonspecialist, this book attempts to bridge the gap from the twentieth century back to the first. Davies is professor of Biblical Theology at Union Theological Seminary.

428 Davies, W. D. THE SERMON ON THE MOUNT. Cambridge, Eng.: The University Press, 1966. 163 pp. $1.65, paperback. Scripture index.

Davies attempts to give us the setting for the Sermon on the Mount by examining Matthew, the Jewish Messianic expectations, contemporary Judaism, the early church, and the ministry of Jesus.

429 Dean, B. S. AN OUTLINE OF BIBLE HISTORY. Cincinnati: Standard Publishing Co., 1912.

A good, brief historical outline showing the unity throughout the Bible. It outlines the books of law and of history from the Old Testament. From the New Testament it gives the gospel and apostolic history, including the founding and spread of the church.

430 Deen, Edith. ALL OF THE WOMEN OF THE BIBLE. New York: Harper & Row, 1955. $4.95.

A popularly written book by a nationally known author on women's affairs. Includes information on all the named women of the Bible and a chronological listing of the unnamed ones. Pertinent information about customs of Biblical times is also included.

431 Deen, Edith. FAMILY LIVING IN THE BIBLE. New York: Harper & Row, 1963. 274 pp. $4.95. Index.

The author presents a detailed study of the origins, relationships, strengths, and activities of the family. Originally written as a master's thesis.

432   Defoe, Daniel. ADVENTURES OF ROBINSON CRUSOE. Chicago: Moody Press, 1965. 256 pp. 89¢, paperback.

This universally familiar tale, first published in 1719, is seldom known as a religious story. The purpose of this edition is to reinsert many passages which appeared in the original work but have been virtually eliminated in the course of many abridgments. These include: Crusoe's recognition of the Holy Spirit working in his life, his realization that he is a sinner, his acceptance of Christ, his recognition of the loving providence of God, and various attempts to convert Friday to faith in Christ.

433   Dennett, Herbert. A GUIDE TO MODERN VERSIONS OF THE NEW TESTAMENT. Chicago: Moody Press, 1966. 142 pp. $2.95. Annotated bibliography. Scripture index.

Seeks to show us how to regard the various translations of the New Testament. The author combines a high view of Scripture as "God communicating with His creatures" with a practical and hard-nosed scholarship that analyzes each of nearly 40 versions for its strength and weaknesses. The first 20 pages explain versions and the process of translation, then each version is examined in detail. There are helpful appendices on the Greek text, concordances, and so on. Dennett recommends no "best" translation but suggests use of several: one quite literal, one colloquial, and one close to the Greek grammar. This book should be useful to the general student.

434   Dentan, Robert C. THE APOCRYPHA—BRIDGE OF THE TESTAMENTS. New York: Seabury Press, 1954. $1.25, paperback.

435   DeWelt, Don. SACRED HISTORY AND GEOGRAPHY. Grand Rapids, Mich.: Baker Book House, 1955. 200 pp. $4.95. No index.

A workbook and teaching manual, chronologically arranged and amply illustrated.

436   Dodd, C. H. THE BIBLE TODAY. New York: Cambridge University Press, 1946. 168 pp. $2.95. ($1.45, paperback.) Scripture index.

Dodd explains the importance and significance of the Bible, and its meaning and place in religious history. Chapters 1–4 examine the Bible and its parts in their historical setting, stressing their unity. Chapters 5–7 deal with the concept of history as revelation and its meaning for men today.

437   Dougherty, John J. SEARCHING THE SCRIPTURES. New York: Doubleday & Co., 1959. 75¢. 239 pp. Paperback. Imprimatur.

This popular guide to the reading and study of the Bible

gives both historical background and theological explanations.

438 Drijvers, Pius. THE PSALMS: THEIR STRUCTURE AND MEANING. New York: Herder & Herder, 1964. 270 pp. $5.50. Index.

The Psalms are grouped according to their purpose (praise, thanksgiving, petition, etc.) and discussed.

439 Dumbauld, Edward. SAYINGS OF JESUS. Scottdale, Pa.: Herald Press, 1967.

A systematic arrangement, classified and organized under appropriate headings so that the reader may have before him at a glance all that Jesus said on any given subject.

440 Dunnett, Walter M. NEW TESTAMENT SURVEY. Wheaton, Ill.: Evangelical Teacher Training Association, 1965. 96 pp. $1.50. Spiral bound.

This is part of the teacher training series described under No. 586. It gives background and surveys the whole New Testament with maps and charts.

441 Dunnett, Walter M. AN OUTLINE OF NEW TESTAMENT SURVEY. Chicago: Moody Press, 1960. 176 pp. $1.75, paperback. Index. Bibliography. Illustrated.

442 Eason, J. Lawrence. NEW BIBLE SURVEY. Grand Rapids, Mich.: Zondervan Publishing Co., 1963. 544 pp. $6.95. Index. Extensive bibliography.

A Ph.D. who was for 36 years a university professor of English and literature here gives us a survey of the whole Bible. Designed primarily for introductory survey courses in Christian colleges. Each book has an introduction, and most or all of the following are given: biography of the author, history and geographical background, illustrations, chronology, synopsis, analysis, interpretation, evaluation, and discussion of meaning and divine purpose. Other reading is suggested for each. A conservative view.

443 Edersheim, Alfred. THE LIFE AND TIMES OF JESUS THE MESSIAH. Grand Rapids, Mich.: Wm. B. Eerdmans, 1953.

This old classic is the work of a lifetime of study. It gives detailed cultural and religious background material for the Gospels.

444 Elder, John. PROPHETS, IDOLS, AND DIGGERS. Indianapolis: Bobbs-Merrill Co., 1960.

Contains information about discoveries made by archaeologists in the Holy Land.

445 Elliot, Melvin E. THE LANGUAGE OF THE KING JAMES BIBLE. New York: Doubleday & Co., 1967. 227 pp. $4.95. Bibliography.

To understand the King James Version today you need this kind of book. Here is an alphabetically arranged glossary of archaic and difficult words. Most helpful where words are still in common use but have changed somewhat in meaning (e.g., "observation": observance—keeping a set of rules—cf. Luke 17:20). The author does omit some difficult words ("concupiscence") while including some obvious ones ("me"). But it is an exceedingly useful book.

446   Ellis, Peter. THE MEN AND THE MESSAGE OF THE OLD TESTAMENT. Collegeville, Minn.: Liturgical Press, 1963. 560 pp. $8.00 ($3.95, paperback). Index. Bibliography. Imprimatur.

Under four headings: "Pentateuch," "Deuteronomist," "Chronicles," and "Didactic," Ellis deals with the types of literature contained in the Bible and attempts to place them in chronological order. Included are exegetical and geographical notes and color maps and charts, also a full-color fold-out timeline. One helpful feature of this book is a listing of significant passages with brief annotations. This will aid the teacher in condensing large portions without missing important facets.

447   Evans, William. OUTLINE STUDY OF THE BIBLE. Chicago: Moody Press, 1941. 59¢, paperback.

This dispensationalist view of the Bible considers the whole and then section by section, with 16 charts.

448   Eversole, Finley. CHRISTIAN FAITH AND THE CONTEMPORARY ARTS. New York: Abingdon Press, 1962. 255 pp. $5.00. Index. Major bibliography.

Part I considers the artist and Part II deals with the arts themselves: poetry, novel, drama (with motion picture and TV), music and dance, painting, sculpture, and architecture—along with cartoons and comic strips.

449   EVERYDAY LIFE IN BIBLE TIMES. Washington, D.C.: National Geographic Society, 1967. 448 pp. $9.95. Index.

This outstanding combination of text and color photos of usual National Geographic quality gives one a vivid journey through Israel today. A treasury of art masterpieces in Biblical archaeology. Done by 7 Bible scholars, with 11 special maps. These include a giant wall map as well as one showing the Exodus route superimposed on a photo taken by an orbiting astronaut.

450   Feidelson, Charles. SYMBOLISM AND AMERICAN LITERATURE. Chicago: University of Chicago Press, 1953. 355 pp. $2.25, paperback.

451   Fenenga, Alica, Haan, Gertrude and Merizon, Beth. THE PILOT SERIES IN LITERATURE. 3 vols. Grand Rapids, Mich.: Wm. B. Eerdmans, 1957. 500 pp. each vol. $5.50.

A series of three literature books designed primarily for junior highers in Christian schools. The guiding idea has been to compile a set of positive, Christian-oriented stories that will aid the student in forming a set of values and discrimination.

The compilers used three criteria for content: spiritual significance, general significance (historical, etc.), and interest appeal. Much well-known as well as some obscure material appears; we have Mark Twain, Walt Whitman, Carl Sandburg, and also John Bunyan, the Book of Common Prayer, and the Bible. Book III contains a number of selections from world literature. These stories were all tested in junior high classes for suitability.

452 Ferguson, George. SIGNS AND SYMBOLS IN CHRISTIAN ART. Washington, D.C.: National Gallery of Art, 1954. 123pp. ½" x 11".

Ferguson discusses the source and use of symbols, with over 350 illustrations (16 in full color) from paintings by Renaissance artists in the Samuel H. Kress Collection.

453 Fosdick, Harry Emerson. A GUIDE TO UNDERSTANDING THE BIBLE. New York: Harper & Row, 1938. 348 pp. $1.75, paperback. General index. Scripture index. Bibliography.

Subtitled "The Development of Ideas with the Old and New Testaments," this book by a liberal Protestant considers God, man, right and wrong, suffering, fellowship with God, and immortality.

454 Frank, John P., and Hogan, Robert F. OBSCENITY, THE LAW, AND THE ENGLISH TEACHER. Champaigne, Ill.: National Council of Teachers of English, 1966, 62 pp. Paperback.

Two papers on the problem of obscenity. One describes an experiment in which "experts" examine and answer questions about "obscene" material. The second argues the view that the best way to defeat pornography is to strengthen the reader with good imaginative literature—not to stamp out the germs, but vaccinate the potential victim.

455 Fraser, Gordon H. ELIJAH THE PILGRIM PROPHET. Chicago: Moody Press, 1956.

A Christian interpretation of Elijah's life and ministry. Somewhat devotional in character.

456 Frye, Roland Mushat. SHAKESPEARE AND CHRISTIAN DOCTRINE. Princeton, N.J.: Princeton University Press, 1963. 314 pp. $6.00. Index. Bibliography.

A research professor at Folger Shakespeare Library in Washington, D.C. here examines Shakespeare's plays in the light of Christian understanding. In addition to an 8-page bibliography the author includes an index to Shakespeare's plays and a subject index. Also available in paperback.

457 Fulghum, W. B. DICTIONARY OF BIBLICAL ALLUSIONS IN ENGLISH LITERATURE. New York: Holt, Rinehart & Winston, 1965. 291 pp. $3.95, paperback.

This book has at least two uses: (1) to identify the meaning of Biblical references or allusions as one comes upon them in literature, and (2) to make available a few representative passages containing the major ones (the word allusion is used here in the broad sense of words or stories). This very well-done book gives a definition of the allusion (arranged alphabetically) by both citing the references and quoting the relevant scripture passages and then listing a few major works alluding to them. The author, who is chairman of the English Department at Central Connecticut State College, uses the King James Version, first because it is in itself a literary work, and secondly because most of the Biblical references with which our language and literature are filled come from this version. This book should also be useful to students of the fine arts because of the large number of references in painting, sculpture, and music.

458 Fuller, Edmund. JOHN MILTON. New York: Seabury Press, 1967. 256 pp. $3.95.

Milton is here brought to life as the passionate, fearless, brilliant man he was—painted large against the rich and turbulent background of his time.

459 Gelin, Albert. THE KEY CONCEPTS OF THE OLD TESTAMENT. New York: Paulist Press, 1963. 94 pp. 75¢, paperback. No index. Imprimatur.

This concise and thoughtful book deals with the concepts of God, His purposes, and personal salvation as they appear in the Old Testament. The author does not try to bring us back to the Old Testament, but rather to glean its ideas and concepts.

460 Gettys, Joseph M. HOW TO ENJOY STUDYING THE BIBLE. Richmond, Va.: John Knox Press, 1945. 72 pp. $1.00, paperback.

A book of practical suggestions.

461 Gettys, Joseph M. HOW TO TEACH THE BIBLE. Richmond, Va.: John Knox Press, 1961. 112 pp. $2.00, paperback. Annotated bibliography.

A combination of Biblical and methodological skills are here combined with great ease.

462 Gilbertson, Merril T. THE WAY IT WAS IN BIBLE TIMES. Minneapolis: Augsburg Publishing House, 1959. $1.75, paperback.

Here is encyclopedic form and nontechnical language is much rich Biblical background material.

463 Ginegan, Jack. HANDBOOK OF BIBLICAL CHRONOLOGY. Princeton, N.J.: Princeton University Press, 1964. 338 pp. $8.50. Index.

The problems of dating Biblical events here receive a very scholarly treatment. Part I discusses the principles of chronology in the ancient world: measurements, the calendar, early attempts at chronology, and so forth. Part II takes up problems of

chronology in the Bible and presents the options available. "The
whole question of how time was reckoned in the ancient biblical world is here reviewed in the fullest possible manner."
Aptly said.

464 Goldberg, David. MEET THE PROPHETS. New York:
Twayne Publishers, 1956. $2.75.
Written at the junior-high level, this fascinating narrative
uses both Biblical history and archaeology to describe the men
who made Judaism great.

465 Goldman, Solomon. THE TEN COMMANDMENTS. Chicago:
University of Chicago Press, 1956. 225 pp. $1.75. Major bib-
liography.
A commentary blending ancient, medieval, and modern rabbinic insight with critical interpretations.

466 Good, Edwin M. IRONY IN THE OLD TESTAMENT. Philadelphia: Westminster Press, 1965. 256 pp. $6.50. Index.
Jonah, Saul, Genesis, Isaiah, and Job are considered as they
use the literary device of irony.

467 Goodspeed, Edgar J. HOW CAME THE BIBLE. New York:
Abingdon Press, 1940. 150 pp. $1.00. Index. Bibliography.

468 Gordis, Robert. THE BOOK OF GOD AND MAN: A STUDY
OF JOB. Chicago: University of Chicago Press, 1966. 389 pp.
$8.50. Index. Bibliography.
Literature and the literary forms of the ancient Semitic
world are used to breathe new understanding into Job. Gordis
provides a summary of each section of the book and shows its
relation to the whole. This able scholar provides a very warm
and human exposition, completed by his own translation of
Job, which brings out the ancient poetry.

469 Grant, Frederick C. AN INTRODUCTION TO NEW TESTA-
MENT THOUGHT. New York: Abingdon Press, 1960. 340 pp.
$1.50, paperback. General index. Scripture index.
A topical study.

470 Grant, Robert M. AFTER THE NEW TESTAMENT. Philadelphia: Fortress Press, 1967. $6.00.
Studies in the literature and theology of the early Christians.

471 Gulston, Charles. OUR ENGLISH BIBLE: NO GREATER
HERITAGE. Grand Rapids, Mich.: Wm. B. Eerdmans, 1960.
232 pp. $1.95, paperback. Index. Bibliography.
A history of the development and translation of the Bible
into English. Subtitled "The Drama of the Birth of the English
Bible."

472 Guthrie, D. NEW TESTAMENT INTRODUCTION. Chicago:
Inter-Varsity Press, THE GOSPELS AND ACTS, 390 pp.,
$5.95. THE PAULINE EPISTLES, 319 pp., $4.95. HEBREWS
TO REVELATION, 320 pp., $4.95. 3 vols.
Guthrie demonstrates his conservative scholarship in this

3-volume set. Each volume contains a general introduction to the books dealt with, and a carefully balanced treatment of evidence and criticism concerning authorship, date, unity, purpose, and so on. The author is very fair to all points of view, pointing out the strengths and weaknesses of each—including his own.

473   Halley, Henry H. BIBLE HANDBOOK, 24th ed. Grand Rapids, Mich.: Zondervan Publishing Co., 1965. $3.95.

This classic surveys the whole Bible. Each book is treated in commentary fashion with major attention given to archaeological discoveries. Many historical tables and maps included. A conservative approach. Useful to high-school students.

474   Hamilton, Kenneth. IN SEARCH OF CONTEMPORARY MAN. Grand Rapids, Mich.: Wm. B. Eerdmans, n.d. 85¢, paperback.

A brief anthology-commentary on several "classic" passages in modern literature which measure the mood of modern man. An introduction to the Contemporary Writers in Christian Perspective series edited by Roderick Jellema (see No. 496).

475   Harned, David Baily. THEOLOGY AND THE ARTS. Philadelphia: Westminster Press, 1966. 200 pp. $5.00. No index.

An attempt at "a systematic interpretation of what artists are doing, why they are doing it, and what it means in the context of the Christian story about man and God." The author examines many of the images that artists use.

476   Harrison, G. B. THE BIBLE FOR STUDENTS OF LITERATURE AND ART. New York: Doubleday & Co., 1964. 506 pp.

Excerpts from the Bible that have affected literature and art.

477   Hawthorne, Nathaniel. THE CELESTIAL RAILROAD. Fort Wayne, Ind.: Religious Instruction Association (4001 Fairfield Avenue—46807), 1967. 8 pp. Free. Pamphlet.

A witty parody on PILGRIM'S PROGRESS, spoofing those who would widen and ease the road to Paradise. Here offered in reprint fashion along with an article suggesting its uses in teaching.

478   Heaton, E. W. EVERYDAY LIFE IN OLD TESTAMENT TIMES. New York: Charles Scribner's Sons, 1956. 240 pp. $4.95.

An account of what life was like during Bible times, written by a fellow at St. Johns College, Oxford, who is a lecturer in theology. It describes the daily life of the ordinary family— meals, work, clothing, amusements—as real people. A rich conversational style and 126 illustrations make the assimilation of a myriad of details enjoyable. However, Heaton does not seem to recognize much diversity within the Old Testament period, from 1250 to 586 B.C.

479   Heidt, William G., *et al.*, eds. OLD TESTAMENT READING

GUIDE. Collegeville, Minn.: Liturgical Press, 1965. 100 pp. Imprimatur. 40¢ ea.

A series of 30 booklets designed to aid the general reader of the Bible.

480 Heim, Ralph D. YOUTH'S COMPANION TO THE BIBLE. Philadelphia: Fortress Press, 1959. 250 pp. $1.95, paperback. No index.

Written for high-school youth, this simple survey of the Bible contains a useful timeline, several maps and pictures.

481 Heinisah, Paul. HISTORY OF THE OLD TESTAMENT. Collegeville, Min.: Liturgical Press. $1.95, paperback.

The author surveys God's dealings with men from Adam to 70 A.D., giving character sketches of the principal personalities. 16 Westminster maps included.

482 Herford, Travers. THE PHARISEES. Boston: Beacon Press, 1924, 1952. 248 pp. $1.75, paperback. General index. Bible index. Rabbinic index.

This scholar and Unitarian minister seeks to reveal the contribution of the much-maligned Pharisees to religion and to show their progressive outlook, reconstructing their faith through a thorough study of the Talmud and the Writings. In trying to find the "real meaning" of the Pharisees, he sees their reaction to Jesus as "shock" at meeting such an unusual person. This is a new interpretation, and rather difficult reading.

483 Hester, H. I. THE HEART OF HEBREW HISTORY. Liberty, Mo.: Quality Press, 1962. 330 pp. No index.

An Old Testament survey.

484 Hester, H. I. THE HEART OF THE NEW TESTAMENT. Liberty, Mo.: Quality Press, 1963. 350 pp.

485 Hollingsworth, J. DISCOVERING THE GOSPEL OF MARK. Chicago: Inter-Varsity Press, 60¢, paperback.

Inductive Bible study principles are used to help the student discover the teachings in Mark. Directions are also given for leading a group discussion on Mark. This book contains 16 studies.

486 Hooper, Stanley Romaine, ed. SPIRITUAL PROBLEMS IN CONTEMPORARY LITERATURE. New York: Harper & Row. 288 pp. $1.95, paperback. Index.

This book considers religion and the artist's situation, means, and beliefs through a series of essays originally presented as lectures at the Institute for Religion and Social Studies of the Jewish Theological Seminary of America. The contributors are from various faiths.

487 Horne, Herman Harrell. JESUS THE MASTER TEACHER. Grand Rapids, Mich.: Kregel Publishers, 1964. 210 pp. $3.50.

488 Howie, Carl G. THE OLD TESTAMENT STORY. New York: Harper & Row, 1965.

The retelling of the Old Testament story with up-to-date scholarship that does not hinder or impede the progress of the reader.

489   Howse, Ernest Marshall. SPIRITUAL VALUES IN SHAKE-SPEARE. New York: Abingdon Press, 1955. 158 pp. $1.25, paperback. General index. Shakespeare index.

Eight plays are explored in the light of the universal moral problems they dramatize.

490   Huffman, J. A. A GUIDE TO THE STUDY OF THE OLD AND NEW TESTAMENTS. Marion, Ind.: Wesley Press, 1963. 176 pp. No index.

This text was adopted for a Biblical literature course in 1926 by the State Board of Education of Indiana. It is an expanded outline of events and personalities, conservative in tone.

491   Hunter, Archibald M. THE GOSPEL ACCORDING TO ST PAUL. Philadelphia: Westminster Press, 1966. 120 pp. $1.65, paperback.

492   Hyatt, J. Philip. THE HERITAGE OF BIBLICAL FAITH. St. Louis: Bethany Press, 1964. 367 pp. $4.50. General index. Scripture index. Annotated bibliography.

An overview of Biblical study.

493   Hymarx Outline Series. THE OLD TESTAMENT. Boston: Student Outlines Co., 1939. 200 pp. $1.50. Also THE NEW TESTAMENT. Same date and price.

These are summaries of the Bible from a liberal perspective for college students as part of the "College Outline Series."

494   Intrater, Aaron, and Spotts, Leon. THE VOICE OF WISDOM. Cleveland: Bureau of Jewish Education, 1965. 200 pp.

A detailed look at the wisdom literature of the Bible—Proverbs, Job, and Ecclesiastes—and a comparison of its teachings. Bibliography with each chapter.

495   Jackson, Warren W. THE NEW TESTAMENT IN THE CONTEMPORARY WORLD. New York: Seabury Press, 1967.

Contemporary obstacles to belief are carefully considered and contrary points of view set forth so that the student may ultimately form his own conviction.

496   Jellema, Roderick. CONTEMPORARY WRITERS IN CHRISTIAN PERSPECTIVE. Grand Rapids, Mich.: Wm. B. Eerdmans, 1966–1968. 48 pp. 85¢ ea.

This ongoing series of booklets has received widespread acclaim. Each seeks to give the reader a better understanding of a given writer's work as seen in Christian perspective. The form and content of the books are, however, specifically oriented to literary criticism. There are volumes on: Albee, Beckett, Bellow, Frost, Lewis, Miller, Salinger, Eliot, Hemingway, and many others.

497 Joekel, Samuel L. FITLY FRAMED TOGETHER. Richmond,
Va.: John Knox Press, 1953.
This inexpensive booklet shows that the Bible is one complete volume, with a continuous plot or design into which each
section and book is fitly framed.

498 Johnson, James. CODE NAME SEBASTIAN. Philadelphia:
J. B. Lippincott, 1967. $4.50.
This intriguing spy novel unfolds the religious dimension of
life in a very interesting fashion. A thoroughly believable work
by a capable author.

499 Kaufmann, Y., ed. THE RELIGION OF ISRAEL. Chicago:
University of Chicago Press, 1960. $8.50.
A translation and abridgment of an 8-volume work dealing
with the history, nature, and literature of pre-exilic Judaism.

500 Kee, Howard Clark, et al. UNDERSTANDING THE NEW
TESTAMENT. Englewood Cliffs, N.J.: Prentice-Hall, 1957,
1965. 490 pp. $7.95. Index.

501 Keller, Werner. THE BIBLE AS HISTORY. New York: William
Morrow & Co., 1956, 1964. 457 pp. $6.95. Bibliography.
This "confirmation of the Book of Books" is written by a
journalist who calls himself a "nontheologian." Keller marshals
archaeological evidence to support the Biblical record. Ur, the
Flood, Egypt, Sinai, the religions of Canaan, Nazareth, the
Dead Sea Scrolls, are but a few of his topics. An excellent book
telling how information uncovered in the Holy Land by archaeologists verifies Biblical history in both Old and New Testaments. Many interesting maps, charts, and excerpts from old
documents add to the value of this work. A major 5-page bibliography includes works in English, German, and French up
to 1955. This book has become something of a classic.

502 Keller, Werner. THE BIBLE AS HISTORY IN PICTURES.
New York: William Morrow & Co., 1964. 360 pp. $7.95.
Bibliography. Biblical index. General index.
A companion book to No. 501, this gives a step-by-step pan-
oramic view of the Bible as history, associating each picture
with a Bible passage. There is just enough text to satisfy curi-
osity about the pictures—and enough pictures to keep one
satisfied for hours: landscape, monuments, sculpture, wall
paintings, excavations, finds, etc. Appendices include a synoptic,
chronological table of Bible history, bibliography, index to
Biblical references, acknowledgments of the illustrations with
comments, and general index. A handsome, well-bound volume.

503 Kelso, James L. ARCHAEOLOGY AND OUR OLD TESTA-
MENT CONTEMPORARIES. Grand Rapids, Mich.: Zonder-
van Publishing Co., 1966. 192 pp. $4.95.
Valuable background material and reference work on Old

Testament personalities is here given in layman's language but
with a scholar's knowledge. This entertaining and informative
book lends insight into the Old Testament characters as real
men. The author proposes to give a Christian understanding to
our Hebrew past and claims to be neither fundamentalist or
liberal, but staunchly conservative. Under such titles as "Amos
a Salvation Army Preacher" he considers nearly a dozen of the
more prominent Old Testament figures. Scholarship is here
combined with the "common touch" in a highly readable
volume.

504   Kennedy, Charles. EARLY ENGLISH CHRISTIAN POETRY.
New York: Oxford University Press, 1963. 292 pp. $1.75.
A general introduction to the historical background, manu-
script sources, content, and meter of medieval poetry.

505   Kenyon, Sir Frederic. THE STORY OF THE BIBLE. Grand
Rapids, Mich.: Wm. B. Eerdmans, 1967. 149 pp. $1.95, paper-
back. Index. Bibliography.
The history, not the origin, of the Bible is Kenyon's concern
here. He gives a concise story of its writing and publishing
from the beginning to the present. This popular account by a
recognized scholar in the original languages and manuscripts
leads the reader through the new discoveries that so aided the
art of translating up to the year 1936. A final chapter by
F. F. Bruce on "The Last Thirty Years" brings the book up
to date as to the Dead Sea Scrolls and recent discoveries.

506   Keyes, Nelson Beecher. STORY OF THE BIBLE WORLD.
Pleasantville, N.Y.: Readers Digest Association, 1962. 208 pp.
$5.95. 7" x 10".
This popular account of the Bible world includes more than
100 photographs of ancient and modern Bible scenes, 30 new
maps in full color, and useful time charts. Useful to both
teachers and students.

507   Killinger, John. THE FAILURE OF THEOLOGY IN MOD-
ERN LITERATURE. Nashville, Tenn.: Abingdon Press, 1963.
239 pp. Index.
Areas of contemporary literature are examined as they relate
to such recurrent themes in the theology of the Christian faith
as: the absence of God, the journey into self, the unredeemed
community, the only way to be cleansed, etc.

508   Kitchen, Kenneth A. ANCIENT ORIENT AND OLD TESTA-
MENT. Chicago: Inter-Varsity Press, 1966. 192 pp. $3.95.
Offers some solutions in coordinating ancient Near Eastern
history with a Biblical text.

509   Kraeling, Emil G. THE DISCIPLES. Chicago: Rand McNally
& Co., 1966. 300 pp. $4.95. Index.
Through an exhaustive study of the New Testament and
other records and legends of early times, the lives of the disciples

and their relation to Jesus are reconstructed in 12 many-hued portraits. Laborious research is here presented to the reader in easy fashion. The author mentions his sources of information so that one may see just how probable the accounts are.

510 Lace, O. Jessie. UNDERSTANDING THE NEW TESTA-MENT. New York: Cambridge University Press. $1.65, paperback.
Deals with the background of the New Testament.

511 Ladd, George Eldon. JESUS CHRIST AND HISTORY. Chicago: Inter-Varsity Press, 1963. 95¢, paperback.
One of a series in contemporary Christian thought.

512 Lanczkowski. SACRED WRITIINGS.
Excerpts from the scriptures of the various world religions. See No. 768.

513 Leach, Charles, and Torrey, R. A. OUR BIBLE. Chicago: Moody Press, no date. 39¢, paperback.
The sources, beginnings, and compilation of the Bible are dealt with here. Part One examines the New Testament Greek manuscripts in ancient versions; Part Two explores the Old Testament as the source; and Part Three considers the English versions from the Anglo-Saxon down to the revised versions of 1890. The appendix by Torrey is called "Ten Reasons Why I Believe the Bible Is the Word of God."

514 Leeb, David. THE OLD TESTAMENT AS LITERATURE. Philadelphia: Educational Research Associates, with Bantam Books, 1967. 220 pp. $1.00. Bibliography. Glossary.
This indexed study guide includes charts, maps, and literary background of the Old Testament. Historical backgrounds, a summary of each book, critical analyses, character analyses, questions and answers, research areas, bibliography, and glossary are also included. Leeb proposes to approach study of the Old Testament as a unique literary achievement, enabling the student to read with background and context, both historical and literary. He recognizes that this "may at times conflict with the interpretation of the Bible as theology" (p. 14), since he is working from a different basis.

515 Lewis, C. S. THE LITERARY IMPACT OF THE AUTHORIZED VERSION. Philadelphia: Fortress Press, 1963. 85¢, paperback.
This professor of medieval literature at Cambridge University argues what is and is not the influence of the King James Version on the English language in literature. Not very exciting reading, but well documented and well written.

516 Lewis, C. S. A PREFACE TO PARADISE LOST. New York: Oxford University Press, 1961. 143 pp. $1.25, paperback.
This major introduction to a masterpiece of literature, by a scholar, is in Lewis' familiar "common man" style. The author

is a Christian (p. 65) who seeks to take Milton as a whole, theology and all.

517 Lewis, C. S. REFLECTIONS ON THE PSALMS. New York: Harcourt, Brace & World, 1958 $3.95. ($1.45, paperback.)

An introductory book which deals first with the difficulties in the Psalms (as: cursings, judgment, and death) and goes on to offer real help with such problems as second meanings— i.e., reading in more than the author knew. Lewis begins by saying, "This is not a work of scholarship. I am no Hebraist, no higher critic, no ancient historian, no archaeologist. I write for the unlearned about things in which I am unlearned myself." He goes on to talk about the difficulties he has met in studying the Psalms and how he has solved them. This helpful work ought to be clear to high-school students.

518 Lewis, C. S. SPACE TRILOGY. New York: Collier Books, 1943.

This is a series of three "science-fiction" novels by one whose view of life was thoroughly Christian. Well done and stimulating to read.

OUT OF THE SILENT PLANET, 95¢, paperback.
PERELANDRA, 95¢, paperback.
THAT HIDEOUS STRENGTH, $1.50, paperback.

519 Lightfoot, Neil R. HOW WE GOT THE BIBLE. Grand Rapids, Mich.: Baker Book House, 1963. 127 pp. $2.50. Bibliography. Index.

520 Lloyd-Jones, D. Martyn. STUDIES IN THE SERMON ON THE MOUNT. Grand Rapids, Mich.: Wm. B. Eerdmans, no date.

A detailed study of each section of the sermon in lecture form by an evangelical Christian.

521 Lockyer, Herbert. ALL THE KINGS AND QUEENS OF THE BIBLE. Grand Rapids, Mich.: Zondervan Publishing Co., 1961. 253 pp. $13.95. Short bibliography. Short index.

Here is a *Who's Who* of the kings and queens mentioned in the Bible, from Mesopotamia, Assyria, Egypt, Babylonia, Persia, Greece, Rome, Palestine, plus a section on the use of kings in prophecy, symbol, etc. A factual account of each, with Biblical references.

522 Longacre, Lindsay B. THE OLD TESTAMENT: ITS FORM AND PURPOSE. Nashville, Tenn.: Abingdon-Cokesbury Press, 1945.

An attempt to see the Old Testament as a whole.

523 Luck, G. Coleman. THE BIBLE BOOK BY BOOK. Chicago: Moody Press, 1955. 250 pp. $1.25.

524 Lynch, Wm. F. CHRIST AND APOLLO: THE DIMEN-SIONS OF THE LITERARY IMAGINATION. New York:

New American Library, 1960. 254 pp. 75¢, paperback. Imprimatur.

Lynch tries to relate literature to the rest of life.

525 MacGregor, Geddes. THE BIBLE IN THE MAKING. Philadelphia: J. B. Lippincott Co., 1967. $6.00.

A history of the Bible from its composition to the most recent translations.

526 MacLeish, Archibald, J. B. Boston: Houghton Mifflin Co., 1958. 153 pp. $1.50, paperback.

A contemporary play based on the Book of Job.

527 Male, Emile. RELIGIOUS ART. New York: Noonday Press (a division of Farrar-Straus & Co.), 1949. 208 pp. $1.75, paperback. Index.

This translation from the French covers religious art from the 12th to the 18th century. 48 black-and-white plates included.

528 Manley G. T. THE NEW BIBLE HANDBOOK. Chicago: Inter-Varsity Press, 1962. 465 pp. $4.95. Index.

Encyclopedia articles deal with inspiration, authority, the canon, modern criticism, history, and geography, with an introduction to each of the Biblical books.

529 Manley, G. T., and Oldham, H. W., eds. SEARCH THE SCRIPTURES. Chicago: Inter-Varsity Press, 560 pp. $4.95.

Offers pointed questions to help you engage in a systematic three-year study of the Bible on a personal basis.

530 May, Rollo, ed. SYMBOLISM IN RELIGION AND LITERATURE. New York: George Braziller, 1960. 253 pp. $1.95, paperback.

Excerpts from Tillich, Burke, Scott, and others are the material used.

531 Maus, Cynthia Pearl. THE OLD TESTAMENT AND THE FINE ARTS, New York: Harper & Row, 1954. Also CHRIST AND THE FINE ARTS and THE CHURCH AND THE FINE ARTS, 1959 and 1960. $5.95 ea. 813 pp.

Here in three separate volumes are anthologies of pictures, poetry, music, and stories covering the periods indicated. Useful source books for illustrative material. An accompanying set of slides is available for the Old Testament from the Visual Education Service, Yale University, 409 Prospect Street, New Haven, Conn., 06511. The set contains 101 slides and costs $45.00.

532 McCormack, Jo Ann. THE STORY OF OUR LANGUAGE. Columbus, Ohio: Charles E. Merrill Books, 1967. 44 pp. $1.00, paperback. Index.

The development of the English language is traced from earliest times to the present, and its relation to other Indo-European languages explored.

533   McKenzie, John L. THE TWO-EDGED SWORD. New York: Doubleday & Co., 1956. $1.65, paperback.

This has been called "the finest, modern interpretation of the Old Testament available today." It is also obtainable from the Bruce Publishing Company in hard-cover form for $4.50.

534   McLeman, James. JESUS IN OUR TIME. Philadelphia: J. B. Lippincott, 1967. 158 pp. $3.95. Index.

McLeman tries to approach history and theology on an equal basis, recognizing that the need to know and the need to believe are equally imperative when taken seriously. Jesus is seen in the light of both historical research and Christian conviction. Not a summary of a majority of opinions, but the author's own critical assessment. The first two chapters trace the church's thinking about Jesus up to the present day and show the need for historical knowledge. The author then considers Jesus historically (well argued but not well documented), and theologically—what does He mean for us?

535   Mead, Frank S. WHO'S WHO IN THE BIBLE. New York: Harper & Row, 1934. 250 pp. $1.45, paperback.

Biographies of 250 Bible personalities, one per page. Not just listed, but given in miniature stories that help to relive their lives. Contrary to the author's disclaimer, he does seek to show their theological significance and thus helps us to understand their importance. References given to where each may be found in the Bible.

536   Mears, Henrietta C. WHAT THE BIBLE IS ALL ABOUT. Glendale, Calif.: Regal Books, 1953, 1966. 675 pp. $2.95.

This layman's commentary, written for Sunday-school teachers, is a strongly conservative Christian explanation of the Bible. Basically an historical summary of each book, with some very good digests that tend to be devotional in tone. Some good maps.

537   Merchant, W. Moelwyn. CREED AND DRAMA. Philadelphia: Fortress Press, 1965. 119 pp. $1.95, paperback. Short bibliography.

This essay in religious drama gives special attention to classical Greece, medieval liturgical dramas, Marlowe's DOCTOR FAUSTUS, Shakespeare and his contemporaries, Milton's SAMSON AGONISTES, Byron's CAIN: A MYSTERY, and Tennyson's BECKET, as well as contemporary trends.

538   Metzger, Bruce. THE NEW TESTAMENT: ITS BACK-GROUND, GROWTH, AND CONTENT. Nashville, Tenn.: Abingdon Press, 1965. 288 pp. $4.75.

An elementary text in New Testament survey adapted to the needs of secondary school students and college freshmen. The author tries to make the complex clear—not "certain"— by presenting the various theories with their strength and weaknesses. Professor of New Testament Language and Literature at Princeton Theological Seminary, he usually writes at the technical level, but here has produced an excellent work for the student. After a brief introduction to the culture, he gives a summary of each book of the New Testament.

539 Miller, Madeleine S., and Lane, J. ENCYCLOPEDIA OF BIBLE LIFE. New York: Harper & Row, 1955. 500 pp: $7.95. General index. Bible index.

540 Mirsky, Jeannette. HOUSES OF GOD. New York: Viking Press, 1965. 235 pp. $8.50. Index.

This lavishly illustrated book deals with the buildings and shrines of the great world religions, going back to the primitives and including Egypt, India, Greece, and Rome; Judaism, Islam, and Christianity.

541 Morris, Leon. THE STORY OF THE CHRIST CHILD. Grand Rapids, Mich.: Wm. B. Eerdmans. 1961. $2.50.

542 Morris, Leon. THE STORY OF THE CROSS. Grand Rapids, Mich.: Wm. B. Eerdmans, 1957. $2.50.

543 Moseley, Edwin M. PSEUDONYMS OF CHRIST IN THE MODERN NOVEL. Pittsburgh: University of Pittsburgh Press, 1962. 231 pp. $4.95. Bibliography. Index.

Moseley considers the Christ-figure in such modern novels as LORD JIM, THE GREAT GATSBY, THE OLD MAN AND THE SEA, and several more.

544 Mould, Elmer W. K. ESSENTIALS OF BIBLE HISTORY. New York: Ronald Press, 1966. 842 pp. $7.75.

Written for introductory courses in the Bible and revised in 1966, this book treats outstanding events in both Biblical and general history. Scriptures are fully discussed from religious, ethical, and literary perspectives. Each book is examined separately. The domestic life and manners of the people are also discussed.

545 Mueller, W. R. JOHN DONNE: PREACHER. Princeton, N.J.: Princeton University Press, 1962. $6.00.

546 Muirhead, Jan A. EDUCATION IN THE NEW TESTAMENT. New York: Association Press, 1965. 95 pp. $2.50.

A scholarly monograph.

547 Murdock, Kenneth. LITERATURE AND THEOLOGY IN COLONIAL NEW ENGLAND. New York: Harper & Row, 1949. 235 pp. $1.50, paperback. Index.

An attempt to outline the relation between the theological ideas of the Puritans and their literary theory and output. Originally given as a series of lectures, these essays show how the Puritan use of literary means enabled them to dominate the intellectual life of New England for a century, and still influences us today.

548 Murray, Victor A. TEACHING THE BIBLE. Cambridge, Eng.:

The University Press, 1955. 232 pp. General index. Scripture
index.

The subtitle reads: "Especially in Secondary Schools." Contains general principles, subject-matter syllabus, and method.

549   Napier, B. D. COME SWEET DEATH: A QUINTET FROM
GENESIS. Boston: United Church Press, 1967.

The author proposes to put new life into the ancient stories
of the Garden of Eden, Cain and Abel, the Flood, the Tower
of Babel, and Abraham, by casting them in a poetic lyrical
style.

550   Nelson, Lawrence E. OUR ROVING BIBLE. Nashville, Tenn.:
Abingdon Press, 1945. $1.45, paperback.

Presents objective and abundant evidence that the Bible has
shaped English and American thinking for centuries at a
rapidly accelerating rate.

551   Newman, Barcley M. THE MEANING OF THE NEW TEST-
AMENT. Nashville, Tenn.: Broadman Press, 1966. 330 pp.
$6.95. Large bibliography. No index.

The author uses the wine-and-wineskin metaphor of Jesus as
a way of expressing the continuity and discontinuity of the
faith of Israel and the faith of the church, since the New
Testament cannot be understood apart from its Jewish backgrounds. This survey gives good background and an outlined
exposition for each book, with the larger context always in
view. 58 interesting maps and illustrations. The closing section
deals with the canon, inspiration, and the authority of the
New Testament. An objective evaluation.

552   Newton, Eric, and Neil, William. 2,000 YEARS OF CHRIS-
TIAN ART. New York: Harper & Row, 1966. 318 pp. $9.95.
Index.

This well-illustrated study by an artist and a theologian covers
8 periods from early Christian times to the present, and
endeavors to show the relation between what was believed
and what was created. A valuable resource book of pictures of
religious significance.

553   Nida, Eugene. GOD's WORD IN MAN'S LANGUAGE. New
York: Harper & Row, 1952. 191 pp. $3.95. Scripture, general,
and language indexes.

A story of the translation of the Scriptures into the languages
of the world.

554   Oursler, Fulton. THE GREATEST BOOK EVER WRITTEN.
Garden City, N.Y.: Doubleday & Co., 1951. $4.95. 360 pp.

This old classic on the Bible is also available in paperback.

555   Oursler, Fulton. THE GREATEST STORY EVER TOLD.
Garden City, N.Y.: Doubleday & Co., 1949, $1.25, paperback.
300 pp.

A chronological story of the life of Jesus from the betrothal of Mary and Joseph to the days after the resurrection. Oursler fills in missing details with imagination guided by what is known from the records.

556 Oursler, Fulton. MODERN PARABLES. Garden City, N.Y.: Doubleday & Co., 1950.

Selected parables from real experience to show that life is stranger than fiction and that things happening to men and women every day are more significant than fables or allegories.

557 Patterson, Alexander. BIRDS' EYE BIBLE STUDY. Chicago: Moody Press, 1911. 130 pp. 39¢, paperback.

Written for the busy layman, this book "is intended to create a desire for Bible study and to aid in prosecuting it." Conservative in approach. 36 chapters survey the entire Bible from a dispensational point of view.

558 Patterson, Charles H. NEW TESTAMENT NOTES. Lincoln, Nebr.: Cliff's Notes, 1965. 100 pp. $1.00, paperback. Bibliography.

The author gives historical background to the New Testament, outlines the life of Jesus, and introduces and comments on each New Testament book in a short, succinct fashion.

559 Patterson, Charles H. OLD TESTAMENT NOTES. Lincoln, Nebr.: Cliff's Notes, 1965. 100 pp. $1.00. Short bibliography.

This professor of philosophy at the University of Nebraska writes an introduction, a short outline of Old Testament history, and a chronology of the writings; and summarizes and comments on the major sections and books of the Old Testament from a basically liberal point of view.

560 Pfeiffer, Charles F. THE BIBLICAL WORLD. Grand Rapids, Mich.: Baker Book House, 1966. 612 pp. $8.95.

The first dictionary of its kind dealing with archaeology and subjects affected by archaeology, this volume is intended to supplement the general Bible dictionary. More than 40 contributors have supplied articles on the whole archaeological field: customs, cities, sites, texts, manuscripts, and major archaeologists. The book seems very complete and has substantial articles on most important topics. 250 photographs are included in this reference work intended primarily for the layman. An excellent addition to any library.

561 Pfeiffer, Charles F. AN OUTLINE OF OLD TESTAMENT HISTORY. Chicago: Moody Press, 1960. 160 pp. $1.75, paperback. No index. Major bibliography.

562 Pfeiffer, Charles F., and Vos, Howard F. WYCLIFFE HISTORICAL GEOGRAPHY OF BIBLE LANDS. Chicago: Moody Press, 1967. $8.95.

Separate chapters deal with Mesopotamia, Egypt, Greece, Asia, Syria, Italy, Cyprus, Phoenicia, Iran, and Palestine. The details of national customs, aspirations, craftsmanship, and religion are discussed. 440 illustrations and 32 pages of maps.

563   Pfeiffer, Robert H. INTRODUCTION TO THE OLD TESTA-
MENT. New York: Harper & Row, 1948. 900 pp. $6.50.

A scholarly work of religious, literary, historical, and critical interest in the Old Testament, intended primarily for the
graduate student or teacher. This liberal scholar tries to convey
the background, style, purpose, thought, and faith of the Old
Testament writers to those unfamiliar with Hebrew. He is concerned about the Bible—date, author, composition, and so on—
rather than with what the Bible actually says.

564   Phillips, John. EXPLORING THE SCRIPTURES. Chicago:
Moody Press, 1965. 288 pp. $3.00.

A rather brief survey of the Bible with an introduction and
outline of each book. Several good maps are included.

565   Phillips, J. B. RING OF TRUTH. New York: The Macmillan
Co. 1967. 125 pp. $2.95.

A defense of the trustworthiness of Scripture written by one
who has devoted most of his adult life to a study of the manuscripts in their original languages.

566   Price, James L. INTERPRETING THE NEW TESTAMENT.
New York: Holt, Rinehart & Winston, 1961. 560 pp. $8.95.
Index.

This has been a popular text for survey courses.

567   Pritchard, J. ARCHAEOLOGY AND THE OLD TESTA-
MENT. Princeton, N.J.: Princeton University Press, 1958.
$5.00.

568   Pritchard, J. GIBEON, WHERE THE SUN STOOD STILL:
THE DISCOVERY OF A BIBLICAL CITY. Princeton, N.J.:
Princeton University Press, 1962. $5.75.

569   Rall, Harris F. THE TEACHINGS OF JESUS. Nashville,
Tenn.: Abingdon Press, 1930. 224 pp. $1.00, paperback. Index.

This book first considers Jesus as a teacher, and his methods,
then looks at his answers to the great questions of life and
meaning.

570   Ramsay, Wm. M. THE CITIES OF ST. PAUL. Grand Rapids,
Mich.: Baker Book House, 1960. 450 pp. $2.95, paperback.

An old classic.

571   Ramsay, Wm. M. ST. PAUL THE TRAVELER AND ROMAN
CITIZEN. Grand Rapids, Mich.: Baker Book House, 1962.
400 pp. $2.95, paperback.

An old classic.

572   Rece, E. H. and Beardslee, William. READING THE BIBLE:
A GUIDE. Englewood Cliffs, N.J.: Prentice-Hall, 1964. 200 pp.
$4.25, paperback. Bibliography.

573   Redding, David A. THE MIRACLES OF CHRIST. Westwood,
N.J.: Fleming H. Revell, 1964. 186 pp. $3.50. Short bibliog-
raphy. No index.

574 Reeves, James. THE HOLY BIBLE IN BRIEF. New York: New American Library, 1954. 320 pp. 50¢, paperback. Index.

A selection of Bible stories and passages from the King James Version, arranged first as history and then as literature. Appendix on how to read the Bible, written by a liberal scholar.

575 Rest, Friedrich. OUR CHRISTIAN SYMBOLS. Philadelphia: Christian Education Press, 1954. 86 pp. $3.50. Bibliography. Index.

A well-illustrated book.

576 Reynolds, William J. CHRIST AND THE CAROLS. Nashville, Tenn.: Broadman Press, 1967. 128 pp. $1.50. No index.

The author shows how the vast wealth of carols we possess point to Christ. He traces the origin of the carol, the different types of carols, and considers many familiar carols as to how and why they were written, what they say, and how they honor Jesus. Easy reading for youth or adults.

577 Rheim, Francis B. ANALYTICAL APPROACH TO THE NEW TESTAMENT. Woodbury, N.Y.: Barron's Educational Series, 1966. 387 pp. $1.95, paperback.

Chapter-by-chapter analysis of the background, purpose, structure, and content of the New Testament books in light of modern scholarship. This nontechnical book introduces the New Testament world geographically and politically and then reviews the Greek philosophies and Judaism in detail. After discussing their acceptance into the canon, the author deals with each book.

578 Russell, Elbert. THE PARABLES OF JESUS. Philadelphia: John C. Winston Co., 1928.

The chapters on the importance of the parables and the principles of interpreting parables are helpful groundwork for literary study.

579 Rutenborn, Guenter. THE SIGN OF JONAH. A play in nine scenes. New York: Thomas Nelson & Sons, 1960. 91 pp.

A contemporary play which uses, and talks about, the Jonah of the Bible as theme.

580 Ryan, Sister M. Rosalie, ed. CONTEMPORARY NEW TESTAMENT STUDIES. Collegeville, Minn.: Liturgical Press, 1965. 487 pp. $5.50. ($3.95 paperback.) Index. Imprimatur.

The 62 essays by 55 contributors on current trends in New Testament studies are addressed to the general reader and consider why and how to study the Bible, approaches to the Bible, background, content, writers, and relevance for today.

581 Sandmel, Samuel. THE HEBREW SCRIPTURES. New York: Alfred A. Knopf, 1963. $6.25. 550 pp.

Here is an interpretation of the literature and religious ideas of the Old Testament by a famous Jewish scholar. A nontechnical introduction to and summary of each book of the Hebrew Bible.

582 Sandmel, Samuel. HEROD, PROFILE OF A TYRANT. Philadelphia: J. B. Lippincott, 1967. $5.95.

This careful history is written neither as a polemic nor as an apology, but as a well-told narrative.

583 Sandmel, Samuel. WE JEWS AND JESUS.

A Jewish interpretation of Jesus. Cf. No. 797.

584 THE SCHOOL DAY BEGINS: A GUIDE TO OPENING EXERCISES. Pittsburgh: Department of Curriculum and Instruction, 1965. 262 pp. Paperback. Bibliography for different grade levels. Index.

These inspirational programs with themes for opening exercises on the different grade levels were developed subsequent to recent court rulings.

585 Schultz, Samuel J. THE OLD TESTAMENT SPEAKS. New York: Harper & Row, 1960. 430 pp. $6.00. Bible, general and map Indexes.

This conservative scholar covers the archaeology, geography, history, and linguistics of the Old Testament in an attempt to let it speak to men today.

586 Schultz, Samuel J. OLD TESTAMENT SURVEY: LAW AND HISTORY. Wheaton, Ill.: Evangelical Teacher Training Association, 1964. 96 pp. $1.50. Spiral bound.

This survey of Genesis through Esther, with charts and maps, is designed as part of a teacher training program for church school teachers. Each section ends with questions, projects, and a bibliography.

587 Scott, Nathan A., ed. THE CLIMATE OF FAITH IN MODERN LITERATURE. New York: Seabury Press, 1964. 237 pp. $5.95. No index. Bibliography.

588 Scott, R. B. Y. THE PSALMS AS CHRISTIAN PRAISE. New York: Association Press, 1958. 94 pp. $1.98. No index.

589 Shepard, J. W. THE CHRIST OF THE GOSPELS: AN EXEGETICAL STUDY. Grand Rapids, Mich.: Wm. B. Eerdmans, 1939. $6.50. 640 pp.

This exhaustive chronological interpretation of the life of Jesus is carefully keyed to the Scriptures. A classic conservative treatment of the life of Jesus which ought to be useful to the teacher of literature.

590 Shepard, J. W. THE LIFE AND LETTERS OF ST. PAUL. Grand Rapids, Mich.: Wm. B. Eerdmans, 1950. 600 pp. $6.00. Index.

A very readable exploration of the life of Paul.

591 Sherwin-White, A. N. ROMAN SOCIETY AND ROMAN LAW IN THE NEW TESTAMENT. New York: Oxford University Press, 1963. 204 pp. $4.00.

592 Shideler, Mary McDermott, THE THEOLOGY OF ROMANTIC LOVE. Grand Rapids, Mich.: Wm. B. Eerdmans, 1966. $2.45, paperback.

This interpretive analysis of the theme of love in the writings of Charles Williams deals with most of his major works. A bibliography of his work is included.

593 Short, Robert L. THE GOSPEL ACCORDING TO PEANUTS. Richmond, Va.: John Knox Press, 1964. $1.50. 127 pp.
An attempt to see the "theological implications" of Schulz's cartoons!

594 Silver, A. H. MOSES AND THE ORIGINAL TORAH. New York: The Macmillan Co., 1949.
This Jewish scholar makes use of the differences between Northern and Southern Israel to interpret early Scriptures.

595 Simon, Marcel. JEWISH SECTS AT THE TIME OF JESUS. Philadelphia: Fortress Press. $2.95, paperback.
An introduction to the Judaism of Jesus' day.

596 Slaughter, Frank G. THE CROWN AND THE CROSS. Cleveland: World Publishing Co., 1949. $4.95. (Also available from Permabooks in a 50¢ paperback.)
Using all the important events in His life, Slaughter writes a moving story of Jesus in His humanitarian role.

597 Sloan, W. W. A SURVEY OF THE OLD TESTAMENT. New York: Abingdon Press, 1957. 334 pp. $1.50, paperback.
A good historical and geographical survey for the "serious layman." This Christian scholar and Bible professor gives a nontechnical account of the Old Testament from a basically liberal position. Helpful test questions, assignments, and selected readings are provided at the end of each chapter. An easily read and well-organized book.

598 Smith, Wilbur M. A BIBLIOGRAPHY OF THE INFLUENCE OF THE BIBLE ON ENGLISH LITERATURE. *Fuller Library Bulletin* Nos. 9 and 10, January–June, 1951, Pasadena, Calif.
A valuable source book for the literature teacher, which lists books directly influenced by the Bible. This is the kind of book that needs to be brought up to date.

599 Speaight, Robert Wm. CHRISTIAN THEATRE. New York: Hawthorn Books, 1963. 140 pp. Selected bibliography.
The author attempts to trace the Christian presence in the more important sections of European drama during the past 700 years.

600 Stalker, James. THE LIFE OF CHRIST. Westwood, N.J.: Fleming H. Revell Co., 1949.

601 Stevenson, Burton. THE HOME BOOK OF BIBLE QUOTATIONS. New York: Harper & Row. $8.95.

602 Stewart, Randall. AMERICAN LITERATURE AND CHRISTIAN DOCTRINE. Baton Rouge, La.: State University Press. 155 pp. $3.50. Index.
Guided by an orthodox view of original sin, the author examines our literary heritage from colonial times to the present day. Special attention is given to Edwards, Paine, Jefferson,

Franklin, Emerson, Whitman, Dreiser, Hawthorne, Melville, James, Eliot, Tate, Warren, and Faulkner.

603   Stott, J. R. W. BASIC INTRODUCTION TO THE NEW TESTAMENT. Chicago: Inter-Varsity Press, 1964. 180 pp. $1.50, paperback. No index.

The author summarizes the main themes and style of the New Testament writers and relates their thought to the overall message of the Bible. Treats not individual books, but men. A good initial introduction to New Testament thought.

604   Stowe, Everett M. COMMUNICATING REALITY THROUGH SYMBOLS. Philadelphia: Westminster Press, 1966. 158 pp. $4.95. No index.

605   Tenney, Merrill C. JOHN: THE GOSPEL OF BELIEF. Grand Rapids, Mich.: Wm. B. Eerdmans, 1948. 320 pp. $4.00. Index. Bibliography.

A conservative treatment.

606   Tenney, Merrill C. NEW TESTAMENT TIMES. Grand Rapids, Mich.: Wm. B. Eerdmans, 1965. 396 pp. $5.95. Major bibliography. Scripture index. Subject index.

Gives the historical background of the New Testament with emphasis upon the tensions in the Jewish and Roman world in which Christianity arose and developed. Shows not only how the Jewish world was in the time of Christ, but how it got that way. The author describes the effect of Judaism, Roman imperialism, and Hellenism on the early church and continues to trace the growth of Christianity under the various emperors. The appendices include a chart of the events of the Biblical world from 312 B.C. to 138 A.D., a chart of the Roman procurators and emperors, and a genealogical chart of Herod. 130 illustrations and 3 original maps.

607   TeSelle, Sallie McFague. LITERATURE AND THE CHRISTIAN LIFE. New Haven: Yale University Press, 1966. $6.50. 238 pp. Index.

This scholarly and theoretical treatise was originally a Ph.D. dissertation. It considers religion and the arts, the nature and function of literature, the nature of the Christian life, and the interrelationships between literature and Christian living.

608   Thomas, Leslie G. AN INTRODUCTION TO THE EPISTLES OF PAUL. Nashville, Tenn.: Gospel Advocate Company, 1955. 247 pp.

Gives historical information on the background of each epistle, an outline of its contents, some information on the author, city, and origin of the church in that city, and other interesting facts.

609   Thomas, W. H. Griffith. HOW WE GOT OUR BIBLE. Chicago: Moody Press, 1926. 39¢, paperback.

Deals with the canonicity, authority, trustworthiness, unity, progression, and purpose of the Bible from a conservative point of view. Each chapter ends with a series of questions.

610 Thomas, W. H. Griffith. METHODS OF BIBLE STUDY. Chicago: Moody Press, 1926. 39¢, paperback.

611 Thompson, Lawrence. MELVILLE'S QUARREL WITH GOD. Princeton, N.J.: Princeton University Press, 1952. 474 pp. $7.50. Index. ($2.95 paperback.)

A controversial interpretation of the religious significance of Melville's work.

612 Tidwell, J. B. THE BIBLE BOOK BY BOOK. Grand Rapids, Mich.: Wm. B. Eerdmans, 1950. 233 pp. $3.95.

A concise outline of every book of the Bible, intended as a guide to Bible study. The author gives brief background information on each book, presents a short analysis, and offers some ideas for study and discussion.

613 Travis, M. Mitchell. THE BIRTH OF A PEOPLE. New York: Vantage Press, 1957.

A modern reconstruction of the Exodus.

614 Trawick, Buckner B. THE BIBLE AS LITERATURE: OLD TESTAMENT HISTORY AND BIOGRAPHY. New York: Barnes & Noble, 1963. 180 pp. $1.25, paperback. Major bibliography. Index.

Includes geographic, historical, and social backgrounds as well as a history of translations. Deals with Hebrew problems and texts. A 2-page chart compares 7 modern translations. The writer makes some good literary observations and comparisons. He is liberal in his approach to the historicity of the Old Testament. A part of the "College Outline Series."

615 Trawick, Buckner B. THE NEW TESTAMENT AS LITERA-TURE: GOSPELS AND ACTS. New York: Barnes & Noble, 1964. Bibliography.

The author summarizes each book with geographic, historical, and social backgrounds provided. A part of the "College Outline Series."

616 Trueblood, Elton. THE HUMOR OF CHRIST. New York: Harper & Row, 1964. 125 pp. $2.50.

Here is an attempt to explain the wry Oriental humor which Jesus used in his teachings (e. g., to "strain at a gnat and swallow a camel").

617 Turnell, Martin. MODERN LITERATURE AND CHRISTIAN FAITH. Westminster, Md.: Newman Press, 1961. 69 pp.

Tries to show the distinctive shape of contemporary literature as well as the problem of belief by a study of selected authors.

618 van Loon, Henrik Willem. THE STORY OF THE BIBLE. New York: Pocket Books, 1950. 450 pp. 50¢, paperback.

This retelling of the drama of the Old and New Testaments is illustrated by the author himself.

619   Via, Dan Otto, Jr. THE PARABLES. Philadelphia: Fortress Press. 1967. $4.00.

A new approach to the literary form of the parables.

620   Watts, Harold H. THE MODERN READER'S GUIDE TO THE BIBLE. New York: Harper & Row, 1949. 540 pp. General index. Biblical index.

A guide to encourage the reader to recognize that the Bible is literature, a monument in the history of culture.

621   Watts, J. Wash. OLD TESTAMENT TEACHING. Nashville, Tenn.: Broadman Press, 1967. 358 pp. $5.95. No index.

This survey has been done as a textbook and includes historical information on each book of the Old Testament. It gives resource readings and a summary of name, theme, authorship and date, plan and purpose, textual notes (key passages in each section), and critical (literary) and theological problems for each book. The notes help the teacher in selecting important parts for study, and the problems are an aid in seeing the whole picture. Though the author does arrive at conclusions, he presents differing views and seeks to lay a foundation on which the student can build his own study of the Old Testament.

622   Weaver, Edwin L. SPIRITUAL LESSONS FROM LITERARY MASTERS. Grand Rapids, Mich.: Zondervan Publishing Co., 1940. 145 pp.

Spiritual truths are drawn from biographical sketches of authors.

623   Wedel, Theodore O. THE DRAMA OF THE BIBLE. Cincinnati: Forward Movement Publications, 1965. 130 pp. 25¢, paperback.

An overview of the Bible.

624   Wegener, G. S. 6,000 YEARS OF THE BIBLE. New York: Harper & Row, 1963. 350 pp. $7.95. Index.

This story of the birth and life of the Bible is told in both words and pictures. The illustrative material is superb.

625   Wehrli, Eugene S. EXPLORING THE PARABLES. Boston: United Church Press, 1963. 126 pp. $1.00, paperback. Short bibliography.

In a way that invites the reader to participate, the author clearly shows the method of understanding a parable, its nature and purpose, and how to "apply" it to one's own situation. He then considers certain of Jesus' parables, trying to find what Jesus meant—not what we can make it mean.

626   Weisser, Francis X. THE HOLY LAND. Collegeville, Minn.: Liturgical Press, 1963. 184 pp. $4.00. Bibliography. Index. Imprimatur.

The author takes us on a tour of the Holy Land and interweaves reference to Biblical events with concrete geographical places and pictures. He deals with some archaeology and gives much information on Biblical geography and history, also a description of the various holy places. No maps.

627 White, Edward J. THE LAW AND THE SCRIPTURES. St. Louis: Thomas Law Book Company, 1935. 420 pp. Index.
The Bible is examined book by book to discover the concepts of law it contains.

628 White, Fred H. MANNERS AND CUSTOMS OF BIBLE LANDS. Chicago: Moody Press, 1953. 336 pp. General index. Scripture index. Bibliography.

629 Wicks, Robert S. ed. THE EDGE OF WISDOM. New York: Charles Scribner's Sons. 1964. 278 pp. $3.95, paperback.
This is a source book for religious and secular writers as they deal with the great religious questions.

630 Wilder, Amos N. THEOLOGY AND MODERN LITERA-TURE. Cambridge, Mass.: Harvard University Press, 1958. 145 pp. $3.00. Indexed.

631 Williams, Albert N. WHAT ARCHAEOLOGY SAYS ABOUT THE BIBLE. New York: Association Press, 1957. 75¢, paperback.

632 Wright, Sara Margaret. A BRIEF SURVEY OF THE BIBLE. New York: Loizeaux Brothers, 1958. 240 pp. $3.00.

633 Yoder, Sanford Calvin. HE GAVE SOME PROPHETS. Scottdale, Pa.: Harold Press, 1964. 250 pp. $4.50. No index.
An introduction to the prophets.

634 Yoder, Sanford Calvin. POETRY OF THE OLD TESTA-MENT. Scottdale, Pa.: Harold Press, 1952. 422 pp. $4.50. No Index.

Versions of the Bible

635 THE AUTHORIZED VERSION. The King James Version. New York: American Bible Society. $1.00, ord. No. 00231.
This classic translation done in 1611 by a team of scholars is probably still the most widely used version of Scripture. It is *the* monument of English literature. Old thought forms and the changing nature of language make it difficult to understand for the average reader. (Cf. No. 445 in this list: THE LAN-GUAGE OF THE KING JAMES BIBLE.) It is available in a number of editions from various publishers, but the one given above is about the least expensive.

636 *King James Version—Scofield Reference Edition.* C. I. Sco-field. New York: Oxford University Press. $4.00 up.
This classic edition includes chain references, summaries of important topics, an introduction and outline for each book, indexes of names, maps, and a limited concordance. It presents a dispensational view of Scripture.

637 *The New Scofield Reference Bible.* E. Schuyler English, ed. New York: Oxford University Press, 1967. $7.25.

A complete revision of the notes and format of the old Scofield reference edition. It maintains Scofield's basic position.

638   *Reference Bible in the King James Version.* New York: American Bible Society, 1962. $2.15, ord. No. 00290.

The text is laid out in paragraph form with section headings, and poetry printed in verse form. A list of alternate readings and a list of words which have changed in meaning add to the value of this edition.

639   *A Digest of the Bible: The Authorized Version Condensed for Easy Reading.* Peter V. Ross. New York: Prentice-Hall, 1938.

640   *Nave's Topical Bible.* O. J. Nave. Chicago: Moody Press, no date. 1615 pp. $9.95. 7" x 10".

Nave arranges the King James Version under topics (more than 20,000) with the references printed in full. Facilitates finding many scriptural passages on any given topic.

641   Richardson, Cyril C. THE POCKET BIBLE. New York: Simon & Schuster, 1936, 1951. 461 pp. 60¢, paperback.

This abridgment of the King James Version is designed to be read—it is arranged in paragraph and poetic verse form without chapter breaks and other disturbing interruptions.

642   THE AMERICAN STANDARD VERSION. Publishers include: Nelson, Lockman, Broadman, Moody, World, 1901. Revised in 1963.

There is much to recommend this version in its accuracy and freedom from archaisms, since it still retains something of the happy atmosphere of earlier versions. Done in paragraph form with internal verse numbering and running heads. Decidedly conservative in style and language.

643   THE AMPLIFIED NEW TESTAMENT. Grand Rapids, Mich.: Zondervan Publishing Co., 1958.

A modern expanded translation which gives not only the most probable, but several meanings for the significant Greek word. Not good for public reading, but helps the private reader know just what the options are. Done in separate verse form with no headings.

644   THE AMPLIFIED BIBLE. Grand Rapids, Mich.: Zondervan Publishing Co., 1965. $9.95.

The Old and New Testament in one volume. The above comments apply.

645   THE BERKELEY VERSION OF THE HOLY BIBLE. Gerrit Verkuyl. Grand Rapids, Mich.: Zondervan Publishing Co., 1945. $7.95.

In paragraph form with side verse numbering; often a good forceful translation into modern English, but not uniformly so. The translators attempt to give the date at the head of each page. The whole Bible was published in 1959, with the assistance of 20 scholars. This is one of the few modern translations of the Old Testament.

646   TODAY'S ENGLISH VERSION. Good News For Modern Man. New York: American Bible Society, 1966. 35¢, paperback.

A forceful and scientific modern translation in simplified English. Helpful for anyone desiring a version which limits vocabulary without sacrificing accuracy and meaning.

647   *The Right Time. The Gospel of Mark in Today's English Version.* New York: American Bible Society. (No. 94530—9¢ each).

In 4¼" x 6¼" format illustrated with line drawings.

648   INSPIRED LETTERS OF THE NEW TESTAMENT IN CLEAREST ENGLISH. Dr. Frank Laubach. New York: Thomas Nelson & Sons, 1956.

In paragraph form with internal verse numberings, using simple words and sentences. A very suitable translation for new literates. Not a literal translation, but special attention is given to the tenses of the verbs.

649   THE JERUSALEM BIBLE. A. Jones ed. Garden City, N.Y.: Doubleday & Co. Inc. 2,000+ pp. $16.95.

A widely acclaimed Catholic translation into fresh and vivid English (via the French), it avoids both slang and archaic expressions. It is done in paragraph form with side verse numbering.

650   LIVING LETTERS. Kenneth Taylor. Wheaton, Ill.: Tyndale House, 1962.

This is correctly subtitled as a paraphrase, since Taylor tries not to translate but to interpret the New Testment epistles. Done in separate verse form with no headings; reads both naturally and well. Other portions of the Bible by Mr. Taylor are now appearing in the same format: LIVING GOSPELS, LIVING PROPHECIES, etc.

651   THE NEW ENGLISH BIBLE: THE NEW TESTAMENT. England: University Presses of Oxford and Cambridge, 1961.

This translation, known for its detail and accuracy, is from a combination of Greek manuscripts. Done in paragraph form with section headings.

652   THE NEW TESTAMENT—A NEW TRANSLATION. James Moffatt. New York: Harper & Row, 1913.

This modern-speech translation is done in paragraph form with side verse numbering and displays a high quality of scholarship. The general style is very good and the author takes great care with tenses and synonyms. The translator says he is "free" of the verbal inspiration theory.

653   THE NEW TESTAMENT—AN AMERICAN TRANSLATION. Edgar Goodspeed. Chicago: University of Chicago Press, 1923.

An attempt to translate the Bible into the American idiom, done in short paragraph form with side verse numbering. Goodspeed is better than average in dealing with the Eastern backgrounds of the New Testament. He has also translated the whole Bible (*The Bible—An American Translation*, 1939.)

654 THE NEW TESTAMENT—AN EXPANDED TRANSLATION. Kenneth Wuest. Grand Rapids, Mich.: Wm. B. Eerdmans, 1956. $2.95, paperback.

In paragraph form, with the translator seeking to add something of the richness of the original Greek by expanding certain words and phrases to bring out shades of meaning or tense. Somewhat stiff and unnatural in style. Much stress is put on the exact force of tenses.

655 THE NEW TESTAMENT—CONFRATERNTY VERSION. New York: Guild Press, 1941. $1.25, paperback. Imprimatur.

A revision of the Challoner-Rheims version under the Confraternity of Christian Doctrine. A modern-language Catholic New Testament in paragraph form with side verse numbering and paragraph headings. Many interpretive footnotes and several maps and charts.

656 THE NEW TESTAMENT IN ENGLISH. Ronald Knox. Publishers include Burns, Oates, Sheed & Ward, 1947. $2.00 up.

This Roman Catholic Version of outstanding merit is translated from the Latin Vulgate with references to the Greek text. Done in long paragraph form with page headings. The style is lively and vigorous and relatively unbiased. Many footnotes give the Roman Catholic interpretation.

657 THE NEW TESTAMENT IN MODERN ENGLISH. J. B. Phillips. New York: The Macmillan Co., 1947.

Done for the benefit of young people in London who found they could not understand the King James Version. It is in vivid, idiomatic language and paragraph form. Phillips has written a valuable introduction which gives the "feel" of the translator.

658 *One Way For Modern Man.* The Gospel of John in the Phillips translation. New York: American Bible Society. (No. 94500—13¢ each.)

This is in a 5" x 7½" format in paragraph form. The little booklet contains full-page contemporary black-and-white photographs facing each page. An interesting presentation.

659 *The Inside Story.* Luke, John, Acts, and Romans in the Phillips translation. New York: American Bible Society. (No. 04521—35¢ each.)

The familiar Phillips translation, arranged with 50 contemporary photographs to highlight the text.

660 THE NEW TESTAMENT IN MODERN SPEECH. R. Weymouth. New York: Harper & Row, 1902.

This modern-speech version is in paragraph form with side verse numbering. It is among the most careful in dealing with tenses of the verb and synonyms, but does not give a clear picture of the New Testament's Eastern background.

661 THE NEW TESTAMENT IN PLAIN ENGLISH. C. Kingsley Williams. Grand Rapids, Mich.: Wm. B. Eerdmans, 1952.

An easily read translation using simple words and sentence construction, in paragraph form with internal verse numbering. There is a brief introduction explaining the basis of the vocabulary chosen. Because of the simple language, Williams fails to render accurately some of the tenses and synonyms.

662 THE NEW TESTAMENT: A TRANSLATION IN THE LANGUAGE OF THE PEOPLE. Charles Williams, Chicago: Moody Press, 1937.

Done in long paragraph form with chapter summaries. A moderately colloquial translation which takes exceptional pains to bring out the exact force of the flexible Greek verb in its various tenses. Though this is somewhat monotonous, it is a helpful translation to serious students.

663 *The New Testament from 26 Translations.* Curtis Vaughan, gen. ed. Grand Rapids, Mich.: Zondervan Publishing House, 1967. 1237 pp. $12.50.

The aim of this volume is to combine in one book the complete text of the King James Version and the most significant and clarifying variations of 25 other versions. E.g., John 3:16: For God so loved the world . . . had such love for the world . . . loved the world so dearly . . . etc.

664 THE NEW WORLD TRANSLATION. New York: Watchtower & Bible Tract Society, 1950.

Published by a particular group, this translation is slanted to their doctrine and the name "Jehovah" introduced in over 200 passages in the New Testament in place of the word "Lord." Long paragraph form with internal verse numbering.

665 REVISED STANDARD VERSION. New York: Thomas Nelson & Sons (and many others), 1946, 1952.

Although less literal than the American Standard Version, this is a very accurate revision. It is done in short paragraph form with captions and reads easily. Now available with a few minor changes in a Roman Catholic edition.

666 *The New Testament with Pictures.* New York: American Bible Society, 1964. 259 pp. $1.00, paperback. 8½" x 11".

Available in either the King James Version or the Revised Standard Version. Present-day photos taken in Bible lands are used to illustrate this volume, which contains 581 pictures and 10 maps. A Catholic edition with the same pictures is available from Liturgical Press, Collegeville, Minn. The Bible Society also produces portions (individual books or sections) in the same 8½" x 11" format at 10¢ each.

667 *A Harmony of the Gospels.* A. T. Robertson, New York: Harper & Row, 1950. 300 pp. $3.75.

Robertson attempts to put the events of Jesus' life in sequential order and to parallel the various Gospel accounts of the same—or similar—incidents.

668 *Harper Study Bible.* Harold Lindsell. New York: Zondervan Publishing Co., 1964. $9.95.

This is a study Bible edited by an outstanding evangelical, using the Revised Standard Version text.

669 *The Holman Study Bible.* Philadelphia: A. J. Holman, 1962.

A study edition of the Revised Standard Version.

670 *The Oxford Annotated Bible.* Herbert G. May and Bruce M. Metzger, eds. New York: Oxford University Press, 1962. $7.95. (College ed. $5.95.)

Helpful explanations are added to the Revised Standard Version text to aid the reader in understanding the Scriptures.

671 *The Oxford Annotated Bible with Apocrypha.* Herbert G. May and Bruce M. Metzger, eds. New York: Oxford University Press, 1965. $10.50. (College ed. $7.95.)

This study edition of the Revised Standard Version includes a special article on the number and names of the books of the Bible, and lists the differences between the Douay Version and the Revised Standard Version.

672 *Westminster Study Bible.* New York: Collins' Clear Type Press, 1965. $12.50.

Helpful and interesting footnotes on each page as well as a general introduction are included in this study edition of the Revised Standard Version.

673 THE SIMPLIFIED NEW TESTAMENT. Olaf M. Norlie. Grand Rapids, Mich.: Zondervan Publishing Co., 1961.

This version is especially recommended for young people and for those unfamiliar with the vocabulary of an ordinary Bible.

674 Wide Margin, Loose-Leaf *New Testament.* New York: American Bible Society. Available in the American Standard Version (No. 02180), $5.95, and in the Revised Standard Version (No. 02390) for $3.55.

This edition is published to fit a standard 8½" x 11" three-ring binder and contains 21 separate sections, each page with a 5" margin. Comes complete with binder.

Commentaries

675 THE ABINGDON BIBLE COMMENTARY. Frederick C. Eiselen *et al.,* eds. Nashville, Tenn.: Abingdon Press, 1929, 1952. 1451 pp. $10.00.

A scholarly but readily understandable one-volume commentary, concise yet complete in every essential respect. The work of 63 scholars.

676 THE ANCHOR BIBLE. W. F. Albright and David Noel Freedman. Garden City, N.Y.: Doubleday & Co., 1964. 38 vols.
Prices vary on individual volumes but are somewhat under $10.00 each.

677 THE CAMBRIDGE BIBLE COMMENTARY. O. Jessie Lace. New York: Cambridge University Press, 1964. 167 pp. $3.50.

678 COMMENTARY ON THE ENTIRE BIBLE. Adam Clark. Ralph Earle, ed. Grand Rapids, Mich.: Baker Book House, 1966. 1356 pp. $11.95.
Dr. Earle here abridges Clark's popular commentary.

679 COMMENTARY ON THE WHOLE BIBLE. Jamieson, Fausset, and Brown. Grand Rapids, Mich.: Zondervan Publishing Co., 1957. 1600 pp. $9.95.
This commentary has been acclaimed for its approach, clarity, and high scholastic standard.

680 THE DAILY STUDY BIBLE. William Barclay. Philadelphia: Westminster Press, 1958. 17 vols. $2.50 each.
A topic-by-topic commentary that is helpful to the average layman and scholar alike.

681 EXPLORE THE BOOK. J. Sidlow Baxter. Grand Rapids, Mich.: Zondervan Publishing Co., $14.94.
A broadly interpretive study course is here bound in one large volume.

682 THE INTERPRETER'S BIBLE. George A. Buttrick, ed. New York: Abingdon Press, 1952. 12 vols. $8.75 each or $89.50 per set.
Probably the most complete commentary available. The writers present a wide range of conservative and liberal viewpoints.

683 THE NEW BIBLE COMMENTARY. Francis Davidson, ed. Grand Rapids, Mich.: Wm. B. Eerdmans, 1954. 1200 pp. $7.95.
This has been called "the finest one-volume Bible commentary in English." Produced by 50 scholars from England, the Continent, and America, it contains a surprising amount of detail. In the historic Protestant tradition.

684 THE WYCLIFFE BIBLE COMMENTARY. Charles Pfeiffer and Everett F. Harrison. Chicago: Moody Press. 1962. 1525 pp. $11.95.
An entirely new commentary on the whole Bible, written and edited by a staff of 48 scholars representing a wide cross section of American Protestant Christianity. It treats the complete text of the Old and New Testaments on a phrase-by-phrase basis. Summaries of the major sections of each book are included. Neither a devotional nor a technical approach, but aims to determine the meaning of the text.

Dictionaries

685   Boyd, James P. BIBLE DICTIONARY. Baltimore: Ottenheimer Publishers, 1958. 283 pp. 49¢, paperback, 2½" x 3½".
A pocket dictionary.

686   Buttrick, George A., ed. THE INTERPRETER'S DICTIONARY OF THE BIBLE. New York: Abingdon Press, 1962. $45.00. 4 vols.
Probably the most exhaustive dictionary of the Bible available today. Names, places, concepts, and background are all dealt with in great detail.

687   Cruden, Alexander. CRUDEN'S COMPLETE CONCORDANCE TO THE OLD AND NEW TESTAMENTS. Westwood, N.J.: Fleming H. Revell Co., n.d. $5.95. ($1.95, paperback.)
A revision of the first edition, published in 1737, with upwards of 220,000 references, notes, and Biblical proper names under one alphabetical arrangement.

688   Davis, John D. WESTMINSTER DICTIONARY OF THE BIBLE. Philadelphia: Westminster Press, 1944. $6.00.
A complete and very useful one-volume Bible dictionary.

689   Douglas, J. D. THE NEW BIBLE DICTIONARY. Grand Rapids, Mich.: Wm. B. Eerdmans, 1962. $12.95.
This work not only records the contents of the Bible as a concordance does, but also presents the results of the scholarship of 134 different writers.

690   Hastings, James, ed. DICTIONARY OF THE BIBLE. New York: Charles Scribner's Sons, 1963.
The revision of a classic work.

691   Miller, M. S. & J. L., eds. HARPER'S BIBLE DICTIONARY. New York: Harper & Row, 1952. $8.95.
A concise encyclopedia of Biblical terms and references useful to the high-school student.

692   Orr, James, et al., eds. INTERNATIONAL STANDARD BIBLE ENCYCLOPEDIA. Grand Rapids, Mich.: Wm. B. Eerdmans, 1952. 5 vols. $37.50

693   Palmer. THE JUNIOR BIBLE ENCYCLOPEDIA.
A simplified Bible encyclopedia for children. Cf. No. 833.

694   Smith, William. SMITH'S BIBLE DICTIONARY. Westwood, N.J.: Fleming H. Revell. 95¢, paperback.
Every person, place, and thing mentioned in the Bible is carefully identified and defined.

695   Tenney, Merrill C., gen. ed. ZONDERVAN PICTORIAL BIBLE DICTIONARY. Grand Rapids, Mich.: Zondervan Publishing Co., 1963. $9.95.
More than 700 pictures and drawings plus 40 pages of full-color maps are included.

696 Unger, Merrill F. UNGER'S BIBLE DICTIONARY. Chicago: Moody Press, 1208 pp. $8.95.

A scholarly and authoritative up-to-date reference work that deals with the archaeology, geography, chronology, and much other Biblical information.

697 Welsh, D. R., trans. THE ENCYCLOPEDIA OF THE BIBLE. Englewood Cliffs, N.J.: Prentice-Hall, 1965. $2.95, paperback.

The work of Dutch Roman Catholic and Protestant scholars, edited by P. A. Marijnen.

Bible Geographies

698 Baly, Denis. THE GEOGRAPHY OF THE BIBLE. New York: Harper & Row, 1957. 300 pp. $5.95. Scripture index. General index. Glossary. Extensive bibliography.

Dr. Baly has a B.A. in geography from Liverpool University and writes here a geography book that takes into account both the whole "environment" of the Bible and its unique message. He tries to show relationships between the two. Contains 97 photographs and 47 especially prepared maps and charts. They concentrate on the less well-known facets of the Holy Land. Part I deals with the general geographical contribution to our understanding of the Bible. Part II gives a geographical survey of the region. Has the detail of a scholar and the interest of a layman, and is suited for advanced study of the geography of Palestine.

699 Baly, Denis. GEOGRAPHICAL COMPANION TO THE BIBLE. New York: McGraw-Hill Book Co., 1963. 200 pp. $6.50. Scripture index. General index.

Compiled by a professional geographer (see above, No. 698). Contains a good section of colored relief maps and a good selection of pictures.

700 Gilbertson, Merrill T. WHERE IT HAPPENED IN BIBLE TIMES. Minneapolis: Augsburg Publishing House, 1963. $1.75, paperback.

An annotated atlas.

701 Grollenberg, L. H. SHORTER ATLAS OF THE BIBLE. New York: Thomas Nelson & Sons, 1959. 200 pp. Biblical index. Subject index.

A well-illustrated book containing 8 color maps.

702 Kraeling, Emil G. HISTORICAL ATLAS OF THE HOLY LAND. Chicago: Rand McNally & Co., 1959. 87 pp. 7" x 10". $2.95. ($1.95, paperback.)

A minimum of explanatory text, with 40 pages of beautiful full-color maps and 25 black-and-white maps, all arranged chronologically and fully indexed. 40 photographs of historical or archaelogical interest and tables on Bible history—Palestine, western Asia, Egypt, and the Western world—add to the value of this little book.

703 Kraeling, Emil G. RAND McNALLY BIBLE ATLAS. Chicago: Rand McNally & Co., 1956. $9.95. 7" x 10".

In addition to the 400 pages of full-color maps, 47 black-and-white maps, and 200 photographs of Biblical interest, this major atlas contains over 400 pages of text.

704 Rowley, H. H. STUDENT'S BIBLE ATLAS. New York: World Publishing Company, 1965. 24 pp. $1.75, paperback. 8' x 10".

Contains 16 pages of color maps with 24 pages of explanatory text. The gazetteer is annotated with definitions and Biblical references, the text is brief and easily understood; the maps are clear and well made. A useful collection.

705 Stirling, John. AN ATLAS OF THE LIFE OF CHRIST. Westwood, N.J.: Fleming H. Revell, 1956. 27 pp. 75¢, paperback. 5½" x 9".

Twenty color maps trace the movement of Jesus in chronological fashion. There are brief annotations on the map and a short accompanying text.

Section C: Books Dealing with

Social Studies, Religion, and Philosophy

(This section begins with No. 715.)

715 Adler, Morris. THE WORLD OF THE TALMUD. New York: Schocken Books, 1963. $1.45, paperback.

Adler attempts to explain, in language intelligible to the layman, what *the* classic of post-Biblical Judaism is all about, how it came into existence, and what its dominant ideas are.

716 Anderson, E. Hutto. ADJUSTMENT. New York: Carlton Press, $2.00.

This comprehensive history and analysis of religion gives special attention to the ancient relationship between Judaism and Christianity.

717 Anderson, Charles S. THE AUGSBURG HISTORICAL ATLAS OF CHRISTIANITY IN THE MIDDLE AGES AND REFORMATION. Minneapolis: Augsburg Publishing House, 1967. 70 pp. $7.50. 11" x 8½". Indexes.

The author's aim, to provide the student with a working set of maps to use in conjunction with his study of the church in these periods, is admirably fulfilled in this book. Truly an atlas, it contains 32 full-color, full-page plates—the details are clear, the text easy to read and profitable to study. Each map contains only elements thought essential to its purpose, and they are in a sequential order. The maps follow the movement and expansion of Christianity and its competitors, as well as the progress of the Reformation in various countries, from 600 to 1650. There is sufficient text to indicate the best use of the maps, but this is a book of maps. A good index to both maps and text.

718 Baird. THE CORINTHIAN CHURCH.
A Biblical approach to urban culture. Cf. No. 386.

719 Berry, Gerald. RELIGIONS OF THE WORLD. New York: Barnes & Noble, 1956. 136 pp. 95¢, paperback. Index.
Berry presents an evolutionary view of religion, and also treats contemporary movements and the state of religion in various countries today.

720 Blau, Joseph, ed. CORNERSTONES OF RELIGIOUS FREE-DOM IN AMERICA. New York: Harper & Row, 1949. 344 pp. $2.25, paperback.
The subtitle of this book is "Selected Basic Documents, Court Decisions, and Public Statements." Contains an introduction by the editor and is simple enough reading for high-school students.

721 Bouquet, A. C. COMPARATIVE RELIGIONS. Baltimore: Penguin Books, 1961. $1.65, paperback.

722 Braden, Charles. THE WORLD'S RELIGIONS. New York: Abingdon Press, 1954. 256 pp. $3.00. Major bibliography. Index.
A simple, concise account of the great religions, at the same time impartial and significant. In addition to the contemporary faiths, space is given to primitive religions, the ancient religions of America, and those of Greece, Rome, and northern Europe. Basically a chronological historical study.

723 Bradley, David. A GUIDE TO THE WORLD'S RELIGIONS. Englewood Cliffs, N.J.: Prentice-Hall, 1963. 182 pp. $1.95, paperback. Major bibliography. Index.
This is not an encyclopedia of gods and men, but a book that proposes to introduce the reader to major contemporary religions in a factual manner, summarizing as accurately as possible the essential teachings of each faith regarding salvation. After an introduction to the land, culture, founder, and scriptures of each religion, the author examines their essential beliefs according to the following categories: cosmos, deity, man, man's plight, salvation, human conduct, and destiny. He also endeavors to show the interrelation of these beliefs so each religion is seen in its integrity. This is followed by a brief summary of the religion's development, spread, and present significance.
The author treats the religion of primitive peoples, of Bible lands, of India, and of China, stressing the uniqueness of each and not trying to blend them together. He is equipped with a Ph.D. from Yale in Biblical Studies and has pursued Oriental and African studies at the University of London. This book

is intended for those with little or no knowledge of world religions and is written in succinct paragraphs by one who has mastered the art of condensation and overview.

724　Bradley, David G. CIRCLES OF FAITH: A PREFACE TO THE STUDY OF THE WORLD'S RELIGIONS. New York: Abingdon Press, 1966. $4.50. 239 pp. General index. Biblical index.

With great tolerance and superb logic, the author shows the various world religions and their vis-à-vis stance as "circles of faith," with some common human overlapping but radically different concepts of God, the good, and the world. Every religious idea stands in a context—a circle of faith—so that even though Buddhist and Christian may agree that it is "good" not to kill, they do so for radically different reasons: the Christian because he is responsible to God, the Buddhist because he must be free from desire of any kind if he is ever to escape the wheel of rebirth. A stimulating prerequisite for anyone teaching about the different religions.

725　Brantl, George. CATHOLICISM. New York: Simon & Schuster, 1961. 277 pp. 60¢, paperback. No index. Imprimatur.

Quotations from the Bible and from great Catholic theologians are interwoven to produce a clear exposition of the range of Catholic teaching. The first four sections deal with the Catholic conception of God, the fifth with the church; seven and eight give an explanation of life for a Catholic, and the last section deals with the hereafter and future events. Presents a clear understanding and basis for the central teachings of the Catholic Church. Part of the "Great Religions of Modern Man" series, No. 749.

726　Brentano, Frances, ed. NATION UNDER GOD. Great Neck, N.Y.: Channel Press, 1957, 1964. 376 pp. $5.95.

This religious and patriotic anthology should be understandable to high-school students.

727　Brow, Robert. RELIGION: ORIGINS AND IDEAS. Chicago: Inter-Varsity Press, 1966. 128 pp. $3.50. Index.

Not another book about the facts of world religions, but an exploration and comparison of the basic philosophies of each and *why* they developed as they did. This introductory survey has the unique gift of handling a multitude of facts in an easily comprehensible manner. Brow works from the hypothesis that monotheism, with informal animal sacrifices, best fits the evidence as the earliest form of religion. He shows how this idea develops into a formal priesthood, priestcraft, magic, and then reform. The author's twenty years in India have given him acquaintance with a wide number of Oriental religions, which he traces in great detail. He is not afraid to bring his conclusions up to date (Bishop Robinson's monism, he says, dates from the sixth century B.C.), but is not militant in tone. He tries only to explain and label—does not attempt to prove or oppose. There are some oversimplifications, but the book covers a necessary groundwork for any study of comparative religion.

728 Brown, Robert McAfee. THE ECUMENICAL REVOLUTION. New York: Doubleday & Co., 1967. 384 pp. $5.95.

The author, an official Protestant observer at Vatican II, traces Protestant and Roman Catholic movements from the 1900's to the present and attempts to interpret them. He does not seek an easy answer and is not afraid to ask hard theological or practical questions concerning ecumenism.

729 Buber, Martin. TWO TYPES OF FAITH. New York: Harper & Row, 1961. $1.45, paperback.

This famous Jewish philosopher examines the distinctive Jewish and distinctive Christian formulations of religious truth.

730 Cairns, Earle E. CHRISTIANITY IN THE UNITED STATES. Chicago: Moody Press, 1964. 190 pp. $1.75, paperback. Bibliographies in text. Index.

A well-written and complete chronological-topical history from the colonial era to the present. It is well arranged and clearly explained. A number of diagrams are used to show interrelated movements, with a short bibliography at the end of each chapter. Cairns seeks to present each position sympathetically.

731 Caplan, Samuel, and Ribalow, Harold U., eds. THE GREAT JEWISH BOOKS, AND THEIR INFLUENCE ON HISTORY. New York: Washington Square Press, 1963. 272 pp. 60¢, paperback. Select bibliography.

Aims to present in popular format the essence of those masterworks of Jewish literature which have most decidedly molded the life of the Jewish people. A dozen major works are considered, including the Bible, Talmud, Siddur, Rashi's Commentaries, and others.

732 Cell, Edward D. RELIGION AND CONTEMPORARY WESTERN CULTURE. New York: Abingdon Press, 1967. 400 pp. $7.95. 7" x 10". Bibliographies. Index.

This exceptionally well-bound book is a scholarly work aimed at the college undergraduate. It seeks to present leading theories of the relation of religion and culture and to show their application to specific areas of Western culture. Designed as an introduction, these 44 readings have been drawn from the theistic Christian position (Roman Catholic, neo-orthodox, postliberal, Tillichian), and from humanist positions (Freudian, Marxist, Existentialist, Positivists). The first chapter, by Cell himself, deals with the question of what is religion. The next section deals with religion and culture and presents nine theories. The last six chapters deal with religion and . . . modern art, modern literature, philosophy, psychotherapy, science, and the socioeconomic and political orders. A number of outstanding men are represented, including Brunner, Tillich, Cox, Freud, Sartre, and Ayer. Cell completely ignores the conservative Christian position as well as the more radical stance of some of the "new theologians." Not easy reading, but certainly profitable.

733   Cohen, Rabbi Harry A. A BASIC JEWISH ENCYCLOPEDIA. Hartford, Conn.: Hartmore House, 1965. 200 pp. $4.95. General index. Hebrew index.

Jewish teaching, practices and personalities are listed in the order of their importance, beginning with Elohim and including all the major Jewish festivals. A handy reference work, prepared for Jewish readers but useful also for teachers and interested persons of other faiths. A whole array of Jewish beliefs and customs are here detailed in a readily understandable manner and labeled according to Orthodox, Conservative, and Reformed positions. The author shows a great understanding of Judaism, but misses the point when he tries to contrast it with Christianity (see pp. 52, 53, 152). Nevertheless, this book is a handy tool for teachers.

734   Cousins, Norman. IN GOD WE TRUST. New York: Harper & Row, 1958. 460 pp. Major bibliography. Index.

Subtitled "The Religious Beliefs and Ideas of the American Founding Fathers," this book contains selected and edited statements, with a commentary by Cousins.

735   Craig, Clarence Tucker. THE BEGINNING OF CHRISTIANITY. New York: Abingdon Press, 1943. 365 pp. $1.75, paperback. General index. Biblical index. Bibliography.

A chronological table from 332 B.C. through 150 A.D. is included.

736   Cronbach, Abraham. JUDAISM FOR TODAY. New York: Bookman Association, 1954. 148 pp. $2.75. Index.

Designed to make Judaism come alive for the reader of today.

737   Cushman, Robert E., and Grislis, Egil, eds. THE HERITAGE OF CHRISTIAN THOUGHT. New York: Harper & Row, 1965. 245 pp.

An anthology.

738   Dawson, Christopher. RELIGION AND THE RISE OF WESTERN CULTURE. New York: Doubleday & Co., 1958. 242 pp. $3.50. (95¢ paperback.) Index.

739   DeVries, Jan. THE STUDY OF RELIGION: A HISTORICAL APPROACH. Chicago: Harcourt, Brace & World, 1967. $2.95. 230 pp. Index. Paperback.

The author studies religion from classical antiquity to the present, from the Odyssey to Freud.

740   Dimont, Max. JEWS, GOD, AND HISTORY. New York: Simon & Schuster, 1962. $7.50. (Also available in paperback.)

741 Dunstan, J. Leslie, ed. PROTESTANTISM. New York: Simon
      & Schuster, 1961. 257 pp. 75¢, paperback. No index.
        Presents the scope of Protestantism in an historical approach,
      without attempting to deal with the divisions within it except
      as they bear on the central stream of development. Protestantism
      owes both its unity and its diversity to its chief tenet: that God
      deals directly with man—salvation is by faith. The author traces
      the story through the writings of representative leaders but does
      not quote much Scripture—shows *what* happened, not why.
      More a history of Protestantism than an exposition of its
      thought. Part of the "Great Religions of Modern Man" series,
      No. 749.

742 Eliade, Mircea. FROM PRIMITIVES TO ZEN. New York:
      Harper & Row, 1967. $8.00.
        This thematic source book on the history of religion deals
      with such major topics as: God, creation, man and the sacred,
      death, afterlife, etc.

743 Elmslie, W. A. L. HOW CAME OUR FAITH. New York:
      Abingdon Press, 1962. 475 pp. $2.25, paperback. Scripture
      index. General index.
        Subtitled "A Study of the Religion of Israel and Its Signifi-
      cance for the Modern World."

744 Ferm, Vergilius, ed. AN ENCYCLOPEDIA OF RELIGION.
      Paterson, N.J.: Little, Adams & Co., 1964. 844 pp. $3.45.
        Contributions by Catholics, Protestants, and Jews represent-
      ing both liberal and conservative opinions.

745 Finegan, Jack. ARCHAEOLOGY OF WORLD RELIGIONS:
      Vol. 1., PRIMITIVISM, ZOROASTRIANISM, HINDUISM,
      AND JAINISM; Vol. 2., BUDDHISM, CONFUCIANISM,
      AND TAOISM; Vol. 3., SHINTO, ISLAM, AND SIKHISM.
      Princeton, N.J.: Princeton University Press, 1952. $2.95 each
      ($7.95 boxed set of 3), paperback.

746 Finkelstein, L. THE BELIEFS AND PRACTICES OF JU-
      DAISM. New York: Devin-Adair Co., 1952.
        This brief survey and interpretation of the basic values of
      Judaism is written by a leading spokesman of the Conservative
      branch.

747 Gaer, Joseph. HOW THE GREAT RELIGIONS BEGAN.
      New York: New American Library, 1956. 237 pp. 60¢, paper-
      back. (Also available in hard cover, $5.00.)
        A history of the beginnings of twelve religions (Protestantism
      is included separately), with biographies of their founders. Each
      chapter begins with a fact sheet of vital information concerning
      that particular faith.

748 Gard, Richard A. BUDDHISM. New York: Simon & Schuster,
      1962, 1967. 252 pp. 75¢, paperback. Index.
        The Buddhist way of life is discovered by looking at its

ideals and practices, its philosophy, moral principles, and political, social, and cultural implications. Section I describes the teaching of Buddha, II deals with the Buddha himself, III with his principles of life, and IV with Buddhist practices; V describes the life of a Buddhist monk, with details on three Buddhist monasteries; while VI is concerned with the social, political, and practical implications of Buddhism and its significance for our understanding today.

749 Gard, Richard A., gen. ed. GREAT RELIGIONS OF MODERN MAN. New York: Pocket Books, 1962.

This 6-volume series is designed to serve as an introduction to each of the great religions. No attempt has been made to compare or contrast them; each is explained by a scholar and/or partisan of that religion as a meaningful and coherent whole. See the annotation on each book: Buddhism by Gard, No. 748. Catholicism by Brandt, No. 725. Hinduism by Renou, No. 790. Islam by Williams, No. 814. Judaism by Hertzberg, No. 756. Protestantism by Dunstan, No. 741.

750 Gaustad, Edwin Scott. A RELIGIOUS HISTORY OF AMERICA. New York: Harper & Row, 1966. 421 pp. $8.95. Index. Annotated bibliography.

Many primary sources are quoted in this detailed history of the religious significance and happenings of American history. Also considered are religious topics such as the Bible in American literature. An appendix includes an elaborate chronology of important religious events between 1492 and 1965. This thorough and well-documented work amply fulfills its aim to describe the role of religion in American life. It is built on the following four propositions: (1) In the American heritage the religions role has always been significant and often crucial. (2) It is necessary to examine that role. (3) Even though it is controversial, it cannot be ignored without being dishonest. (4) Controversy is often good. The excerpts and illustrations are especially good. This ought to become a standard reference work.

751 Gilbert, Arthur. A JEW IN CHRISTIAN AMERICA. New York: Sheed & Ward, 1966. $4.95.

A series of personal essays clearly sets forth the position of the Jew in today's America. Gilbert goes on to chart the path by which Jew and Christian can transcend their often bitter common history and accept all the implications of American pluralism.

752 Goldberg, David. HOLIDAYS FOR AMERICAN JUDAISM. New York: Bookman Associates, 1954. 182 pp. $2.75. Index.

An explanation of the Jewish calendar and major feasts.

753 Gouker, Loice, ed. DICTIONARY OF CHURCH TERMS

AND SYMBOLS. Norwalk, Conn.: C. R. Gibson & Co., 1964. 70 pp. 50¢, paperback.
Short annotations for terms and symbols are given in dictionary form.

754 Gulston, Charles. OUR ENGLISH BIBLE. A history of its development. Cf. No. 471.

755 Hartt, Julian N. A CHRISTIAN CRITIQUE OF AMERICAN CULTURE. New York: Harper & Row, 1967. $8.50.

756 Hertzberg, Arthur, ed. JUDAISM. New York: Simon & Schuster, 1961. 260 pp. 60¢, paperback. No index.
Under such topics as people, God, the Torah, the year, the land, doctrine, and prayer, this author tries to establish the essential unity of the various expressions of Jewish faith. After a short introduction, he weaves extensive quotations from Jewish writings into his own brief commentary. An easily-read account, enlightening to the general reader with some background in Judaism. The key contribution Rabbi Hertzberg makes is in the unity of the presentation.

757 Hitt, Russell, ed. HEROIC COLONIAL CHRISTIANS. Philadelphia: J. B. Lippincott, 1967. $4.95.
The lifework and character of four men of the Great Awakening are explored: Jonathan Edwards by Courtney Anderson, Gilbert Tennet by Russell T. Hitt, David Brainerd by Clyde S. Kilby, and John Witherspoon by Henry W. Coray.

758 Holmes, A. F. CHRISTIANITY AND PHILOSOPHY. Chicago: Inter-Varsity Press, 1960. 40 pp. 95¢.
A study of the nature of Christianity and of philosophy, and their relation in contemporary philosophical movements.

759 Howard, D. THE THREE TEMPTATIONS: MEDIEVAL MAN IN SEARCH OF THE WORLD. Princeton, N.J.: Princeton University Press, 1966. $7.50.

760 Howard, Thomas. CHRIST THE TIGER (A Postscript to Dogma). Philadelphia: J. B. Lippincott, 1967. $4.50. ($2.25, paperback.)
An autobiographical record of the difficulties encountered by one who comes from a background of dogmatic orthodoxy when he realizes his vision is altogether too small.

761 Hudson, Winthrop S. RELIGION IN AMERICA. New York: Charles Scribner's Sons, 1965. 447 pp. $7.95 ($3.95, paperback.) Index.
A well-written popular history of religious life in America from colonial times to the present.

762 Hume, Robert Ernest. THE WORLD'S LIVING RELIGIONS. New York: Charles Scribner's Sons, 1959. 335 pp. $4.50. Bibliography. Index.
Hume gives special attention to the sacred scriptures of the

major world religions and tries to reveal them in comparison with Christianity.

763   Hutchins, Robert M., and Adler, Mortimer J. THE GREAT IDEAS TODAY. New York: Encyclopedia Britannica, 1967. $10.00.

Part I gives a debate on the secularization of theology, with Harvey Cox for and E. L. Mascall against. Martin Marty and M. D. Chenu also comment. There is a section on developments in theology this year by Langdon B. Gilkey.

764   Jurji, E. J., ed. THE GREAT RELIGIONS OF THE MODERN WORLD. Princeton, N.J.: Princeton University Press, 1946. $7.50. ($2.95, paperback.)

765   Kilby, C. S. CHRISTIANITY AND AESTHETICS. Chicago: Inter-Varsity Press, 1961. 43 pp. 95¢, paperback.

Kilby relates art and creativity to the image of God in man. He stresses morality, subjectivity, and the Christian's need for creative insight.

766   Kuiper, B. K. THE CHURCH IN HISTORY. Grand Rapids, Mich.: Wm. B. Eerdmans, 1964. $5.95.

A textbook designed to be used in Christian schools, by the National Union of Christian Schools.

767   Lanczkowski, Gunter. SACRED WRITINGS: A GUIDE TO THE LITERATURE OF RELIGIONS. New York: Harper & Brothers, 1956. 150 pp. $1.45.

An introduction to the Christian, Muslim, Indian, and Chinese holy books.

768   Landis, Benson Y. RELIGION IN THE UNITED STATES. New York: Barnes & Noble, 1965. 120 pp. $1.25, paperback. Index. Glossary.

This book describes current religious bodies from Adventists to Zen Buddhists, gives a brief statistical summary, and provides a quick reference guide to religious issues.

769   Lawson, John. COMPREHENSIVE HANDBOOK OF CHRISTIAN DOCTRINE. Englewood Cliffs, N.J.: Prentice-Hall, 1966. 287 pp. $7.75.

An outline of Christian thought. Without oversimplifying, the author presents parallel views of Roman Catholic, Orthodox, and Protestant theologians. Intended as an introductory work for colleges and seminaries, but useful to the layman.

770   Lewis, C. S. THE GREAT DIVORCE. New York: The Macmillan Co., 1946. $3.95. (95¢, paperback.)

Blake wrote "The Marriage of Heaven and Hell." Here is Lewis' reply with his own theological position. The author shows a powerful poetic imagination and keen psychological insight in this fantasy, as a busload of people from Hell arrive at the edge of Heaven and meet experiences according to their temperament.

771 Lewis, C. S. MIRACLES. New York: The Macmillan Co., 1947. 95¢, paperback.
A philosophical defense of the possibility of miracles.

772 LIFE magazine staff. THE WORLD'S GREAT RELIGIONS. New York: Golden Press, $2.45, paperback.
The basic beliefs and rites of Hinduism, Buddhism, the Chinese philosophies, Islam, Judaism, and Christianity are presented in a text enhanced by many photographs and paintings, most of them in full color.

773 Link, Henry Charles. THE RETURN TO RELIGION. New York: The Macmillan Co., 1936.
An eminent American psychologist describes the elements of his education that estranged him from religion, and the experiences responsible for his return.

774 Lortz, Joseph. HOW THE REFORMATION CAME. New York: Herder & Herder, 1964. 113 pp. $2.95. No index. Imprimatur.
A Catholic view of the Reformation.

775 MacGregor, Geddes. THE HEMLOCK AND THE CROSS. Philadelphia: J. B. Lippincott, 1963. $5.50.
An account of the conflict and collaboration of the Christian and humanist traditions.

776 MacKay, D. M. CHRISTIANITY IN A MECHANISTIC UNIVERSE. Chicago: Inter-Varsity Press, 1965. $1.25, paperback.

777 Menkus, Belden, ed. MEET THE AMERICAN JEW. Nashville, Tenn.: Broadman Press, 1963. $3.75. ($1.25, paperback.)
Eleven essays by prominent Jewish writers on the status of contemporary Jews.

778 Mixter, Russell L. EVOLUTION AND CHRISTIAN THOUGHT TODAY. Grand Rapids, Mich.: Wm. B. Eerdmans, 1959. 220 pp. $4.50.
Various biological data are here considered in the light of theology.

779 Mueller, Barbara. POSTAGE STAMPS AND CHRISTIANITY. St. Louis: Concordia Publishing Co., 1964. 90 pp. $1.95, paperback. Bibliography.
A book that combines two "how to's": how to collect stamps, and how to use stamps with religious meaning. Information on stamps with religious significance and a 15-page supplement of pictures of such stamps from around the world are also included.

780 Murdock. LITERATURE AND THEOLOGY IN COLONIAL NEW ENGLAND.
An attempt to see their interrelationship. Cf. No. 552

781 National Council of Churches. THE HANDBOOK OF THE NATIONAL COUNCIL OF CHURCHES OF CHRIST IN

THE U.S.A., 1967-68-69. New York, 1966. 125 pp. $1.00.
This guide to the history, purposes, and programs of the
National Council is factual and informative.

782   Nida. GOD'S WORD IN MAN'S LANGUAGE.
The story of how translation is done. Cf. No. 559.

783   Noss, John B. LIVING RELIGIONS, 3d ed. New York: The
Macmillan Co., 1963. $7.95. (Also available from United
Church Press in paperback for $1.95.)
This objective presentation points out the similarity and dis-
similarity of other religions to Christianity.

784   Olmstead, Clifton E. RELIGION IN AMERICA: PAST AND
PRESENT. Englewood Cliffs, N.J.: Prentice-Hall, 1961. 172 pp.
$1.95, paperback. Index. Bibliography.
This survey of organized religion from the beginning of
colonialization traces men, movements, revivals, theology, and
education, and ties them together very well.

785   Otto, Rudolf. THE IDEA OF THE HOLY. New York: Oxford
University Press, 1958. 253 pp. $5.75. ($1.75, paperback.)
Man's feeling of awe in the presence of an unseen force,
the *numinous,* is used to show the reality of that force. An
investigation of the relation between rational and nonrational
factors in the idea of the Divine.

786   Posener, George, *et. al.* DICTIONARY OF EGYPTIAN CIV-
ILIZATION. New York: Tudor Publishing Co., 1961. $7.95.
Hundreds of entries cover 3500 years of Egyptian history,
art, culture, religion, persons, and places. Illustrated.

787   Potter, Charles Francis. THE GREAT RELIGIOUS LEADERS.
New York: Simon & Schuster, 1962. 496 pp. 90¢, paperback.
From Akhenaten to Mary Baker Eddy, Potter gives short
historical sketches of the great religious leaders of the world.

788   Qualben, Lars P. A HISTORY OF THE CHRISTIAN
CHURCH. New York: Thomas Nelson & Sons, 1933, 1961.
648 pp. $4.00. Index.
A complete survey of church history up to modern times by
a Lutheran, with a select bibliography for each chapter.

789   Redfield, Robert. THE PRIMITIVE WORLD AND ITS
TRANSFORMATIONS. Ithaca, N.Y.: Cornell University Press,
1953. 185 pp. $1.95, paperback. Index.
Originally given as six lectures by this prominent anthro-
pologist.

790   Renou, Louis, ed. HINDUISM. New York: Simon & Schuster,
1961, 1967. 226 pp. 75¢, paperback. Index. Bibliography.
The author first gives a general introduction to Hinduism,
its practices, beliefs, sects, and so on. The major part of the
book is given over to a selection of texts from primary sources,
both Sanskrit and others, arranged historically from the earliest
hymns to modern times. Selections are prefaced by explanatory

introductions. A concluding section considers the role of Hinduism in Indian society today. Because of the number of unfamiliar terms, this may be rather rough going for the beginner.

791 Reynolds. CHRIST AND THE CAROLS. Stories of popular carols. Cf. No. 585.

792 Ringgren, Helmer. ISRAELITE RELIGION. Philadelphia: Fortress Press, 1966. $7.50.
A history up to the time of rabbinic Judaism.

793 Ross, Floyd H., and Hills, Tynette. THE GREAT RELIGIONS BY WHICH MEN LIVE. Greenwich, Conn.: Fawcett Publications, 1956. 192 pp. 60¢, paperback. Index.
This exposition of the 7 great living religions measures each by its best ideals. A syncretistic approach.

794 Ross, Nancy Wilson. THREE WAYS OF ASIAN WISDOM. New York: Simon & Schuster, 1966. 222 pp. $7.50. Major bibliography. Index. Glossary. 7" x 10".
The three ways are Hinduism, Buddhism, and Zen. The author, a Westerner, seeks to interpret these religions to the Western mind as being helpful in the present East-West confrontation. Each section is complete with 16 pages of pictures on the art of that religion. Not designed as a comparison, but as an explanation of each, showing history, tenets, and practices. The author gives very sympathetic presentations, especially of Zen. She does not seem to be so kind or objective regarding Christianity (p. 187). This is a popular and informative book.

795 Rosten, Leo. RELIGIONS IN AMERICA. New York: Simon & Schuster, 1963. 415 pp. $1.95, paperback. Glossary. Index.
This handbook of the faiths, churches, and denominations in the U.S. brings together much factual and interpretive data according to the following scheme: Part I, "Religious Beliefs" ("What is a—")—about half the book. Part II, "Facts, Figures, and Opinions" (membership, attendance, preference, clergy, mergers, religious education, American history, sociological data). Part III, "Selected Reading and Reference List" (books on religion, facts about the Bible, comparison chart of Protestants, Catholics, and Jews, comparison of 16 denominations, church holy days, church headquarters). A wealth of information.

796 Russell, Bertrand. WHY I AM NOT A CHRISTIAN. New York: Pocket Books, 1967. 266 pp. $1.45, paperback.
Russell presents his own statement of faith in reason. Other essays on religion are also included.

797 Sandmel, Samuel. WE JEWS AND JESUS. New York: Oxford University Press, 1965. 164 pp. $5.00. Index. Annotated bibliography.
With warmth toward Christianity but loyalty to the tenets of his faith, the author writes of Jesus as seen by modern

Judaism. This nontechnical survey presents the scholarship of both Jews and Christians on the early Christian roots within Judaism, the meaning of the Messiah, and the search for the historical Jesus. Here a liberal rabbi writes for Jews, especially of college age, and tends to stress Jesus' basic loyalty to Judaism. He assigns to Paul the real departure from the Law of Moses. This book will be informative to both Jews and Christians alike.

798 Schoeps, Hans-Joachim. THE RELIGIONS OF MANKIND. New York: Doubleday & Co., 1966. $5.95.

A thorough yet nontechnical treatment of the origins, basic concepts, and historical growth of mankind's various beliefs in divine powers.

799 Sherman, Bezalel. THE JEW WITHIN AMERICAN SOCIETY. Detroit: Wayne University Press, 1965. $2.50, paperback.

800 Smith, Daniel H. NEW VISUAL RESOURCES IN HISTORY OF RELIGIONS. Syracuse, N.Y.: Syracuse University, n.d. 33 pp.

This catalog lists 2″ x 2″ black-and-white slides of terms, proper names, and diagrams for use in courses on Indian and Chinese religions. A majority relate to Hinduism—only a few are on Islam. A "standard set" of 150 cardboard-frame slides is $35.00. Individual slides cost 50¢ each, with a minimum order of $10.00.

801 Smith, Horace Greeley. THE WORLD'S GREATEST STORY. New York: Rand McNally & Co., 1965.

Smith discusses the spiritual meaning of the nativity.

802 Smith, Huston. THE RELIGIONS OF MAN. New York: Harper & Row, 1958. 328 pp. $5.75. Paperback, $1.95. Index.

A survey of the world's major religions.

803 Smith, Wilfred Cantwell. THE FAITH OF OTHER MEN. New York: New American Library, 1962. 128 pp. 60¢, paperback. No index.

A basic symbol is chosen to present the essence of each of 4 great oriental religious traditions. This symbol rather than a systematic approach to beliefs or customs, is used to try to understand not only the religions but the people back of them.

804 Steinberg, Milton. BASIC JUDAISM. New York: Harbinger Books (Harcourt), 1947. $2.50, textbook. ($1.75, paperback.)

Here is a stimulating description of the tenets of Judaism.

805 Stevenson, William. THE STORY OF THE REFORMATION. Richmond, Va.: John Knox Press, 1959. 200 pp. $1.95, paperback. Index.

806 Tarshish, Allan. NOT BY POWER. New York: Twayne Publishing Co., 1952. $3.95.

This one-volume history of the development of Judaism up to recent days is written at the high-school level.

807 Thomas, George F. RELIGIOUS PHILOSOPHIES OF THE

WEST. New York: Charles Scribner's Sons, 1965. 454 pp.
$3.95, paperback. Index. Bibliography.
A critical analysis of the major philosophers from Plato to
Tillich.

808 Tillich, Paul. THEOLOGY OF CULTURE. New York: Oxford
University Press, 1959, 1964. 224 pp. $4.75. ($1.45, paperback.)
The many spheres of man's cultural activity are examined
for their religious significance.

809 Toynbee, Arnold. CHRISTIANITY AMONG THE RELI-
GIONS OF THE WORLD. New York: Charles Scribner's Sons,
1957. $2.95. ($1.25, paperback.)
These lectures interpret what is right from the standpoint of
other faiths.

810 Wach, Joachim. THE COMPARATIVE STUDY OF RELI-
GIONS. New York: Columbia University Press, 1961. $1.95,
paperback.

811 White. THE LAW AND THE SCRIPTURES.
Concepts of law in the Bible. Cf. No. 627.

812 Wicks. THE EDGE OF WISDOM.
A source book of great writers as they deal with religion.
Cf. No. 629.

813 Weiss, Benjamin, ed. GOD IN AMERICAN HISTORY. Grand
Rapids, Mich.: Zondervan Publishing Co., 1966. $4.95.
Government documents and speeches which refer to God
or have other religious significances are here compiled.

814 Williams, John Alden, ed. ISLAM. New York: Simon & Schuster, 1961. 240 pp. 60¢, paperback. Index.
Williams organizes his material to give an overall view of
the Muslim and his world, guiding our attention to his basic
beliefs and important writings. After introducing the subject
and summarizing, he quotes extensively from the Qur'an
(Koran) and the Muslim theologians. He also deals with the
divisions within Islam. This may be a little hard to read for
those unfamiliar with the many technical terms.

Section D: Books Dealing with

Children, Youth, and Elementary Schools

815 Arch Books. BIBLE STORIES. St. Louis: Concordia Publishing
Co. 35¢ each. 6 for $2.00, paperback.
Familiar Bible stories are told in verse and prose, with bril-
liant color illustrations on every page. The 18 titles include
THE GOOD SAMARITAN, THE BOY WHO RAN AWAY,
THE RICH FOOL, NOAH'S ARK, THE BOY WITH A
SLING, A BABY BORN IN A STABLE, and many others.
These very attractive 7" x 8" books have durable paper covers.

816   BASIC BIBLE READERS (Series) Cincinnati: Standard Pub-
       lishing Co., 1952. 128 pp. $2.50 each.
          This graded series of Bible Readers includes a glossary of
       new words and has the following titles: Primer: I LEARN TO
       READ ABOUT JESUS. Grade 1: I READ ABOUT GOD'S
       LOVE. Grade 2: I READ ABOUT GOD'S GIFTS. Grade 3:
       BIBLE ADVENTURES. Grade 4: BIBLE HEROES. These
       stories and vocabulary are especially selected for the various
       age levels.
817   Bradford, Barbara Taylor. CHILDREN'S STORIES OF THE
       BIBLE. Toronto: Lion Press, 1966. $4.95. 128 pp. 8" x 11".
          Selected Bible stories told in eloquent but simple language
       in biographical form. The author tries to stay close to the
       Biblical text, but some interpretation is necessary for children.
       This book should be appropriate for children nine years and
       above, and probably understandable by younger children.
818   Dearmer, Percy, et al. OXFORD BOOK OF CAROLS FOR
       SCHOOLS. New York: Oxford University Press, 1956. 56 pp.
       Piano ed., $2.75. Voice ed., 75¢.
          These selections are arranged for use in singing from the
       Oxford Book of Carols.
819   De Vries, Anne. CHILDREN IN THE BIBLE. St. Louis: Con-
       cordia Publishing Co., 1966. $3.95.
          Interestingly told stories about children mentioned in the
       Bible.
820   De Vries, Anne. THE CHILDREN'S BIBLE. St. Louis: Con-
       cordia Publishing Co., 1963. $3.95.
          The Bible is recast into children's words and illustrated.
821   Fenega. PILOT SERIES IN LITERATURE.
          A junior-high anthology of Christian-oriented literature. Cf.
       No. 451.
822   Goldberg, David. STORIES ABOUT JUDAISM. New York:
       Twayne Publishing Co., 1954. $2.75.
          The basic ideas and concepts of Judaism are presented
       through the personalities of those who played the leading roles
       in their formulation. For children 11–13.
823   HOW AND WHY WONDERBOOKS. Columbus, Ohio: Charles
       E. Merrill Books, $1.60 each. No. 3032, LOST CITIES. A
       junior-high interest level book about archaeology in Bible lands,
       with a lower reading level. No. 5050, OLD TESTAMENT.
       The story of the Old Testament in the same series as above.
          These are part of a larger series (60 titles in all) dealing
       with science, history, famous people, and other topics.
824   Jones, Mary Alice. KNOW YOUR BIBLE. New York: Rand
       McNally & Co., 1965. 71 pp. $1.95.
          This book of facts about what the Bible is, how it was
       written, and what it means today contains maps, charts, and

colored illustrations. Suitable for the middle elementary grades.

825 Jones, Mary Alice. LIFE IN BIBLE TIMES. New York: Rand McNally & Co., 1967. 48 pp. $1.95. 8½" x 11".
This book covers the land; life in the countryside, at home, and in the cities; living together and living with God.

826 Komroff, Manuel. HEROES OF THE BIBLE. New York: Golden Press, 1966. 144 pp. $4.95.
These biographical sketches of Biblical personalities in prose form stick fairly close to the Biblical style. But more than 70 full-color illustrations in a fluidly dramatic style are the distinctive features of this book.

827 Korfker, Dena. MY PICTURE STORY BIBLE. Grand Rapids, Mich.: Zondervan Publishing Co., 1960. 512 pp. $4.95.
270 simple Bible stories retold, with 24 full-color illustrations and many black-and-white drawings.

828 Lewis, C. S. THE NARNIA TALES. New York: The Macmillan Co., 1951–1956. $3.95 each. Also available in paperback from Penguin books.
From a thoroughly Christian understanding of life, Lewis writes imaginative tales of a different world and of children who travel back and forth. For ages 9–13 (although enjoyed and appreciated by many adults), the titles include: THE LION, THE WITCH AND THE WARDROBE; PRINCE CASPIAN; THE MAGICIAN'S NEPHEW; THE VOYAGE OF THE DAWN TREADER; THE SILVER CHAIR; THE HORSE AND HIS BOY; THE LAST BATTLE.

829 Luckhardt, Mildred Corell, ed. THANKSGIVING FEAST AND FESTIVAL. New York: Abingdon Press, 1966. 350 pp. $5.95.
Written for older children.

830 Mack, Sara R. INSPIRATIONAL READINGS FOR ELEMENTARY GRADES. Kutztown, Pa.: Kutztown Publishing Co., 1964. 106 pp. $2.00, paperback. Index.
These inspirational readings, done since the Supreme Court decision, are divided for primary and intermediate; further divided into year-round, special days, lands, and so forth.

831 McGavran, Grace. STORIES OF THE BOOK OF BOOKS. New York: Friendship Press, 1960. $1.95, paperback.
A book about the Bible written for middle elementary school children.

832 Moody Press. MOODY BIBLE STORY BOOK. Chicago: Moody Press, 1953, 1965. 639 pp. $4.95. Biographical index.
408 stories arranged chronologically with 32 full-color pictures and 164 black-and-white illustrations. Bible events are retold so close to the original as to be a paraphrase in simplified language. Readable by a child of 8 and over, except for names and places.

833   Palmer, Geoffrey. THE JUNIOR BIBLE ENCYCLOPEDIA.
       Cleveland: World Publishing Co., 1964. 140 pp. $2.95.
       This well-illustrated book contains simple, short annotations
       based on the King James Version.
834   Rubin, Alvan D. A PICTURE DICTIONARY OF JEWISH
       LIFE. New York: Behrman House, 1956. 25 pp. $1.95.
       This is a simple book done for young Jewish children in
       large format.
835   Sawyer, Ruth. JOY TO THE WORLD, CHRISTMAS LEG-
       ENDS. Boston: Little, Brown & Co., 1966. 100 pp. $3.95.
       Six stories from all parts of the world are here told for
       children. Illustrated.
836   White, Marian. THROUGH THE BIBLE WITH FINGER
       PLAYS. Grand Rapids, Mich.: Baker Book House, 1965. 60 pp.
       $1.00, paperback. Index. Illustrated.
837   Wright, Kathryn S. LET THE CHILDREN PAINT. New York:
       Seabury Press, 1966. 170 pp. $4.50. Bibliography.
       This book contains both theoretical and practical helps on
       the use of art in religious education.

Magazines

838   AMERICAN LITERATURE. P.O. Box 6697, College Station,
       Durham, N.C., 27708. Subscription: $5.00 a year.
       Published quarterly by Duke University Press in cooperation
       with the American Literature section of the Modern Language
       Association of America. Contains articles, notes, and book
       reviews on themes in American literature; also indexes to doc-
       toral theses in progress and articles on American literature in
       current publications. About 120 pages per issue.
839   THE BIBLE TODAY. Collegeville, Minn., 56321. Subscrip-
       tion: $5.00 a year.
       Published monthly by the Liturgical Press, this Catholic
       periodical promotes "the popular appreciation of the Word of
       God," with articles designed to speak to the layman on Bibli-
       cal topics. About 60 pages per issue.
840   THE FOURTH R JOURNAL. 4603 Greenwood, Lincoln,
       Nebr., 68504. Subscription: $5.00 a year.
       Published four or more times a year by the Fourth R Foun-
       dation, this magazine contains articles to promote the instruc-
       tion of religion in the public schools. It supports the Supreme
       Court decision. About 35 pages per issue.
841   INTERNATIONAL JOURNAL OF RELIGIOUS EDUCA-
       TION. 475 Riverside Drive, New York, N.Y., 10027. Sub-
       scription: $5.00 a year, $9.00 for two years, $12.00 for three
       years, $18.00 for five years.
       Published monthly (except August) by the Department of

Educational Development, National Council of Churches of Christ in the U.S.A. Issues are usually dedicated to some facet or theme of religious education. Contains articles, book reviews, news notes, and monthly worship resources for church school departments. Approximately 44 pages per issue.

842 JOURNAL OF THE AMERICAN ACADEMY OF RELIGION. Harry M. Buck, managing editor, Wilson College, Chambersburg, Pa., 17201. Subscription: $10.00 a year. Student $4.00 a year.
Published quarterly by the American Academy of Religion. Contains articles on comparative religion and problems in Biblical study, also a few on the sociology of religion. Nearly half the magazine is given to extended reviews of current books by scholars in their respective fields. Approximately 110 pages per issue.

843 A JOURNAL OF CHURCH AND STATE. Box 258, Baylor University, Waco, Tex., 76703. Subscription: $3.50 a year.
Published three times a year by the J. M. Dawson studies in church and state of Baylor University. Indexed in the INDEX TO RELIGIOUS PERIODIC LITERATURE. Contains articles on current church-state problems and theories. Has a major section on book reviews and doctoral dissertations. Also a section of "notes" on church-state affairs around the world, including the U.S.A. Approximately 200 pages per issue.

844 RELIGIOUS EDUCATION. 545 West 111 St., New York, N.Y., 10025. Professional membership—including subscription —$8.50 a year. Student $4.00 a year.
Official publication of the Religious Education Association. Published bimonthly and indexed in the Education Index, it "seeks to present on an adequate, scientific plane, those factors which make for improvement in religious and moral education." It does not defend particular views; the opinions are those of the writers alone. Contains articles and book reviews on theological and religious educational programs by Catholics, Protestants, and Jews. Nearly 20 pages of book reviews. Approximately 80 pages per issue.

WESTMAR COLLEGE LIBRARY